Grappling
Masters

Grappling Masters

JOSE M. FRAGUAS

 UNIQUE PUBLICATIONS
Burbank, California

Disclaimer
Please note that the author and publisher of this book are NOT RESPON-SIBLE in any manner whatsoever for any injury that may result from prac-ticing the techniques and/or following the instructions given within. Since the physical activities described herein may be too strenuous in nature for some readers to engage in safely, it is essential that a physician be con-sulted prior to training.

First published in 2003 by Unique Publications.

Library of Congress Catalog Number: 2002 155302
ISBN: 0-86568-212-7

Unique Publications
4201 Vanowen Place
Burbank, CA 91505
(800) 332-3330
First edition
05 04 03 02 01 00 99 98 97 1 3 5 7 9 10 8 6 4 2

Printed in the United States of America.

Editor: Todd Hester
Design: Patrick Gross
Cover Design: George Chen

"What we believe to be the motives of our conduct are usually but the pretext for it. At times to be silent is to lie. You will win because you have enough brute force. But you will not convince. For to convince you need to persuade. And in order to persuade you will need: reason and right."

—Miguel de Unamuno (1864–1936)
Spanish philosopher and writer

Dedication

To the memory of my father who passed away on Christmas 2002.

Acknowledgments

Writers, like fighters, need commitment, stamina, and a good team in their corner. Whenever my enthusiasm and energy for this book showed signs of flagging, I knew I could depend on the help and encouragement of some marvelously dedicated people to keep me going. Without them, I couldn't have gone the distance.

At the top of the list is Todd Hester, editor of the work and an enthusiastic supporter of this project from the very beginning. He not only tirelessly spent long hours editing but also kindly contributed additional information of his own to make the work more complete. Also of particular assistance were Ed Ikuta (one of the world's greatest martial arts photographers); John Steven Soet (editor and writer), who unselfishly spent many hours polishing the manuscript on my behalf; Aaron Chang from San Diego, the best professional surf photographer in the world and a dedicated Brazilian jiu-jitsu practitioner; Matt Midyette, owner of Powerhouse Gym in West Los Angeles for his sincere friendship and support throughout the whole project; Markus Boesch, close friend and talented photographer; Tami Goldsmith, for allowing me to use photos from her personal archives; Kid Peligro (Brazilian jiu-jitsu black belt and columnist for the two best grappling magazines in the world—*Grappling Magazine* and *Gracie Magazine),* who kindly supplied additional information and interviews; and finally Curtis F. Wong, a true visionary who supported the grappling arts in America long before the first Ultimate Fighting Championship, and who spread the word about the grappling revolution when all others ignored it.

I would further like to give my most heartfelt gratitude to all the masters and fighters appearing in this book. Not only did they generously give me an enormous amount of personal time for the long interviews, but they also provided me with wonderful photographs to illustrate the book as well. Without their work ethics, sacrifice, and commitment to martial arts, this work would not exist.

Finally, this book would have never been completed without the unwavering support of my family. I especially wish to thank my wife, Julie, for more love and understanding than anyone could reasonably expect.

—Jose M. Fraguas

Contents

About the Author

Born and raised in Madrid, Spain, Jose "Chema" Fraguas began his martial arts studies with judo, in grade school, at age 9. From there he moved to taekwondo and then to kenpo karate, earning black belts in both styles. During this same period he also studied shito-ryu karate and eventually received a fifth-degree black belt. He began his career as a writer at age 16 by serving as a regular contributor to martial arts magazines in Great Britain, France, Spain, Italy, Germany, Portugal, Holland, and Australia. Having black belts in three different styles allows him to better reflect the physical side of the martial arts in his writing. "Feeling before writing," Fraguas says.

In 1980, he moved to Los Angeles and met grappling legends such as Gene LeBell, Wally Jay, Larry Hartsell and studied wrestling, judo, and jiu-jitsu. Seeking to supplement and expand his personal training, he researched other disciplines such as muay Thai, kickboxing, French savate, Chinese kung-fu, and jeet kune do from such well-know masters as Jun Chong, Benny Urquidez, Hawkins Cheung, Dan Inosanto, et cetera.

In 1986, Fraguas founded his own book and magazine company in Europe, authoring dozens of books and distributing his magazines to 35 countries in three different languages. His reputation and credibility as a martial artist and publisher became well known to the top masters around the world. Considering himself a martial artist first and a writer and publisher second, Fraguas feels fortunate to have had the opportunity to interview many legendary martial arts teachers. He recognizes that much of the information given in the interviews helped him to discover new dimensions in the martial arts. "I was constantly absorbing knowledge from the great masters," he recalls. "I only trained with a few of them, but intellectually and spiritually all of them have made very important contributions to my growth as a complete martial artist."

Jose Fraguas started his training in Brazilian jiu-jitsu in the late '80s with several members of the Gracie family and continued for over a decade. "The art was not as big as it is today," Fraguas recalls, "and there was a feeling of being on the cutting edge of something significant and important. Years later, when I met Helio Gracie for the first time, I realized that the easy-going attitude and high technical level his sons displayed was simply a direct reflection of his own expertise and personality."

While Fraguas will not reveal his BJJ rank, he does admit that it is considerably below black belt. "I would love to mention the members of the Gracie family who spent so many hours in private and group classes sharing the art with me," Fraguas laughs, "but I'm afraid that naming them as being responsibility for my grappling skills would make them feel more pain than pride. They know who they are, and they know how much I appreciate their patience."

Steeped in tradition yet looking to the future, Fraguas understands and appreciates martial arts history and philosophy and feels this rich heritage is a necessary stepping stone to personal growth and spiritual evolution. His desire to promote both ancient philosophy and modern thinking provided the motivation for writing this book. "If the motivation is just money, a book cannot be of good quality," Fraguas says. "If the book is written to just make people happy, it cannot be deep. I want to write books so I can learn as well as share."

The author currently lives in Los Angeles, California, where he is the General Manager of CFW Enterprises, the world's leading martial arts publishing company.

He can be contacted at: **mastersseries@yahoo.com**

Introduction

Some of my best days were spent interviewing and meeting the masters appearing in this book. There is little I enjoy more than "gnawing" on a great interview while time slows and sometimes even seems to stop. Having the opportunity to meet and interview the most relevant and prestigious martial artists of the past four decades is something that every martial artist doesn't have the chance to do. Hopefully, in some small way, this will help make up for that.

Meeting the masters and having long conversations with them that were published in magazines around the world allowed me to do more than simply "scratch the surface" of the technical aspects of their respective styles, but to also research and analyze the human beings behind the teachers. Some of the dialogues and interviews began by simply commenting about the superficial techniques of fighting, and ended up turning into a very uncommon spiritual conversation about the philosophical aspects of the martial arts.

Although they are all very different, considering their respective styles and backgrounds, they all share a common thread of the traditional values such as discipline, respect, positive attitude, dedication, and etiquette.

For more than 25 years I've faced the long odds of interviewing these fighters and martial arts masters, one-on-one, face-to-face, and with no place to run if I asked a stupid question. Many times, it was a real challenge to not just make contact with them, but also how to make the interview interesting enough to bring out the knowledge that resided inside them. In every interview I tried to absorb as much knowledge as I could, ranging from their training methods, to their fighting methods, and to their philosophies about life itself.

Their different origins and cultural backgrounds heavily influenced them but never prevented them from analyzing, researching, or modifying anything that they considered appropriate. They always kept an open mind to improving both their arts and themselves. From a formal philosophical point of view many of them follow the wisdom of Zen and Taoism—others just use common sense.

They devoted themselves to their arts, often in solitude, sometimes to the exclusion of other pursuits most of us take for granted. They worked themselves into extraordinary physical condition and stayed there. They ignored distractions and diversions and brought to their training a great deal of concentration. The best of them got as good as they could possibly get at performing and teaching their chosen art, and the rest of us watched them and, leading our "balanced lives," wondered how good we might have gotten at something had we devoted ourselves to whatever we did as ferociously as these masters embraced their arts. In that respect they bear our dreams.

It would be wonderful to find a single martial artist who combined all the great qualities of these fighters—but that's impossible. That, however, was one of the things that inspired me to write this book. I wanted to preserve some things that were said a long time ago, of which not many people today are aware.

If you read carefully between the lines, you'll see that these men either trained hard to personify their personal idea of what it means to be "the best fighter in the world," or dedicated time and knowledge to create the most devastating martial arts system known to man. Interestingly enough, at the same time they also focused on how to use the martial arts to become better human beings. There are many links that once discovered open a wide spectrum of possibilities, not only to martial arts, but to a better existence as individuals.

The interviews often lasted as long as three or four hours of non-stop talking. I would begin at their school and finish the conversation at a restaurant or coffee shop. A lot of information in these interviews had been never published before and some had to be trimmed either at the master's request or edited to avoid creating senseless misunderstandings later on. It is not the questions that make an interview. An interview is either good or bad depending on the answers given. Considering the masters in this book, I had an easy job. My goal was to make these masters comfortable talking about their life and training—especially those who trained under the founders of original systems. In modern time, there are not many who have had the privilege of living and learning under the legendary founders.

"The masters are gone," many like to say. But as long as we keep their teachings in our heart, they will live for ever. To understand the martial arts properly it is necessary to take into account the philosophical and psychological methods as well as the physical techniques. There is a deep distinction between a fighting system and a martial art, and a general feeling in the martial arts community is that the roots of the martial arts have been de-emphasized, neglected, or totally abandoned. Martial arts are not a sport—they are very different. Someone who chooses to devote themselves to a sport such as basketball, tennis, soccer, or football, which is based on youth, strength, and speed chooses to die twice. When you can no longer do a certain sport, due to the lack of any one of those attributes, waking up in the morning without the activity and purpose that has been the center of your day for twenty-five years is spooky. Martial arts can and should be practiced for life. They are not sports, they are a "way of life."

A true martial arts practitioner—like an artist of any kind—be this a musician, painter, writer or actor, is expressing and leaving parts of themselves in every piece of their craft. The need for self-inspection and self-realization of who they are becomes the reason for a journey in search of that perfect technique, that great melody, that inspiring poetry, that amazing painting or that Academy Award performance. It is this motivation to reach that "impossible dream," that allows a simple individual to become an exceptional artist and master of their craft.

Many of the greatest teachers of the fighting arts share a commonly misunderstood teaching methodology. They know the words that could be used to pass their personal experience to their students have little or no meaning. They know that to try "self-discovery" in quantitative or empirical terms is a useless task. A great deal of knowledge and wisdom (the ability to use knowledge in a proper and correct way) comes from what is called the "oral traditions," which martial arts, like every other cultural aspect, has. These oral traditions have been always reserved for a certain kind of student and have been considered "secrets." I believe these secrets are such because only few very special students, perspicacious and with a keen sense of introspection, have the minds to attain them. As Alexandra David-Neel wrote: "It is not on the master that the secret depends but on the hearer. Truth learned from others is of no value, the only truth which is effective and of value is self-discovered...the teacher can only guide to the point of discovery." In the end "The only secret is that there is no secret," or as Kato Tokuro, probably the greatest potter of the last century, a great art scholar, and the teacher of Spanish painter and sculptor Pablo Picasso (1881–1973) said: "The sole cause of secrets in craftsmanship is the student's inability to learn!"

As human beings, we are always tempted to follow straight-line logic towards ultimate self-improvement—but the truth is that there are no absolute truths that apply to all. You have to find your own way in life whether it be in the martial arts, in business, or in cherry picking. Whatever path you pursue, you have to distill your personal truths to what is right for you, according to your own life. The quest for perfection is actually quite imperfect and is not in tune with either human nature or human experience. To have any hope of attaining even a single perfection, you have to concentrate on a single pursuit and direct all your energies towards it. In this sense, perfection comes from appreciating your endeavors for their own sake—not to impress anyone—but for your own inner satisfaction and sense of accomplishment.

Martial arts are a large part of my life and I draw inspiration from them, both spiritually and philosophically. I really don't know the "how" or the "why" of their effect on me, but I feel their influence in even my most mundane activities. It's not a complex thing where I have to look deep into myself to find their influence. All human beings have sources or principles that keep them grounded, and martial arts is mine. I believe that is when the term "way of life" becomes real. In bushido, the self-discipline required to pursue mastery is more important than mastery itself—the struggle is more important than the reward. A common thread throughout the lives of all the masters is their constant struggle towards self-mastery. They realized that life is an ongoing process, and once you achieve all your goals you are as good as dead. But this process is not all driven by action. Often the greatest action is inaction, and the hardest voice to hear is the sound of your inner voice. You need to sit alone and collect your thoughts, free from all forms of technology and distraction, and just think. It is perhaps the only way to achieve mental and spiritual clarity.

I don't believe that great books are meant to be read fast. I've always thought that really good writing is timeless, and that time spent reading doesn't detract anything from your life, but rather adds to it. So take your time. Approach the reading of this book with either the Zen "beginner's mind" or "empty cup" mentality and let the words of these great teachers help you to grow not only as a martial artist but as a human being as well. ☯

Bas Rutten

Clean and Shaved

BAS RUTTEN STARTED HIS MARTIAL ARTS CAREER AT THE LATE AGE OF 21 AND QUICKLY DISCOVERED THAT PROFESSIONAL FIGHTING WAS HIS CALLING IN LIFE. WITHIN ONE-AND-A-HALF YEARS HE HAD EARNED HIS FIRST DEGREE BLACK BELT IN TAEKWONDO. ONE YEAR LATER HE RECEIVED A FIRST DEGREE BLACK BELT IN KYOKUSHIN KARATE. HE PRESENTLY HOLDS A SECOND DEGREE BLACK BELT IN TAEKWONDO AND A FIFTH DEGREE BLACK BELT IN KYOKUSHIN KARATE.

WHILE HE WAS DOING THESE TWO SPORTS HE ALSO STARTED TO COMPETE IN THAI BOXING. HE BECAME THE DUTCH CHAMPION AND FOUGHT 16 THAI BOXING MATCHES, WINNING 14 BY KO. IN 1993 RUTTEN WAS CONTACTED BY THE PANCRASE ORGANIZATION OF JAPAN AND ASKED TO COMPETE. HE FOUGHT HIS FIRST PANCASE FIGHT ON SEPTEMBER 21, 1993, AND WON THE FIGHT IN 43 SECONDS.

FROM THAT MOMENT ON, BAS RUTTEN BECAME ONE OF THE FAVORITE FIGHTERS OF THE JAPANESE AUDIENCE. IN 1995 HE WON THE PRESTIGIOUS KING OF PANCRASE BELT IN THE NIPPON BUDOKAN IN TOKYO. HE SUCCESSFULLY DEFENDED THAT TITLE TWO MORE TIMES AND THEN RESIGNED AS THE WORLD CHAMPION IN ORDER TO COMPETE IN THE BIGGEST NO-HOLDS-BARRED EVENT IN THE WORLD—THE UFC. HE WENT UNDEFEATED IN THE OCTAGON AND BECAME THE UFC WORLD HEAVYWEIGHT CHAMPION IN MAY OF 1998.

AFTER WINNING THE UFC CHAMPIONSHIP, RUTTEN FELT IT WAS THE RIGHT TIME FOR HIM TO RETIRE AS A PROFESSIONAL FIGHTER. HE NOW LIVES IN THE UNITED STATES AND WORKS AS AN ACTOR AND FIGHT COORDINATOR IN THE MOTION PICTURE AND TELEVISION INDUSTRY.

Q: How long have you been practicing martial arts?
A: Since I was 21—a late age, I know. I started when I moved out of my parent's house. They never wanted me to train martial arts because they let me train taekwondo when I was 14, and after two weeks I broke somebody's nose in a street fight. So when I moved out I immediately started training taekwondo and kyokushin karate. I have my second degree black belt in taekwondo and fifth degree in kyokushin karate.

"Fighting moves came very natural to me. I had my first degree black in taekwondo within one year, and my black belt in kyokushin within two— which is very fast by European standards."

As a kid I was very sick. I had a very bad skin condition and asthma. If I had an asthma attack I would be in bed for two weeks and couldn't even get up to go to the bathroom. For my skin condition, I wore gloves which made me a target for the other children to pick on. That resulted in many street fights which, by the way, I never lost. I climbed trees a lot and was a loner. I would climb in a tree in the beginning of a forest very close to my house, and then I would swing from tree to tree to the other side of the forest. It came in handy when there were gangs of guys looking to bully me.

Fighting moves came very natural to me. I had my first degree black in taekwondo within one year, and my black belt in kyokushin within two—which is very fast by European standards. I was also good in general athletics. I was a good high jumper, long jumper, shot putter, discus and javelin thrower. I had to stop that, however, because I blew out my knee every time I competed—I guess my knee didn't match my leg strength.

Q: How has your personal fighting style developed over the years?
A: When I started taekwondo and kyokushin, I already felt that there was more. Even though kyokushin is very tough, there was no hitting to the head. So after six months or so I also started to train in Thai boxing. Three weeks after I signed up for my first class I fought my first Thai boxing match. In 1991, Chris Dolman, a famous free fighter from Holland saw me and a friend of mine doing martial arts demonstrations for television and asked me if I wanted to train with him. I went over to his gym and had the worst experience in my life! I was a good Thai boxer, but when I

rolled around with his students they killed me! When I drove home I pulled off the road, called my wife and told her that I was going to sleep in the car. When I came home my wife laughed because I couldn't eat because I got choked so many times! At the time, I thought that I could hold off a choke with my neck muscles and throat. I was wrong and I couldn't eat for a couple of days.

My wife thought that would be the end of my training there, but I told her that I was going to go back and learn enough to make those guys pay for what they did to me. A few months later, two Japanese fighters named Suzuki and Funaki came to Holland with several other Japanese grapplers to find fighters for a new organization they were starting called Pancrase. Chris called me and I went there for a try out. One of the Japanese tried to hurt me during our sparring and that resulted in him going to the hospital for some

"One of the Japanese tried to hurt me during our sparring and that resulted in him going to the hospital for some stitches in his head. Instead of being upset at me, they made me an offer to fight. Two months later I fought my first Pancrase fight."

stitches in his head. Instead of being upset at me, Suzuki and Funaki were very excited and made me an offer to fight. Two months later I fought my first Pancrase fight, which I won by KO in 43 seconds. Man, that was an experience. Overnight, people recognized me on the street in Japan.

After another KO, the Pancrase fighters soon realized that stand-up was my game. I had just started training submission so I was totally new to the ground game. So my third opponent was Funaki, and he took me down and nearly broke my ankle with a toe hold. Then I won a few more and lost a few more. The last loss that I had against Ken Shamrock in

"Everything changes and uses new ideas to improve—human languages add news words, cars get more horsepower, tennis players hit harder, and runners move faster. The same thing is true with martial arts. We now all think that mixed martial arts is the best way to fight—but that could change too."

February 1995, made me decide to forget about striking training and concentrate on more ground work. I found a really good training partner named Leon van Dijk, and we started to train together two times a day, just trying to tap each other. Chris Dolmans' Amsterdam school was far away from me but I also went there once in a while. I never lost a fight again after making that decision to train heavily in grappling.

Q: How does full contact karate compare with kickboxing and mixed martial arts?
A: I love full contact karate. I think it is one of the toughest martial arts in the world. I love to watch Thai boxing—especially the K-1. I love to see great fighters like Aerts, Hoost, Mike Bernardo—pretty much all the K-1 fighters are super! I am a big fan of Ramon Dekkers, who, for me, is the greatest Thai boxer to ever compete. The UFC is super and Pride is sensational. I love to watch everything that is full-contact oriented.

All martial arts events are positive as long as you grow and don't keep your eyes shut and deny that the old way of semi-contact and point karate is the best, because it is not. Full contact is far closer to reality and you have to change or be left behind. Everything changes and uses new ideas to improve—human languages add news words, cars get more horsepower, tennis players hit harder, and runners move faster. The same thing is true with martial arts. We now all think that mixed martial arts is the best way to fight—but that could change too. Only God knows what's next.

Q: What was Pancrase like?
A: Pancrase is not as big as other events in Japan—K-1 for example—but it is very popular and it was out there a long time before the UFC. I competed in it for a long time but they made me resign my title because I couldn't fight due to my daughter's birth. But I never lost my title to anyone and I had the opportunity to fight against very good opponents. At a certain point I was fighting too much—31 times in four years! I have always been open to good offers to participate in any kind of fighting event. One thing I don't really like in NHB these days is the lack of technique that there used to be in the early Pancrase and UFC shows. Martial arts techniques are just not there anymore. Now it's just two guys throwing each other down and pounding away. I feel that in the end that's going to affect the way the sport is perceived by the fans and hurt its popularity.

"Traditional martial arts are from the East but right now the West has many world champions in every martial art. Still, it is very special to go to Asia and see the people there compete in their own styles. The East has this special feeling. They have ancient traditions that they still live by."

Q: Do you think Western fighters have caught up with Eastern fighters?
A: I really think that the West has caught up. Traditional martial arts are from the East but right now the West has many world champions in every martial art. Still, it is very special to go to Asia and see the people there compete in their own styles. The East has this special feeling. Also, I think that martial arts is still more in the souls of the Eastern fighters. They have ancient traditions and still live by them.

Q: Martial arts are considered a sport these days. Do you like that?
A: I do. I consider it more of a sport than throwing darts, for example, where they drink beer during the game and never even break a sweat. I think it is one of the best man against man competitions. I really think

"My strength training is sport-specific. Sometimes I gain a lot of strength and muscle mass very quickly, so I have to cut back my training. I don't feel comfortable carrying around too much weight—it slows me down."

that you have to get tired in order to call anything a sport. Look at auto racing; it requires super mental concentration and a strong body to drive four hours or more.

People who say martial arts fighting is barbaric are totally wrong. Guys who say that they don't like fighting or don't want to be good fighters are not being honest with themselves. If they are walking on the street with their wife, and they get bullied by some punks who are looking for trouble, they will suddenly pray to God that they could fight so that they can teach them some respect. If they deny this, well, they are lying.

Q: What is your training regimen?

A: When it comes to training I am a pretty simple guy. When something works for me, I won't change it. I personally don't believe in training six or seven hours per day; it's too much for your body. To be honest, as far as weight training goes I only do biceps and triceps exercises. The rest of the time I use my own body weight to develop power—such as push-ups and squats. I use weights more when I want to gain some weight. Generally, I do it three times a week as part of my power training.

My strength training is sport-specific. For example, I don't push a weight above my shoulders in training because I don't do that in the ring. I want to do exercises that are going to strengthen my fighting skills. Sometimes I gain a lot of strength and muscle mass very quickly, so I have to cut back my training. I don't feel comfortable carrying around too

much weight—it slows me down. For my legs, I don't do weight training at all, only running, biking, and kicking drills. On the technical side, four times a week I train grappling and three times a week I train punching and kicking. I also do a lot of heavy bag work on my own.

Diet and nutrition are very important aspects of a fighter. I believe in consistency so I don't change eating habits as I get close to a fight. This means that I always have to control what I eat. I have a real tendency to eat junk food! Also, if I consume dairy products such as milk or cheese, I cannot work out. I eat things like this only at night. I eat my last meal five hours before a fight and in the hours before the fight I only drink water. I don't use supplements at all.

Q: How do you approach cardiovascular conditioning and flexibility?
A: Cardiovascular conditioning is the most important aspect in a fighter's routine. If your cardio is not good, it's like a car without gas—it's that simple. It doesn't matter if you have all the techniques in the world, if you don't have air then you're out of business. A good fighter needs to know that he will be able to go the distance with full power. I like to work my cardio into my punching and kicking training. What I do the most of the time is combine grappling with a partner for two minutes and then kick the bag for one minute. Then, I repeat this routine

"It doesn't matter if you have all the techniques in the world, if you don't have air then you're out of business. A good fighter needs to know that he will be able to go the distance with full power. I like to work my cardio into my punching and kicking training."

for eight rounds. My partner rests as I kick the bag, so when I go back he's fresh and I am more tired. It takes a lot out of me. As far as flexibility goes, I stretch the whole body. When you are young you don't need it as much as when you get older!

Q: Would you explain the training system that you have developed?
A: This is not something that I am trying to sell for somebody else—I really trained on this program for the last five years. Every fighter that came to train with me loved it and asked me for a copy—fighters like Peter Aerts,

"Don't do something just because somebody says so. See if you can find out if it's good and then use it. People are sometimes like a flock of sheep—if one person does it then everybody does it!"

Marco Ruas, Pedro Rizzo, Ian Freeman, Duane Ludwig, Amir Rahnavardi, Mark Kerr, et cetera. It started out as a warm up routine, because I really didn't like skipping rope. So I put my own voice on a tape telling me what to do. I liked it so much that after a short time I started to rewind the tape and do it over and over again and made a workout out of it. The first tapes were an all-around fighting tape and a boxing tape with very simple instructions. The tapes that I made for the workout are way better then the ones I used to train on, plus I made more workouts. The *Bas Rutten Mixed Martial Arts Workout* is a box that contains four audiocassettes, an instructional booklet, and a videocassette that explains how to do the exercises. I also put highlights of my fighting career on it as a little bonus. It is easy to understand for everybody but you have to be right handed! The four tapes are boxing, Thai boxing, all-around fighting, and an all-round workout. The best thing about them is that you can do them anywhere, as long as you have a tape player. If I don't have time to go to a gym, I do it right in my backyard. The last four times I went to Japan to do the commentary for Pride, I did the workout in my hotel room to stay in shape. You can do it all by yourself as a shadow-boxing routine, in the gym on the bag, or with a partner using focus mitts or Thai pads. The tapes will improve your stamina and power, your speed, your reflexes, your coordination between hearing and executing, and will enable you to throw out combinations like you never did before. My students are training on it and I see vast improvements in their fighting abilities. They are throwing combinations now, that they never did before. I can't tell you they make you a good fighter because they won't—you need to spar with partners for that. But besides sparring, they will do everything for you. Try them out and I am sure that you will use them a lot.

Q: Where did you learn your grappling skills?

A: In the very beginning I basically learned from watching tapes. When I decided to focus on grappling I got together with a good friend of mine, Leon van Dijk. We used to work out twice a day in grappling. It was during these sparring sessions that we found a lot of useful movements and techniques. Sometimes a person may know a lot of techniques but these won't all work in a real situation. I know all the techniques I use in practice work in a match. It is better to know fewer techniques that actually work than many techniques which are useless. Every move I make works—either in the ring or in the street. I train very hard so the fight will be easy.

Q: What is the most important aspect for a fighter to have?

A: Mental flexibility—keep your mind open to everything. Don't do something just because somebody says so. See if you can find out if it's good and then use it. People are sometimes like a flock of sheep—if one person does it then everybody does it! Just because somebody wrote something down or put it on a video doesn't make it right.

"If you train, do it 100 percent. Don't train, come home, and then not think about it anymore. Lock it up in your mind; go over it again and again. If you really want to learn how to fight, then think about fighting night and day. Almost every day that you train, you learn something new if you keep your mind open."

In the past, an instructor of mine would tell me to do something a certain way because the master who invented it had a fifth degree black belt. So what? If he never tried it in a real fight then I'm not interested in learning it. I'm also very skeptical about claims that because a street fighter has 1,000 wins,

his technique must be good. So what? I can make a record of 50-0 in one night in a bar if I want. People on the street are not trained fighters, so that also is a dumb comment. You have to try a technique for yourself and see if it works for you.

If you train, do it 100 percent. Don't train, come home, and then not think about it anymore. Lock it up in your mind; go over it again and again. If you really want to learn how to fight, then think about fighting night and day. When I was competing, I used to write down things that popped up in my head. There were many times that I woke up at night, woke up my wife, and then submitted her with some technique that I just made up in my sleep. I would ask her if it hurt, and if she said yes I would write it down and try to use it the next day in training. Almost every day that you train, you learn something new if you keep your mind open. If you're never out-learned, you'll never be out-fought.

"When I was competing I stayed motivated because I wanted to be the best and I hated to lose. That is the only good motivation. My advice is to stay open-minded, load everything up in your mind that you see in other fights, and then use it in training."

Q: How should someone new approach training?

A: I would tell him to take submission fighting or jiu-jitsu classes, take boxing classes, and take wrestling classes—do all three together. Then later on go to a good shootfighting school and learn how to kick. Punching, ground fighting, and taking somebody down or defending a takedown is the most important combination of skills. I wished that we had wrestling schools in Holland and that I had learned that with the rest of my martial arts.

When I was competing I stayed motivated because I wanted to be the best and I hated to lose. That is the only good motivation. My advice is to stay open-minded, load everything up in your mind that you see in other fights, and then use it in training. Only then can you decide if you want to keep using it or if it is useless for you. Don't do something just because you read it, saw it on a video, or somebody told you. Find out if it really works first. This is important for any person who wants to train in martial arts. The rest is just to maintain consistent eating habits and train as hard as you can.

Q: What is the future of NHB?
A: I think it is on the right track. In the United States, I think fighters should be allowed to kick their opponent when he is down; they also need to do something about a stand-up rule. Right now in the UFC there is no stand-up rule because of the round system, but I think that they should stand the fighters up if nothing happens on the floor. If the fighter on top does nothing to improve his position or to win the fight they should put the fighters on their feet again. Also, forget about the one-inch punches from the guard—those will never

"Everything changes and uses new ideas to improve—human languages add news words, cars get more horsepower, tennis players hit harder, and runners move faster. The same thing is true with martial arts. We now all think that mixed martial arts is the best way to fight—but that could change too."

bring a KO. So if that is the only thing a fighter does then stand them up! People don't want to see two guys just laying on each other for 15 minutes. Without fans, the sport of no-holds-barred fighting will die. ↻

Masters Techniques

Bas Rutten is attacking from his opponent's right side (1). Bas slides his left arm under his opponent's neck (2), and grabs his left arm (3), leaving room to place his left arm next to his opponent's head (4). Supporting himself with both arms (5), Bas moves his left leg around (6), places it next to his own left arm (7), grabs his opponent's head (8), and applies pressure for the finishing neck crank.

*Bas Rutten is trapped from behind by an opponent who has both hooks in (1).
As soon as Bas feels his opponent move his right arm to apply the rear choke (2),
he grabs the right wrist with his left arm (3), then hooks his right arm and grabs
his own neck at the same time, pushing towards the right and executing a painful
arm-lock (4).*

Bas Rutten's opponent falls backwards and tries go for a leg lock (1). But to get it, he has to hold his right leg (2). With his elbow, Bas pushes to the left (3), then guides his opponent's leg all the way down, opening his right thigh to create space (4). Holding the leg down, Bas now grabs his heel, making sure that he has leverage so his thigh is catching his toes and his hand is grabbing his heel (5). Bas lets gravity do the work and holds his heel with his two hands and drops backwards to the submission (6, close-up).

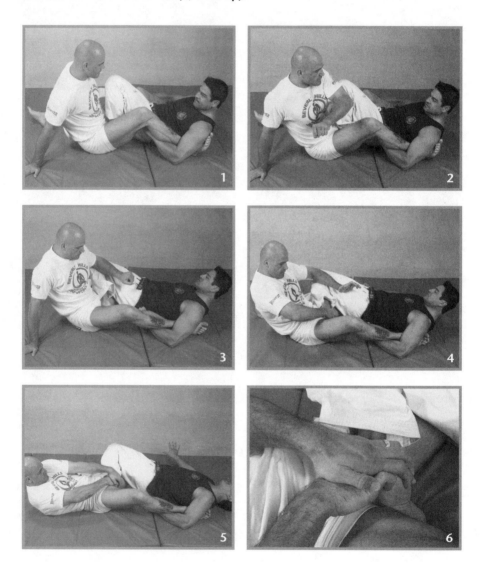

Bas Rutten holds his opponent's triceps with the left hand and also makes sure that his right hand grabs the back of his own knee (1). Bas grabs his opponent's right leg with his left hand (2), then grabs all the way up his own leg, just underneath the knee (3). Bas finishes by pushing his knees together and holding his opponent (4).

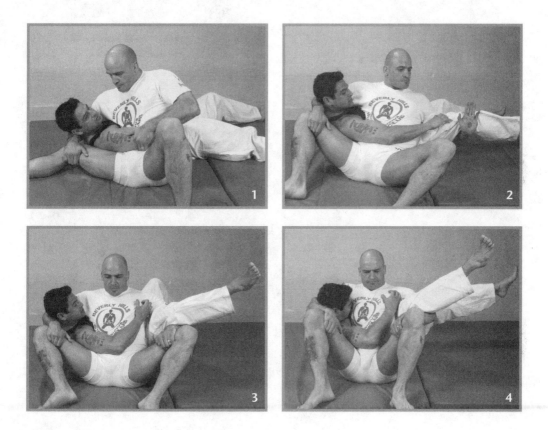

Carlos "Caique" Elias

The Possible Dream

RELATIVELY LITTLE HAS BEEN WRITTEN ABOUT THIS MAN KNOWN SIMPLY AS "CAIQUE"—BUT ANYONE WHO SPENDS ANY AMOUNT OF TIME RESEARCHING THE GRAPPLING ARTS KNOWS THAT HE IS ONE OF THE TOP BRAZILIAN JIU-JITSU INSTRUCTORS IN THE UNITED STATES.

A DIRECT STUDENT OF RELSON AND RICKSON GRACIE, CARLOS "CAIQUE" ELIAS' EXPERTISE AND KNOWLEDGE OF THE TECHNICAL ASPECTS OF JIU-JITSU ARE SECOND TO NONE. MANY YEARS OF HARD TRAINING AND COMPETITION AGAINST THE WORLD'S ELITE HAVE PROVIDED HIM WITH AN IMMENSE UNDERSTANDING OF THE COMPLETE GROUND GAME. WHEN HE MOVES, IT IS WITH PRECISION AND DIRECTION; ALL HIS ENERGY FOCUSED TOWARD THE END RESULT—TO SUBMIT HIS OPPONENT USING THE "GENTLE" PERSUASION OF JIU-JITSU.

BUT JIU-JITSU, TO CAIQUE, ISN'T ALL ABOUT CHOKES AND LOCKS; IT IS ABOUT RELATIONSHIPS, FRIENDSHIPS AND STRONG BONDS WITH HIS STUDENTS. OUT OF ALL THE MARTIAL ARTS INSTRUCTORS IN NORTH AMERICA, CAIQUE IS ONE OF THE MOST REVERED AND RESPECTED BY THOSE HE TEACHES. HOLDING NOTHING BACK, CAIQUE HAS NO "HIDDEN" OR "SECRET" TECHNIQUES—WHEN A STUDENT IS READY TO LEARN, HE TEACHES. AND THIS TEACHING EXTENDS TO LIFE AS WELL AS TO THE DEVASTATING ART OF JIU-JITSU. CURRENTLY LIVING AND TEACHING IN SOUTHERN CALIFORNIA, CAIQUE TEACHES HIS STUDENTS WITH THE SAME PATIENCE AND DEDICATION THAT HE USED TO BECOME A CHAMPION IN HIS NATIVE BRAZIL.

"THE KEY," SAYS CAIQUE, "IS TO BALANCE EVERY SINGLE ELEMENT IN YOUR TRAINING SO THAT ONE ASPECT WILL HELP THE OTHERS. YOU DON'T WANT TO BE UNBALANCED IN JIU-JITSU. REMEMBER THAT THE SECRET IS BALANCE, NOT ONLY IN MARTIAL ARTS BUT IN LIFE AS WELL. TO BE SUCCESSFUL YOU HAVE TO HAVE GOALS AND WORK IN THAT DIRECTION. YOU HAVE TO TRAIN HARD AND SMART—OTHERWISE EVERYTHING YOU WANT WILL JUST BE A DREAM. A GOAL IS AN IMPOSSIBLE DREAM IF YOU DON'T TAKE THE NECESSARY STEPS TO MAKE IT HAPPEN."

Q: How did you begin your martial arts training?
A: I began my training in judo. My teacher taught the art in a very street-fighting oriented format. It was not sport judo but a self-defense

"One of the most important things that you take with you in the martial arts journey is the atmosphere of the places where you train. In the long run, the techniques are important, but the environment and the memories of the other students stay with you forever."

approach. He really emphasized the street element. Then I started jiu-jitsu with Relson Gracie and also trained extensively with Rickson Gracie. They are the two people I should mention here. They not only gave me an extensive amount of technical knowledge but also spent a lot of time educating me in the different aspects of jiu-jitsu. The training was tough. It was not as easy as these days but I remember the atmosphere. One of the most important things that you take with you in the martial arts journey is the atmosphere of the places where you train. In the long run, the techniques are important, but the environment and the memories of the other students stay with you forever. I have many memories that have stayed with me. I remember once, a very famous black belt came to the school and he sparred with me—I was a purple belt at that time. He literally ran over me; it wasn't him making me tap, not at all, he ran over me. Helio Gracie was there and in the end he called Rickson. Rickson talked to his father and said, "This is the last time he does that to you. From now on you are going to make him tap every single time." Under his tutelage I made that guy tap every single time after that night. I became one of Rickson's top students for many years.

Q: Is it important to specialize in a few techniques or have a wide repertoire?
A: Everything boils down to what you are looking for in your martial arts training. If you decide to compete then you need to have a wide understanding of many techniques, although not necessarily to use them all.

You need to know them and understand the way they work so you can counter them with your specialties— that is the key. You may have five or six special moves, but it doesn't mean these five or six techniques are the only thing you know. However, you must know many different ways of using your special moves or pretty soon all your opponents will know how to stop you before you even think about trying. You need to have a variety of ways to apply your submission techniques and keep your opponent guessing what's going to be next. You must have a complete game and develop an under-

"You need to have a variety of ways to apply your submission techniques and keep your opponent guessing what's going to be next. You must have a complete game and develop an understanding of the advantageous positions and how to get into them."

standing of the advantageous positions and how to get into them— because regardless of the instructor's approach, the principles and concepts involved in maintaining and escaping from each of the main positions are universal.

Q: Why do you think people are attracted to jiu-jitsu?
A: It is very interesting to see how the interest of the so-called "gentle" art has emerged. I think that we can look at this from two different points of view. First, jiu-jitsu has always been a self-defense system, not a sport. As a self-defense method the practitioner has to rely on those techniques that do not require a lot of strength and physical power to be effective. The overall idea is to allow the student to train as hard as possible without getting injured, while still maintaining the effectiveness necessary to defend himself on the street. But that's not the reason why people today are training in Brazilian jiu-jitsu. People today are interested in jiu-jitsu because of the UFC and the need to complete their martial arts training with knowledge about how to deal with aggression on the ground. That's the main reason.

"Today jiu-jitsu is both a self-defense art and a sport. Brazilian jiu-jitsu meets both those requirements. It is not a martial arts system that hides behind a veil of mysticism, but instead deals with the realities of combat with no exaggerated claims."

Today jiu-jitsu is both a self-defense art and a sport. Brazilian jiu-jitsu meets both those requirements. It is not a martial arts system that hides behind a veil of mysticism, but instead deals with the realities of combat with no exaggerated claims. A lot of martial artist from other styles realized that their arts were lacking ground strategies and techniques that could be very valuable in a real situation. Therefore, they came to Brazilian jiu-jitsu to get this knowledge. I think is great when people have no fear in learning something that is valuable and can make them better.

Q: How does jiu-jitsu apply to a no-holds-barred fight?
A: NHB is a completely different game than a real fight. In an NHB fight, weight counts for a lot and the environment is totally different. NHB is a sport and not a real fight—you use different kinds of techniques because of the nature of the sport and concern for the safety for the fighters. It's about winning a trophy and not about self-defense. You have to train specifically for that because the individual in front of you knows how to fight, how to counter your movements, and how to create an opening to apply his techniques. This creates a completely different situation. You have to prepare for this kind of event in a very specific way.

Q: How different from NHB is sport jiu-jitsu?
A: It's important to understand that the main self-defense methods are very dangerous. This is not only applies to jiu-jitsu but to other arts such

as karate or kung-fu. People do not always get involved in martial arts because of self-defense. Even if self-defense was the main reason for them to initially train, one day they will enjoy doing it just for the fun and satisfaction, and not because of the self-preservation aspect. Then the sport element becomes more relevant. People like to train and compete in a more relaxed atmosphere than is encountered in a real streetfight. The simple fact that the training makes them feel at peace with themselves is what really counts at the end of the day. Historically speaking, the original self-defense techniques of jiu-jitsu were extremely dangerous and could not be executed during normal training sessions. So in times of peace the sport aspects took over from the self-defense methods needed during times of war.

"People do not always get involved in martial arts because of self-defense. Even if self-defense was the main reason for them to initially train, one day they will enjoy just doing it just for the fun and satisfaction, and not because of the self-preservation aspect."

Q: How effective, then, is modern Brazilian jiu-jitsu for self-defense?
A: For self-defense purposes you have to evaluate what is really happening in a streetfight, and then choose the style or method that will deal with the circumstances. Jiu-jitsu is expressed in the way the techniques are executed, not in the effect these techniques have upon the opponent. You may decide to control the aggressor by neutralizing him, or you might decide to take it a step further and immobilize him, or even put him into submission hold. It's up to you decide the degree of pain you'll inflict on the opponent. For instance, you can throw your opponent to

"My opinion is that mixing styles confuses the student and puts them in a very difficult situation if they face a real self-defense situation."

the ground and he will be hurt. Or you can decide to control the throw and immobilize him with an arm lock on the floor after the throw has been applied. You may even decide to apply more pressure and break the arm. There are different degrees of execution. In contrast to jiu-jitsu, if you strike to your opponent's body—such as a kick to the groin—that's going to hurt regardless of the power behind the technique. If you attack the eyes, it will hurt the same whether it is done soft or hard. It's almost impossible to calculate the damage with punches and kicks, especially under the stress of a real fight. And legally you can be accountable for that. I have seen a lot of people mixing different styles of martial arts— but that is very difficult. It is one thing to take elements from other methods to make what you are already doing better, and it is another thing to mix styles thinking that you are going to become better. My opinion is that mixing styles confuses the student and puts them in a very difficult situation if they face a real self-defense situation.

Q: Why are there so many similarities between Japanese judo and Brazilian jiu-jitsu?
A: Just do a little research into the history of both arts and you'll find out. Nobody can deny the historical facts. Judo is a direct descendent of the traditional Japanese jiu-jitsu systems, so there are bound to be some similarities. Personally, I believe the changes that Jigoro Kano made to jiu-jitsu, when he turned it into judo, left judo with only a surface similarity to the original art. Judo became a sport and its inclusion into the Olympic Games definitely pushed the art in a new direction. Today judo is not Japanese anymore, but belongs to the world. Soccer, for example, was

created by the British but today is an international sport. We don't call it "British soccer," but simply "soccer."

Today, "Brazilian jiu-jitsu" is the term used to describe a certain style of jiu-jitsu that is not Japanese—and I think this is good because not all the jiu-jitsu styles are the same. Like in karate, you have different styles such as shito-ryu, shotokan, goju-ryu, and more. So it's important to know what kind of karate or jiu-jitsu you are practicing. It's like being knowledgeable about your family tree—you'd better know what your last name is.

"Today, 'Brazilian jiu-jitsu' is the term used to describe a certain style of jiu-jitsu that is not Japanese—and I think this is good because not all the jiu-jitsu styles are the same. It's like being knowledgeable about your family tree—you'd better know what your last name is."

Q: Do you think the rules used in sport competition condition the way the instructors teach Brazilian jiu-jitsu?
A: I would like to say no, but the truth is that due to the emphasis on sport competition, the real answer is yes. For instance, if you know that a certain technique only gives you one point and another will score three, it's logical that you'll place more emphasis on those techniques that will result in a bigger amount of points. That's the game and you have to play it. As an instructor, though, I recommend training in every single aspect equally. Keep balance in your training. As a competitor, there is nothing wrong with focusing on a few chosen techniques as long as you know how to switch and react under other circumstances with the appropriate technique. By that, I mean that if you have to protect yourself in a real encounter don't try to use the techniques that you use in a competition—they may not work and might put you in a very difficult situation. There is nothing wrong with the sport aspect of jiu-jitsu; just keep in mind that it is only a sport and not a real self-defense situation. If you do that, you'll be perfectly fine.

"Competition is what raises the level of any sport—be it basketball, jiu-jitsu, karate, or football. The need to get better and improve is what makes athletes look for new techniques and approaches. This raises the bar of any sportive activity."

Q: Do you think it is important to continually evolve jiu-jitsu techniques?

A: I think evolution is important in everything in life, not only in jiu-jitsu. If you only train a little bit for self-defense then there are hundreds of movements that you don't need to know—basically because you only need a very direct and simple approach for self-protection. But if you are training and competing in sport jiu-jitsu, that's another story. Competition is what raises the level of any sport—be it basketball, jiu-jitsu, karate, or football. The need to get better and improve is what makes athletes look for new techniques and approaches. This raises the bar of any sportive activity. NBA basketball is not the same as it was 20 years ago, and it will definitely be different 20 years from now. The same is true with jiu-jitsu; if you win a world champion and don't compete for three or four years you can bet that you won't win. Why? Because the evolution of the sport has created a totally new environment, and the techniques that were current years ago will be obsolete now. All Brazilian jiu-jitsu practitioners are developing new techniques all the time, and if you are not aware of this then you won't be winning. It's that simple. If your main goal is just to protect yourself, then develop a very strong base with the fundamental techniques and don't go crazy trying to learn 1,000 different techniques. Stick to the basics because is out of the basic techniques that any new maneuver will come.

Q: So for self-defense, simpler is better?

A: Yes. I see many practitioners who spend a great amount of time and energy trying to learn the latest techniques developed by the top fighters and don't pay attention to the basics. The only reason why these top fighters can pull off these new moves is because of the great technical foundation they have already. Every practitioner needs to evaluate their training and know where they are going and what they really need to work on. There are many important elements that a practitioner has to develop before they get into a more complex technical approach.

"Every practitioner needs to evaluate their training and know where they are going and what they really need to work on. There are many important elements that a practitioner has to develop before they get into a more complex technical approach."

Q: What are the most important basic elements of jiu-jitsu?

A: There are many: body position, leverage, body feel, the ability to read the opponent's intent at the very early stages of the physical movement, breath control while executing the technique, and more. All these elements are basics you need to have before taking your game to a higher level. If you are not aware of these things, and you try to play the advanced games, then you are just wasting your time. Sorry to say that, but that's the truth. Unfortunately, there are many practitioners these days who pay too much attention to the advanced techniques when they should be working on the basics.

Q: What kind of supplementary physical training do you recommend?

A: Jiu-jitsu is jiu-jitsu. What I mean by that is that if you have a limited amount of time to train, then put as much time as you can into developing your technique. Forget about anything else. Jiu-jitsu should be your

"Try to strike a balance between muscle mass and the flexibility needed to perform jiu-jitsu techniques. For a martial artist, a supple body is more important than a bodybuilder physique. Try to stretch every day."

main goal. Then after you have reached a certain level of technical skill you can do some other activities to supplement your jiu-jitsu. I recommend running, swimming, yoga and some kind of resistance and strength training. If you get involved in weight training just do it as a supplementary activity and don't make the mistake of developing huge muscles. The more muscle you have, the more limited your joint range-of-motion is. Try to strike a balance between muscle mass and the flexibility needed to perform jiu-jitsu techniques. For a martial artist, a supple body is more important than a bodybuilder physique. Try to stretch every day. The key is to balance every single element in your training so that one aspect will help the others. You don't want to be unbalanced in jiu-jitsu. Remember that the secret is balance, not only in martial arts but in life as well. To be successful you have to have goals and work in that direction. You have to train hard and smart—otherwise everything you want will just be a dream. A goal is an impossible dream if you don't take the necessary steps to make it happen.

Q: Is any style better than the rest?
A: The truth is that if you are happy practicing a particular style, then that is the best style for you. Period. We should respect the fact that people train martial arts for different reasons and in the end it is the person who makes the style work. Respect for other styles is very important—even if you don't agree with their approach to combat you should respect them and not criticize them. Without respect there is nothing. Respect is a problem we all face in our lives. Instructors of all styles and systems should strive to preserve the ethics and traditions that the martial arts were based on.

Q: Is there anything today's martial arts lack?
A: I would like to see more respect between practitioners. In the Japanese arts you have the "*do*" element which his brings philosophy, ethics,

morality, and honesty into the practitioner's life. In Brazilian jiu-jitsu we don't have that aspect. Unfortunately, people just stick to the physical training and forget all the other important elements such as respect, courtesy, and proper attitude. Whether you win or lose, you have to control your emotions and act in a decent way. You don't have to bow, but it doesn't mean you shouldn't respect your opponent or that you don't have to graciously acknowledge his superiority if you lose. Behave yourself in a proper way at all times, regardless of the situation. I think that all the practitioners of the more combat-oriented systems should look deep into the philosophy of the more classical martial arts and adopt

"Martial arts is not only about winning a championship or beating someone up, but rather about making friends and developing good relationships with everybody. That's the real meaning of the martial arts."

their moral aspects. These elements will only make us a more well-rounded individuals. The "art" within the martial arts means the ability to practice self-control and to think within yourself. No matter how difficult a situation is, or how bad it may appear to be, you have the power to control yourself. Martial arts is not only about winning a championship or beating someone up, but rather about making friends and developing good relationships with everybody. That's the real meaning of the martial arts.

Q: What do you think is necessary to take Brazilian jiu-jitsu to the next level?
A: I believe we need to be more organized. We need to get together because the number of practitioners is very large, but for some reason we are all divided. It would be great to see a unity between European, American, Japanese and Brazilian organizations. That unity would change the direction of the sport. I guess it is very difficult, but if we really want to take the sport to the next level, that's the only way it will occur. I hope it will happen someday because it would be great for everybody in the art. ↻

Masters Techniques

Carlos "Caique" Elias is trapped in a guillotine choke (1). Caique grabs his opponent's back to relieve the pressure on his neck (2), steps to the side to get a better attack angle (3), forces his opponent backwards (4), and then takes him to the ground in side control (5). Freeing his head by applying pressure to his opponent's neck (6), Caique traps the wrist (7), and applies the Americana submission (8).

Caught in a foot-lock, Carlos "Caique" Elias hooks his opponent's knee with his leg (1), then throws him to the ground (2). Grabbing his opponent's arm to relieve the pressure on his ankle (3), Caique then stands up (4), and puts his weight on his trapped foot to break the lock (5). Sliding his foot backwards, Caique then takes the mount (6), traps the wrist (7), and applies the mounted Americana lock (8).

Carlos Gracie Jr.

Heir to the Throne

CARLOS GRACIE JR. IS THE PRESIDENT OF THE CONFEDERATION OF BRAZILIAN JIU-JITSU, AND IS THE PRIME MOVER BEHIND THE GROWING WORLDWIDE MOVEMENT TO ORGANIZE OF THE ART.

FOR DECADES, PEOPLE FROM ALL AROUND THE WORLD HAVE BEEN ENCHANTED WITH BRAZIL—A LAND FAMOUS FOR BEAUTIFUL BEACHES, THE STRING BIKINI, AND UNCONTROLABLE PASSION FOR "FUTEBOL" (SOCCER). BUT THOSE THINGS ARE ALL SECONDARY TO THE WORLD'S MARTIAL ARTISTS—THEY NOW TRAVEL TO BRAZIL TO TRAIN IN THE METHOD OF FIGHTING AND SELF-DEFENSE CREATED BY CARLOS GRACIE, KNOWN THROUGHOUT THE WORLD AS BRAZILIAN JIU-JITSU. AND WHO BETTER TO LEARN FROM THAN THE SON OF THE FOUNDER?

CARLOS GRACIE JR., KNOWN TO ALL IN THE JIU-JITSU WORLD AS "CARLINHOS," IS A WORTHY NAMESAKE OF THE MAN WHO STARTED IT ALL. HE CONDUCTS HIMSELF THE SAME WAY THAT HE PERFORMS THE TECHNIQUES DEVELOPED BY HIS FATHER—WITH FLEXIBILITY AND ADAPTABILITY, ALWAYS HAVING A FIRM GOAL IN MIND. A RELAXED AND THOUGHTFUL MAN WHO ALWAYS ORGANIZES HIS THOUGHTS BEFORE SPEAKING, CARLOS GRACIE JR. LIVES IN A VERY HECTIC WORLD AND APPRECIATES THE INFREQUENT "QUIET TIME" HE GETS.

"BECAUSE OF MY DUTIES IN THE CONFEDERATION, I HAVE A VERY FAST-PACED LIFE," CARLINHOS ADMITS, "BUT TO CREATE AND DEVELOP NEW AND IMPORTANT THINGS YOU NEED ISOLATION TO CALM YOUR MIND DOWN. AFTER ALL, THE MIND IS LIKE A LAKE, YOU CAN ONLY SEE THE BEAUTY OF THE LAKE IF IT IS CALM. GOOD IDEAS ONLY COME WHEN YOUR MIND IS RELAXED. ONLY THEN CAN YOU FIND THOSE THREE OR FOUR THINGS THAT WILL REALLY CHANGE YOUR LIFE. BECAUSE AFTER ALL, THAT'S WHAT LIFE IS ALL ABOUT: THREE OR FOUR DEFINING MOMENTS THAT WILL CHANGE EVERYTHING FOREVER."

Q: How did you get started in jiu-jitsu?
A; Jiu-jitsu training was a very natural thing at my home. Practicing jiu-jitsu was like eating, brushing my teeth, or sleeping. No more, no less— something natural and logical to be done on a daily basis. I didn't have a true appreciation of what the art was all about until I was around 14 or 15 years old. That's when I became more interested in technical develop-

"When you are a child you do what you're told without really understanding why—like going to school. But when I reached my teens my whole perception of jiu-jitsu changed. I became aware of the responsibility of carrying the Gracie name and of the many things expected of me."

ment, competition, and in improving my game.

Before that it was simply a physical activity and a chore, because I had no understanding or purpose. My father made sure I was training, but for me it just wasn't that important. When you are a child you do what you're told without really understanding why—like going to school. But when I reached my teens my whole perception of jiu-jitsu changed. I became aware of the responsibility of carrying the Gracie name and of the many things expected of me.

Q: How did your father, Carlos Gracie, come to learn jiu-jitsu?
A: The jiu-jitsu method my father learned was very Japanese in nature, but definitely not the modern Japanese jiu-jitsu you can see today. It was the old method that influenced the judo techniques later on. My father learned that method and modified certain aspects of what was taught to him; but it was his brother, my uncle Helio, who made great improvements in the defensive aspects of the art. The jiu-jitsu learned by my father had all the necessary attacking components. The offensive techniques were really strong and barely needed any improvement. The old jiu-jitsu was strong on attacking techniques, but weak on defense. Due to his physical limitations, Helio, who was very small and light in stature, came up with new ways of controlling the opponent and developed new strategies for the defensive aspects of jiu-jitsu. How to control a bigger and stronger opponent became the main point of the defensive maneuvers. This completely new defensive approach took the art to a higher level. Helio proved through all his vale tudo fights that the jiu-jitsu developed by the Gracie family had the tools

to control and defeat bigger opponents, wearing them down and putting them into submission. My father was much older than his younger brother Helio, so it was Helio who went out and fought against anyone who doubted the effectiveness of Brazilian jiu-jitsu.

Q: How did Helio defeat bigger and stronger opponents?
A: If you match two people with the same technical knowledge and training experience, and one of them is bigger than the other, for sure the bigger and heavier man will win. But if the bigger man does not know how to handle an opponent on the ground and the smaller man takes him down to the ground, the bigger man will lose because the weight difference that is so relevant when standing up will became nullified once they are on the ground. This is because there is no body weight to put behind punches

"Vale tudo was created by my father, Carlos Gracie. The only reason he did it was to prove to everybody that the art of the Gracie family was an effective system of fighting. At that time, the people's perception of hand-to-hand combat was two men standing. Ground fighting and grappling was something people didn't understand."

and kicks. Of course, if both men are knowledgeable in jiu-jitsu and they have the same technical level then weight will be a factor. That's the reason we have weight divisions in sport jiu-jitsu. Practitioners are athletes and they have extensive technical knowledge, so we do the right thing and put them in a fair competition environment. A small jiu-jitsu man will defeat a bigger opponent who doesn't have the same jiu-jitsu knowledge, but if the bigger man is also good at jiu-jitsu then that's another story.

Q: What was the reason for starting vale tudo fights?
A: Vale tudo was created by my father, Carlos Gracie. The only reason he did it was to prove to everybody that the art of the Gracie family was an effective system of fighting. At that time, the people's perception of hand-to-hand combat was two men standing. Ground fighting and grappling was something people didn't understand, let alone accept as an effective

"Jiu-jitsu practitioners don't need to fight anymore to prove that Brazilian jiu-jitsu is an effective self-defense and fighting method. Everybody knows it is. I remember my father sitting and telling me that once jiu-jitsu was accepted, there was no reason to keep doing challenges and vale tudo matches anymore. They did it for respect and recognition, not for money or fame."

fighting method. My father realized that the only way to prove jiu-jitsu was effective was to make vale tudo fights. That's the reason vale tudo was created. Once everybody in Brazil accepted what jiu-jitsu was about, it became unnecessary to keep challenging people. The point was proven. My uncle Helio did many of these fights and became a national hero in Brazil.

A similar thing happened here in the United States. Royce Gracie, through the UFC, proved to everybody that the jiu-jitsu method developed by the Gracie family was effective in no-hold-barred fights, and that having knowledge of grappling was not just advisable but necessary. After that point was proved and accepted by all martial artist in America, all vale tudo fighting afterwards became solely motivated by business factors. When my father created vale tudo he was not making money. When my uncle Helio was fighting bigger and stronger opponents it was not for money. The reason they put themselves on the line was more important than money to them—it was prestige and recognition of their art. Nowadays, vale tudo events around the world are just a good way for fighters to make money. It has became a show and a business—and the goal is different.

Jiu-jitsu practitioners don't need to fight anymore to prove that Brazilian jiu-jitsu is an effective self-defense and fighting method. Everybody knows it is. I remember my father sitting and telling me that once jiu-jitsu was accepted, there was no reason to keep doing challenges and vale tudo matches anymore. They did it for respect and recognition, not for money or fame.

Q: Is jiu-jitsu harder or easier to learn now than in the old days?
A: Methods of teaching and training have to be continually improved so students can learn as quickly and easily as possible. The beginning students should be patient and hang in there until they get good results,

otherwise they will not succeed in jiu-jitsu. If you quit early in your training, you are apt to be discouraged and developed a negative attitude towards yourself. Throughout your life, the tendency to give up prematurely will stifle the development of the self-confidence which comes from accomplishment. Anyone who undertakes jiu-jitsu training must be determined to stay, otherwise they will lose something very important—the opportunity to know themselves, their potential, and their personal abilities.

Q: Is there anything missing in Brazilian jiu-jitsu today?
A: Today Brazilian jiu-jitsu is well known and everybody is aware of how effective the fighting method is. But when I look at the technical state of the art I see something very important is missing. I see thousand of great athletes who are capable of showing hundreds of technical variations and modifications, but who lack maturity in the basic and fundamental movements of jiu-jitsu. For instance, in the past we had ten different "raspadas" (sweeps), and now there are 100 modifications because the sport has greatly evolved during the last two decades.

I see champions who are able to display a great amount of technique, but who lack high technical skill and understanding of the basics. In the basic techniques, you have the necessary tools that will open doors for a more evolved technical game. But if you spend less and less time on the basics because you need to catch up on all the new modifications, you'll end up with many weak positions and few strong ones. You'll be able to perform your personal specialties very well—maybe four or five movements, but you'll lack the necessary basic structure to improve and grow in the art as you get older. This is simply because you don't have the right knowledge of the foundations of the art.

My advice to students is to spend more time on the basic techniques instead of diversifying your training into an endless number of techniques that will bring you momentary recognition. You'll be able to display more techniques than other practitioners of your same rank, but the consequence after years of training will be that you become incapable of developing a more mature and stronger jiu-jitsu game, simply because you never spent the necessary time developing the basics. No basics, no nothing. It's that simple.

Q: Has competition affected the way the art is evolving?
A: Competition has affected the way many practitioners train jiu-jitsu, and the perception of the outside world is that jiu-jitsu is simply competition

due to the way most instructors teach it. The sportive aspects are an important part of the whole art—a part where the best compete against the best and raise the technical level of the art. My advice to those who teach Brazilian jiu-jitsu, however, is that they should incorporate more classes for those people who are not athletes. There are many people out there who don't have the physical attributes of these athletes—people who are normal citizens, who go to work, have family lives and who would like to learn the art for fun and exercise. Teachers should incorporate more classes into their academies where the training is more relaxed and more natural—where the emphasis relies on learning proper basic techniques and the physical demands are not like those for people who are going to compete.

Jiu-jitsu has to be accessible to the regular individual, and progressively bring these people into a more demanding kind of training. The classes should be separated. You cannot have in the same people who will compete in the national championships, training with people who simply want to learn jiu-jitsu for personal fun and enjoyment. I would like to see more classes where the true essence of jiu-jitsu is being taught. This is what will allow jiu-jitsu to attract the general public. Otherwise, the sport will die out and fewer and fewer students will come to train.

Competition classes and training for athletes who are going to compete should be addressed outside the normal classes. It is something specifically for those individual who spend a lot of time in jiu-jitsu. These people should be trained differently. Not everybody should receive competition training. Many people are not interested in competition, but they are interested in receiving the benefits that Brazilian jiu-jitsu can bring into their lives.

Q: What are the benefits?
A: Ultimately, the greatest benefit of all martial arts training, not only jiu-jitsu, is self-understanding. Many of the people training jiu-jitsu never try to understand their own condition or limitations. It is through jiu-jitsu training that they can get a clearer picture not only of their own physical abilities, but also of their mental limitations. They will find out by themselves what these are, what they are capable of accomplishing if they put their mind to it, and will want to continue their training. Jiu-jitsu training is very similar to life itself. To receive the most out of your training you have to be capable of seeing these similarities.

For instance, when you enter a jiu-jitsu school, everybody makes you tap. You lose to all the people who have been training there for years. It's normal; you don't know much and you are a beginner. After years of training, it happens that now you are the one making people tap. You are a black belt, and by having an extensive knowledge of the art you are capable of defeating other jiu-jitsu practitioners with less experience. Now you are on the top, but as the time goes by, new and younger athletes come up and you get older. Once again, you see how these newcomers are faster and stronger than you— you come full circle. If you don't accept this simple fact, you'll probably quit jiu-jitsu training all together and won't be capable of reaching the highest levels of the art.

Q: What is that higher level?

A: Once you find yourself in a position where you can't overcome an opponent because he is younger and stronger, that is when the real and authentic jiu-jitsu will come out. This usually only occurs when you can't rely on strength and power because you are not that young anymore. I often train with students of mine who are bigger and stronger than me. What I try to do is to find out how to neutralize their strength and physical power. I need to find

"I often train with students of mine who are bigger and stronger than me. What I try to do is to find out how to neutralize their strength and physical power. Only when you have a strong base, and deep understanding of the foundation of the art, can you use certain technical aspects that would be fatal if you didn't have that knowledge."

out by trial and error what amount of physical energy is necessary to keep the opponent in a position where he is vulnerable. I don't want to use more energy than necessary because he is younger and stronger, so I must conserve my energy and use it in the proper way. This concept involves a very deep understanding of the basic techniques of jiu-jitsu, because that understanding will show you the way to reach that higher level. Only when you have a strong base, and deep understanding of the foundation of the art, can you use certain technical aspects that would be fatal if you didn't have that knowledge.

"We need to organize the overall structure of the sport worldwide. This is what I, as the main individual responsible for the Brazilian Jiu-Jitsu Confederation, plan to do. First of all Brazil, and eventually all other countries, will have an official national team, much like in World Cup soccer. There will be only one national team per country. "

Q: Some people believe that weight divisions should not exist in Brazilian jiu-jitsu or vale tudo events. What is your opinion?

A: Let me put it this way. The effectiveness of the jiu-jitsu developed by my family is proven. Everybody knows and accepts that fact. Number one, there is no reason to do vale tudo for that purpose and if vale tudo events still exits is it because it is now a business. Number two, everybody who fights in vale tudo knows jiu-jitsu to some extent. They may punch and kick but they know Brazilian jiu-jitsu as well. If you put two skilled jiu-jitsu practitioners in a jiu-jitsu sport event, the heavier one will probably win because weight, when skill is equal, is definitely a factor. If the smaller fighter is better than the heavier one, then the smaller will win—but if they are technically the same, weight is an issue. Sport was developed to compare relative skills on a level playing field. This is the reason why there are weight classes in jiu-jitsu, boxing, karate, taekwondo, judo, et cetera. We do it to level the playing field. From a sportive point of view it is simply logical. It is a combat sport, not a real self-defense situation.

Q: What will it take for the sport of Brazilian jiu-jitsu to grow in the future?

A: We need to organize the overall structure of the sport worldwide. This is what I, as the main individual responsible for the Brazilian Jiu-Jitsu Confederation, plan to do. First of all Brazil, and eventually all other countries, will have an official national team, much like in World Cup soccer. In the World Cup, there is only one national Brazilian team. The members of each national team will be chosen by their competition records in city, state, regional, and national tournaments. This way, the corporate sponsors and government agencies who are not interested in spending big

amounts of money sponsoring private academies and schools, will be motivated to put up money for the national team.

This is the way other big international sports like basketball and *futebol* (soccer) have been successfully organized. Jiu-jitsu needs to do the same. Later on, every country will use the same format to come up with a national team of its own, and a World Brazilian Jiu-Jitsu Federation will control the sport to ensure fairness.

Q: Will this improve sponsorship involvement?
A: Absolutely, because there will be only one national team per country. The sponsors will put their money into that team and the members of the team. This way, the members of the team won't have to work eight or ten hours per day at their daily jobs and go to train at night to improve their jiu-jitsu. They will have money to become professionals so they can dedicate all their time to training and competition—similar to Olympic athletes. The members of the Olympic team do not work for four years; they simply train. The money for the Olympics comes from the various governments.

Q: Although you live in Rio de Janeiro, Brazil, you keep close contact with family members residing in the United States, particularly the Machado brothers. What do you think has made them so successful in spreading jiu-jitsu in America?
A: The Machado brothers came to the United States a long time ago, although other members of the Gracie family were already in the country. They have been together all these years and never stopped supporting each other. This simple fact reflects their attitude and personality and how reliable they are as individuals. They were well trained and achieved exceptional recognition as competitors in Brazil. Once they moved to America they kept training, teaching, and competing—and succeeded in all these areas. It is very difficult to teach and compete at the same time. Their students are among the best in the country and nobody can deny their teaching ability and their friendly and accessible personalities. It's no wonder that the top American martial artists and movie stars have come to them for instruction in Brazilian jiu-jitsu.

Q: You have recently started a terrific international program, offering interested practitioners worldwide the chance to compete in something called "Gracie Camp." What exactly is that?

A: The idea of the Gracie Camp came because I was receiving a large amount of solicitations from foreign students wanting to train at my school, Gracie Barra, in Rio de Janeiro. People would come from around the world and stay in hotels way too far from the school, and from the nice beaches and the fun and safe Rio areas. Gracie Camp is not only about learning jiu-jitsu, but also about enjoying and experiencing an entire Brazilian adventure. This encompasses jiu-jitsu training, good restaurants, nice beaches, and a lot of fun. Many people were coming to Rio de Janeiro for training but because they didn't know the city, the transportation and the society, they ended up expending huge amounts of money, staying in hotels at very bad locations, and spending a lot of money and time on transportation and basically having a real nightmare there. My idea was to offer these dedicated practitioners and students, of any skill level from white belt to black belt, a safe opportunity to enjoy jiu-jitsu and the Brazilian culture and lifestyle, with us taking care of them. We pick them up at the airport, take them to hotels located very close to the Gracie Barra Academy, and within walking distance of the famous beaches, nice restaurants, and nightclubs where they can have a great time.

The technical level of the classes is designed to fit any practitioner's skill level. If you are a blue belt you'll have a training program specifically for your rank, plus a lot of additional techniques and training that will increase your skill. The same applies for purple, brown and black belt. There is special training for every person and every rank. Nobody is going to force you to train eight hours a day. If you want to go to the beach in the morning, train in the afternoon, and have fun at night, you'll be able to do it. If you want to train all day long, skip the visit to the beach, and then party at night, you'll be able to do that too. You're the boss of your time.

Knowing how to safely find your way around without problems, especially in a developing country like Brazil, can be tough. So everyone can enjoy all the facilities and personal help we provide at the Gracie Camp.

Q: What is the essence of Brazilian jiu-jitsu?

A: Brazilian jiu-jitsu has a good reputation as a combat method. We don't need to do crazy things to prove that anymore, because everybody knows it. All instructors should try to teach the art in the right way, emphasizing the basics and fundamentals that will allow the practitioner to evolve in their future years. They should also keep in mind that the way they behave outside the school will affect the public perception not only of jiu-jitsu, but also of our reputation as martial artists in general. We should all keep in mind that giving is a way of receiving. Once you have gained skill and a position of responsibility, it is your obligation to help others to grow. Blue belts should help white belts, purples should help blues, and brown and blacks should help everyone.

"All instructors should try to teach the art in the right way, emphasizing the basics and fundamentals that will allow the practitioner to evolve in their future years. We should all keep in mind that giving is a way of receiving. Blue belts should help white belts, purples should help blues, and brown and blacks should help everyone."

As president of the Brazilian Confederation of Jiu-Jitsu, it is my responsibility to help younger competitors find their way, and to make things easier for them to succeed in the sport. This involves working for the good of others, not only for myself. In the big picture of jiu-jitsu, we all share that responsibility. We need to put our own selfish interests aside and do things for the benefit of others and for the benefit of the sport. That's what a good leader does—care for others and do things so others can benefit. We are all the leaders of our own lives, so we should all do this. This is the how the sport of jiu-jitsu, with all of us working together, can leave a mark in history. This is the true way of Brazilian jiu-jitsu. ☽

Carlos Gracie Jr. works against his opponent's open guard (1). Throwing his opponent's legs to the side (2), Carlos Jr. puts his knee on the stomach and under-hooks the arm (3). Pulling the arm up to control it, Carlos Jr. spins around (4), then falls to the ground and extends the arm for the submission (5).

Carlos Gracie Jr. is trapped inside his opponent's open guard (1). Throwing his opponent's leg down and moving to the side (2), Carlos Jr. prepares to pass (3). When his opponent defends the pass (4), Carlos Jr. secures the ankle and then lays back and applies pressure for the painful submission (5).

Masters Techniques

Carlos Gracie Jr. works against his opponent's open guard (1). Supporting himself with one hand on his opponent's belt, and the other hand on the collar (2), Carlos Jr. jumps to the side (3), where he lands and controls his opponent's actions (4). He then grabs the right arm (5), and applies a bent arm-lock (6).

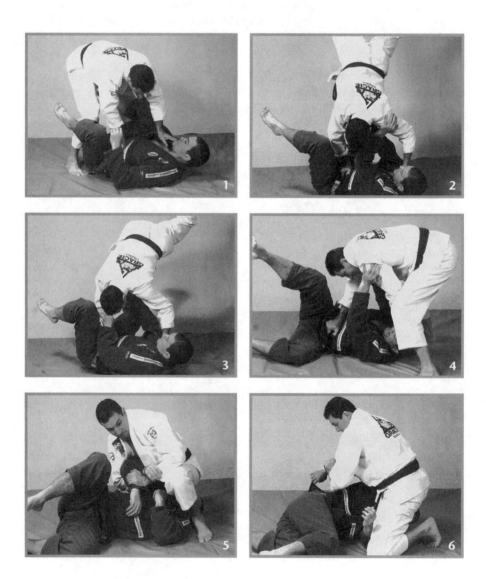

Carlos Gracie Jr. is attacking from his opponent's back (1). Grabbing the gi under the armpits (2), Carlos Jr. pulls to bring the opponent's body up and create space (3). He then inserts both of his legs (4), applies the hooks (5), and finishes with a rear choke (6).

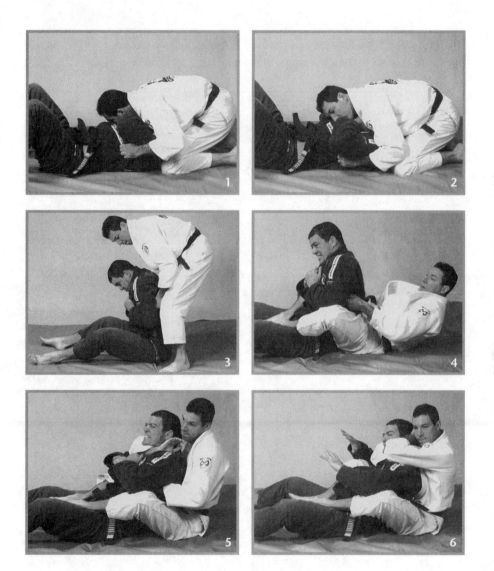

Erik Paulson

The Real Deal

ERIK PAULSON GAINED WORLDWIDE RECOGNITION WHEN HE COMPETED IN THE INTERNATIONAL "WORLD COMBAT CHAMPIONSHIPS" WHERE HE REFUSED TO CUT HIS HAIR FOR THE SEMIFINAL MATCH AGAINST JAMES WARRING. HIS OPPONENT GRABBED HIS HAIR, PREVENTING HIM FROM APPLYING HIS BEST TECHNIQUES. HE LOST BUT HIS INCREDIBLE PERFORMANCE BROUGHT HIM A HANDFUL OF PROPOSALS. A PIONEER IN COMBINING DIFFERENT GRAPPLING STYLES TO CREATE AN EFFECTIVE FIGHTING METHOD, PAULSON MADE HISTORY ON MAY 7, 1996 WHEN HE DEFEATED THE SHOOT WRESTLING ("SHOOTO") WORLD CHAMPION, JAPANESE KENJI KAWAGUCHI, TO BECOME THE VERY FIRST CAUCASIAN TO TAKE THE LIGHT HEAVYWEIGHT TITLE BELT OUT OF JAPAN.

UNTIL HIS RETIREMENT AS WORLD CHAMPION, ERIK PAULSON KEPT FIGHTING IN AMERICA AND JAPAN, BECOMING ONE OF THE MOST RESPECTED MARTIAL ARTISTS IN THE EMPIRE OF THE RISING SUN. THESE DAYS HE IS ONE OF THE MOST KNOWLEDGEABLE MIXED MARTIAL ARTS INSTRUCTORS IN THE WORLD AND SPENDS A GREAT DEAL OF HIS TIME TRAVELING AROUND THE GLOBE SHARING HIS EXPERIENCE WITH THOUSANDS OF STUDENTS.

Q: Erik, how did it all begin?
A: I started training in 1974 in Minneapolis, Minnesota, when I was in 4th grade. I was diagnosed with ADD and my mother thought that it would be a good idea to get me involved in some kind of physical activity, so she signed me into judo classes. My brother was already wrestling so for me the idea of grappling with another guy wasn't strange at all. To be totally honest, judo was the last thing I wanted to do at that time. I enjoyed playing other sports like hockey, baseball and football but judo…no way. Well, I ended up there. Because my brother was involved in wrestling, I was a very competitive individual and loved to spar at the end of the class with everybody there. I was really excited about it. I had a great time. I remember the teacher asking a volunteer to demonstrate the most important aspect of judo. I jumped to help him to demonstrate. He threw me on the floor so hard I was sore for over a week! I didn't know that

"All the kicking and punching made my body terribly sore. Punching and kicking is a whole different thing than wrestling and grappling and my body wasn't used to it. During the first month, every single muscle in my body hurt after class."

the most important aspect of judo is to know how to fall properly. He threw every person in class after he demonstrated with me. Of course after that day, I never volunteered for anything else!

On other hand, there were a lot of bullies in my hometown in Minnesota. I got picked on a lot. Once, I was jumped by three guys. Two held my arms while the third hammered my face. After I recovered, I said to myself, "This is never going to happen to me again!"

Q: Did you feel comfortable doing judo or did you enjoy kicking techniques more?
A: Judo was very natural activity for me because of my grappling with my brother. What was really hard were my first days in tae kwon do training. I didn't know what I was getting into. All the kicking and punching made my body terribly sore. Punching and kicking is a whole different thing than wrestling and grappling and my body wasn't used to it. During the first month, every single muscle in my body hurt after class. Now it would probably be the easiest workout but back then it was really hard. I trained in tae kwon do for 13 years. Actually I was winning a lot of tournaments at that time and there was a tournament to qualify for the Olympics. Dana Hee was there at that time. I tore my knee and couldn't make it. The doctor told me I couldn't kick anymore.

Q: But you kept kicking, right?
A: Yes. Three years later I won my first pro-fight. I got into wrestling and boxing and got involved in Shooto. I remember the first time I saw a Shoot Wrestling fight I thought: "I want to do that!" I was hooked immediately to the exciting combination of punching, kicking, throws and submissions techniques in one single package. One interesting thing is I was already

using my hands like a boxer even before starting in Shooto. I always felt this way of using the hands was more natural than the tae kwon do way of punching. I felt really comfortable with the way of boxing. Combinations are more powerful and flow more naturally—at least for me, that is. During my first boxing classes I tried to kick the guy in the stomach and the coach had to keep telling me to use my hands only to knock the guy out.

"When I went to Japan for training I realized that at that time I was already doing the same kind of training. But after my study with the Japanese teachers everything became more systematized, more compact as far as technical structure goes."

Q: Are you a competitive individual?
A: Yes, I have always been a very competitive person and I think that's the reason why I have always been involved in competitive activities. For instance, I love skiing and I also competed in it. Competition brings the best of me and it's under pressure that I give the best. It may be a psychological thing, I guess.

Q: How have your personal training and teaching methods evolved through the years?
A: My method has become more systematized. When I went to Japan for training I realized that I was already doing the same kind of training. But after my study with the Japanese teachers everything became more systematized, more compact as far as technical structure goes. There were a lot of focus mitts drills and pads workouts. I had the punching, the kicking and the groundwork to some extent but the part I was missing was the takedowns. Knowing how to use the takedowns offensively and defensively gave a complete dimension to what I was doing. Of course, shootfighters are excellent in submissions and I added a lot of those as well. I'm a counter-fighter by nature, so learning how to wait for the opponent to attack me was my main interest. I let the guy come close to punch me, kick me or trying to take me down and then it is when I

"In jiu-jitsu competitions it was not well accepted—the idea of getting your opponent with leg locks—but things are changing these days, although I know still some people don't like to incorporate the leg lock into the jiu-jitsu arsenal."

reverse the situation and I come up on top. I'm not a 100 percent offensive fighter. I like to counter my opponent actions so I can use my own strong techniques on him.

It happened to me a couple of times that I studied tapes of my opponent to know his strengths and weaknesses, and I ended up defeating him with his own "favorite" move! Why? Because I studied it so much first to avoid it, then I wound up becaming good at it and I used at the right time. That's what happened in my first fight in Japan and they said that I got lucky. They invited me again and I won again, and they said I got lucky again; the only problem is that this time I won the World Championship! It was fun anyway. I remember the Shooto Instructor Yori Nakamura said to me that my body was perfect for grappling, that my physical structure was ideal for grappling arts, my bone structure is thick and dense, the body fat percentage was appropriate for a grappler and my quickness necessary for getting the job done.

Q: Shooto is well known for its amazing amount of legs locks and you are very knowledgeable about them. Did you incorporate some of them when you were training in jiu-jitsu?
A: Definitely! I think this is a good thing to do. In jiu-jitsu competitions it was not well accepted—the idea of getting your opponent with leg locks—but things are changing these days, although I know still some people don't like to incorporate the leg lock into the jiu-jitsu arsenal. I remember one day at the time I was training at Rickson Gracie's school. I recorded a tape with a lot of groundwork and leg locks from Shoot fighters and I gave it to Rickson to watch. The next day he came by the school and I asked him what he thought about the tape and he mentioned that

"there were good things that he really liked there but the groundwork was very weak." Then he started the classes and in the end we did some sparring. Rickson made everybody tap using only leg locks! It was really interesting to see how he was using that stuff with such amazing level of skill. I never saw him to do that before. I'm sure he knew some of the techniques already but what really impressed me was the fact that he was using one technical aspect like leg locks to make everybody tap at will. That was the level he was on.

"I think the jiu-jitsu instructors have realized how useful leg, knee and ankle locks are and they are not only incorporating these techniques in the arsenal but also allowing the students to use them in competition."

Q: Did you ever use any of them in jiu-jitsu competition?
A: Yes, I have an interesting experience with leg locks in jiu-jitsu competition. I was fighting in the Pan American championships and my opponent swept me and score a point. Then my coach yelled "30 seconds!" That's one of the training drills I used at the time. It consisted of the trainer yelling the time left, then you needed to go for a submission before the match ends. So when I heard "30 seconds," I instinctively went for what I had closer at that moment and it happened that it was the leg, so I applied a leg lock. I won the match and I remember the Machado brothers telling me "nice leg lock"...but all the people in the stadium booed me. Like I said, at that time it was not "accepted" but I think the jiu-jitsu instructors have realized how useful leg, knee and ankle locks are and they are not only incorporating these techniques in the arsenal but also allowing the students to use them in competition. There is a major danger in leg locks and it is that when you feel the pain, it's already too late. You are injured. They are very dangerous moves because the fighter thinks the leg can take it and all of a sudden with feeling a "progressive degree of pain," your knee pops and you have a prob-

"I did train and still train under Dan Inosanto. In many ways I owe him all that I have achieved in the martial arts because he taught me how to look at things and how to improve my own way of doing things. His teaching is always focused in showing and sharing experiences with the student so the student find his own personal way of expressing himself in martial arts."

lem. I truly think that leg locks are part of grappling regardless of your style.

Q: It's a fact that the UFC, as a mixed martial arts event, influenced the world of martial arts. What's your view on it?

A: It is very interesting to see how martial arts mentality has changed in recent years since the beginning of the UFC. Using the cross-training approach is something very common among the practitioners these days. Even tae kwon do and karate practitioners are learning grappling to supplement their groundwork. I think this proves that people are not as closed-minded as 15 years ago. Things have changed and there is nothing wrong with learning and using what is truly useful and adapting that to your own personality and game.

Q: You have trained under Dan Inosanto for several years. Are you also involved in other arts like kali and silat?

A: Yes, I did train and still train under Dan Inosanto. In many ways I owe him all that I have achieved in the martial arts because he taught me how to look at things and how to improve my own way of doing things. His teaching is always focused in showing and sharing experiences with the student so the student find his own personal way of expressing himself in martial arts. He never imposes his way or orders you to follow blindly. It's true that I'm certified in Jun Fan Martial Arts (Jeet Kune Do) by Guro Inosanto but I'm a professional fighter. Of course, I use part of the elements from Jun Fan but mainly tactics and fighting strategies. My techniques are a combination of several fighting arts and combat sports. As a "ring" fighter I need to look for different things. I truly enjoy

going back to the traditional kali and silat and practicing *djurus* but my main goal is to be 100 percent good at what I do and what I teach. So if I still feel that I need to improve my double leg take down...I don't go back and practice a djuru but make 1,000 repetitions on that double leg take down until I feel comfortable with it. I personally use part of the JKD philosophy adapting things to what I'm doing today.

I'm a very focused person and I know what I want and what it works in the ring. Professional fighters know and this is something that I want to pass to my students; that knowledge of what it works and why it does. Probably that mentality passed to me by Dan Inosanto is what made me be open mined about incorporating techniques and moves from Wrestling to Brazilian jiu- jitsu, and from jiu-jitsu to sambo, and from savate to Thai boxing, et cetera. I don't see any problem or any boundaries as long as

"Regardless of how many years of training you have, you need to have that mentality to expose yourself in someone else's art (class) and learn, and at the same time place yourself in a vulnerable position to learn more, with the same passion and desire of a white belt (beginner)."

they create and fit into a compact and cohesive fighting structure that can be used in a fight against a skilled opponent.

Q: What is the most important characteristic of your training under Inosanto?
A: I already mentioned his open approach to training but above everything else and in order to make that work, you need what I call "white belt" mentality. Regardless of how many years of training you have, you need to have that mentality to expose yourself in someone else's art (class) and learn, and at the same time place yourself in a vulnerable position to learn more, with the same passion and desire of a white belt (beginner). That is an amazing attitude Inosanto displays in everyday of his life. It's inspirational for all of us.

"Do your best in every training session, in every drill in every move, because when you give your 110 percent then you know that you are ready. Knowing that you are ready will automatically bring confidence within your mind and that's the key ingredient to overcome fear: confidence."

Q: Why do you think jiu-jitsu people try the "no-gi" competition such as Abu Dabhi?

A: Today we have "gi-competitions" and "gi-less competitions." In sport jiu-jitsu there is not too much money and some practitioners like to try "gi-less" tournaments and championships so they can eventually move to the major competitions like Abu Dabhi and make some good money. This is okay and it's good for the sport. They are two different approaches to the art and everybody is free to choose the one he likes and enjoys most.

Q: Are you one of those fighters who doesn't know what the word "fear" means?

A: No, I'm not. I always feel fear. It's a natural thing and a human sensation. If you say you don't feel fear I think you are lying. It's not a fear that won't allow you to move a finger but it's that sensation about the unknown what keeps you wondering and keeps you going. What is important is how a fighter deals with that sensation, how he faces those feelings and makes them work positively for him. There is a psychological process behind this and that's the reason why professional boxers have psychologists in their training camps. The mind is the most powerful tool but also the most dangerous. If five minutes before a fight your mind goes in the wrong direction and starts thinking the wrong things, chances are you'll end up losing the fight. I have found that a great way of overcome that fear sensation, if we agree on calling it fear, is to prepare yourself in the best possible way. Do your best in every training session, in every drill in every move, because when you give your 110 percent then you know that you are ready. Knowing that you are ready will automatically bring confidence within your mind and that's the key ingredient to overcome fear: confidence.

Q: Japan was accepted as the number one country in martial arts and Brazil was considered the leader in jiu-jitsu. Do you think they still are the number one in the charts or that other countries like the United States have caught up with them?

A: In the West the evolution has been remarkable. It is true that we don't have the same kind on mentality but technique-wise, the Western fighters are at the same level that the Oriental counterpart. Something similar happened in the vale tudo and NHB field. The Brazilians surprised everybody and they were the kings of the hill for many years but now you see Americans and Europeans taking over and defeating the Brazilians in the own game. I believe that the main reason for this is the open-minded approach the American fighters have been using. America is an eclectic country by nature, it's a tapestry of many cultures and I guess that's the attitude that opens your eyes and doesn't make you feel guilty if you change something from the past in order to make it better. Fighters don't have a problem training and teaching other fighters moves of their own. Olympic wrestlers do that all the time. They train together and they compete against each other. The only thing you may gain by using this open mind attitude is to get better in whatever you do. On the other hand, if you think of all the new instructional tools that we have in the market these days, you'll see that there are no secrets anymore. Videotapes, CD-Roms, DVD, et cetera full of techniques, counters, and moves that you can't imagine are at your hand anytime you want. Of course, the beginner won't be able of absorbing a lot from a videotape but if you give a professional fighter a tape, you can be sure he is going to absorb a lot of stuff from it and make it his own.

"America is an eclectic country by nature, it's a tapestry of many cultures and I guess that's the attitude that opens your eyes and doesn't make you feel guilty if you change something from the past in order to make it better. Fighters don't have a problem training and teaching other fighters moves of their own."

"You better know how to deal with weapons because in a real life situation you are going to need that knowledge. You have to watch out for those unpractical techniques that may look great in the school and in the magazines but that in real life will send you to the hospital if not to the grave."

Q: You seem to enjoy giving your students freedom to go and train under other instructors. That's not a common attitude in a martial arts teacher.

A: As an instructor who cares for his students, I'm perplexed to see how other instructors are extremely concerned about giving their students freedom to go and train in other systems. Personally, I don't have any problem with that. It's true that I was "raised" with that mentality. Students should be free to visit other schools and learn material from whoever they want without getting a resentful feeling from their instructors. The only reason why an instructor can behave that way is due to an insecurity in what he knows. If he is not secure about his knowledge then I can see the reason because he is afraid to lose the students.

Q: As result of your training with Inosanto, how much kali and JKD do you have in your personal fighting system?

A: Kali for me is a more artistic thing and Jun Fan/JKD has been very useful from a conceptual and strategic point of view. As a professional fighter I look at the art more like a sport or a competitive activity. I go out there, do my thing and go back home. I don't hate my opponent; it's not a personal thing. I try to win but not in a mean way. I don't make it personal. I know some people need to find a personal reason to step into the ring and that's fine if that triggers their motivation to win. But on my part, I just don't need to hate my opponent. That's why I consider it more like a sport. In football, baseball or basketball you don't hate the members of the other team but you really want to win. You need that killer instinct but in good way.

After I retired from Shooto, I had to find a different approach to what I was doing. It's bad when you go to train and your shoes are still wet from the previous workout or your gloves have no time to dry out. You train,

you eat, you sleep and go back to train again. Suddenly you reach a point where is not fun to train anymore. You loose that passion, it becomes a job and the eye of the tiger is no longer in you. You are not hungry for it. Then you have to analyze the reason why you are doing what you are doing and if you don't find a good one, you'll quit. It's that simple. In teaching I found a new venue. I always loved to teach but being a fighter leaves almost no time to share your knowledge with others. You have to be selfish and think about yourself at all times. So for me, training in other arts such as kali and silat is a way of keeping my personal motivation going but if I can't do well a double leg take down, I won't go and learn a few disarms for an stick attack. What I do is my job and I want to be good at it so I focus on it. The rest is an enjoyable part of my martial arts quest but not my butter and bread.

Q: How important is weapons training to self-defense on the streets?
A: You better know how to deal with weapons because in a real life situation you are going to need that knowledge. Since I was a kid, conflicts have been coming to me for some kind of strange reason. In the street the most of the time you are going to face someone with a knife, a club or even a gun. It has nothing to do with a match in the ring. You need to have an understanding of how these weapons work in order to be able of defending against them. What is extremely important is that whatever method you are learning to deal with these weapons better be a realistic one or you'll be in trouble. I have seen a lot of what is being taught out there and believe me, it won't work and it will probably get the person killed. You have to watch out for those unpractical techniques that may look great in the school and in the magazines but that in real life will send you to the hospital if not to the grave.

Q: How demanding are you with yourself?
A: Personally, I always push myself to train harder than my students. Maybe this is a residual attitude of my professional days. I use a lot of the training aspects and methodology that I use with my students in my personal training. I also like to train with them. I have no problem at all getting on the mat and rolling with them or sparring with them. I believe this makes them better and also makes me better. The instructor's personal training has to be different than the teaching aspect because it's a different thing. Your training can't be your teaching in class. Training and performing while you teach is great and will keep you going but your

personal training has to take you to the next level, a higher level that can't be achieved just by training with your students while you are imparting knowledge to a class. As an instructor your goal is to make your guys better and as a fighter your goal is to make yourself better. These two goals, although maybe complementary to each other, have to be approached separately.

Q: Do you think instructors sometimes don't teach all they can to their students? Are they holding some knowledge back from them?
A: Unfortunately yes. Many teachers out there don't fully try to make their students better than they are. If you are an honest teacher your goal has to be make your students reach a higher level than your own. Some instructors are afraid to teach their students shortcuts and ways of being better than they are. I truly don't understand why they act that way but I assume they are afraid of their students and their behavior is not more than a reflection of their own insecurities not only in martial arts but in life as well. They don't even know it but their own fears are controlling their relationship with their students and consequently it will affect their student's life. That's why I believe an instructor has a tremendous responsibility with those who he is imparting classes because his influence goes beyond the limits of the school's walls. They are not dedicated to their student's improvement but to the care and feeding of their egos.

Q: How structured is your teaching program and association?
A: My association is completely structured in levels not only for students but also for instructors to keep evolving and improving. Of course, we have a separate program for the fighters—the "Demolition Team"—because a fighter needs certain things to be able to step into the ring as opposed to a student who is not planning to fight professionally. We also separate aspects of fighting so the student can go into what he enjoys more and the things with which he feels more comfortable. For instance we have two methods of submission—Submission Grappling and Submission Fighting. They are different because one person may feel interested in going to a straight grappling event like Abu Dabhi to compete and another may decide to jump into UFC. We use a lot of drills in our training. Drilling is the key to fighting since a fighter can't be fighting all the time. You can be grappling everyday but you can't be sparring full contact in kickboxing in every training session. You have to be smart. Not even the professional NFL players play a game in every practice ses-

sion. They use drills to improve those aspects and qualities they need for the real game. I have a teaching method that I describe as: "Technique Repetition Isolation Grappling" or TRIG. I'm always looking for ways and methods to cut the training time down for my students to improve and many times I wish I could have been trained with this methodology during my fighting days. I was doing a lot of things that I didn't know if they were applicable or not, and I guess I wasted a very valuable time until I finally could figured things out. I want my students to be able of reaching a high level of skill in the shortest possible time and in order to achieve that we have to use proven scientific training methods.

"As an instructor your goal is to make your guys better and as a fighter your goal is to make yourself better. These two goals, although maybe complementary to each other, have to be approached separately."

When I train fighters I do the same way but focus more on the specific of their individual strengths and weakness. It's the same training method but the approach and the structure of the sessions are a little bit different.

Q: Who is the person you would have loved to have trained with, but never did?
A: Definitely Juanito (John) LaCoste. The way Dan Inosanto talks about him makes me want to train with him but unfortunately he is dead. Also I would have liked to train with Bruce Lee, not because of the movie thing but because he was ahead of his time and he was a pioneer in the martial arts and I truly like these kind of individuals. I am not talking about technical stuff but how people present material and how their approach to the arts is different from the rest. That's the reason why I really feel inclined to those two men, because the way they presented their approach to martial arts.

"The art you train in displays your mentality as an individual. Regardless of your chosen direction in the arts, discipline and hard training are what bring to you a feeling of joy. You need to put yourself 100 percent in your training."

Q: What would you tell someone who wants to start training in martial arts?

A: I would ask this person what he or she wants to get from it. It depends what the goals are. Everything else is based on that simple point. Tell me what you want and then I'll tell you the direction to achieve your goal. Want self-defense? Then there are ways of improving in that direction. Want to become a professional fighter? Then you have to use a different approach. That's simple. If you enjoy simply the philosophical approach more than the pure fighting maybe other arts like aikido would fit more into that but your are not going to get the same results if you are looking for that and you train in Thai boxing. The art you train in displays your mentality as an individual.

Regardless of your chosen direction in the arts, discipline and hard training are what bring to you a feeling of joy. You need to put yourself 100 percent in your training. If you are a fighter even more than 100 percent. In life you get back what you put in and martial arts is not an exception. Also I would recommend following a healthy diet—eating properly—and have the right amount of rest (hours of sleep). These two simple but tremendously important elements will not only improve your daily life but your performance in the arts as well.

Q: How positive is mixing styles?

A: It's positive as long as you know where you are going and how to do it. If your goal is to be a complete fighter, well-rounded competitor in mixed martial arts or NHB then you need to approach your training with a very open mind. You need to have kickboxing skill and grappling elements that you can combine in a complete package. You must know how to

make work each one of these elements and how to nullify kickboxing with grappling and vice versa. Regardless of what may be your personal preference you need to be well-rounded. Period. There is no other way around it. For many years, people have been questioning and asking why I don't use trapping in fights. Well, put the gloves on, begin to spar and let's see how many trapping combinations you can really do against a professional fighter. Trapping as addressed in Chinese styles such as wing chun and JKD is one aspect of fighting but I don't think it is very practical in a fight against a skilled opponent in an NHB environment. Don't get me wrong, it not only happens with trapping but with other combat elements from other styles I studied, such as the sweep from silat, "straight blast" from JKD, et cetera. People ask me "Why you didn't do this or that?" Oh, well…get up there, step in the ring and tell me later. That's all I can say.

Q: These days we see athletes with huge bodies. Do you think steroids are part of MMA and NHB?
A: Nope! That's the result of protein shakes, creatine and a lot of egg whites!!! Just kidding! Come on, what do you think? There is no way a human being can develop that amount of muscle and put pounds and pounds of lean muscle in few months or in a very short time. It's simply not possible for a human being to do that. Period. I think that is an issue that should be regulated in some way for the benefit of the sport. Drug and steroid tests should be part of our sport.

Q: What does the future hold for Erik Paulson?
A: I really enjoy teaching and sharing with others my knowledge and experiences. I love to travel around the world and give seminars. Teaching is a big part in my life and I hope I can keep doing for a long time. It's a great sensation, a great feeling but it also brings a tremendous responsibility because people will follow what you tell them, so in many ways you are responsible for these people's growth. I get a lot of motivation from the idea of making my students better fighters and better martial artists. That's my "fuel," that's my reason to keep going. As far as fighting, you never know. Maybe a good offer will bring me back from retirement but that's something that nobody can predict. But there is something I can say; I miss fighting and I know I still have a couple of good fights in me. If these will ever take place, only time will tell! ○

Erik Paulson controls his opponent from the top mount (1). Erik's opponent keeps his elbows in and his face covered, making any offensive move difficult (2). Erik jumps out off the top mount (3), and moves his left leg out to sit on his opponent's left side. He then hooks the opponent's left leg with his own foot (4), crosses his right leg over his left, and applies a straight leg-lock (5).

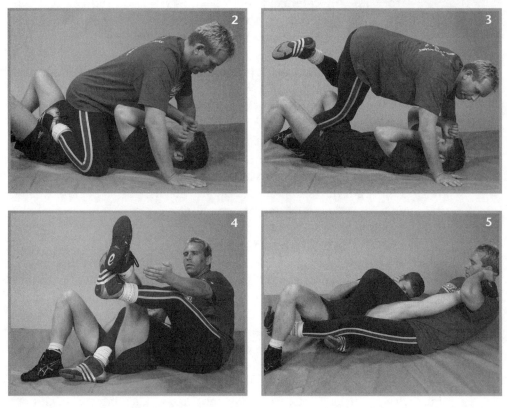

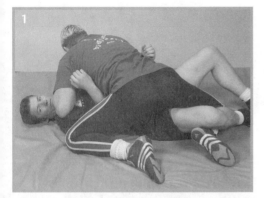

Erik Paulson controls his opponent from the side mount (1). Erik moves to the left side, releasing some control but gaining a better attacking position (2). He then spins and moves his right leg to the back (3), hooks the opponent's left leg (4), and applies a finishing leg-lock (5).

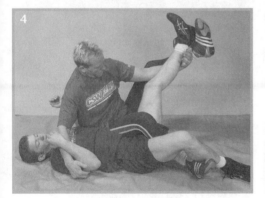

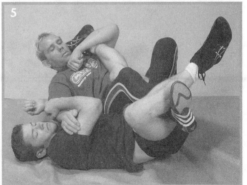

Erik Paulson has his right knee on his opponent's chest (1). Erik grabs the opponent's right arm (2), turns his body sideways (3), spins around (4), and sits on his opponent's stomach, trapping both legs (5). Erik then releases one leg, grabs the other (6), and applies a finishing leg-lock (7).

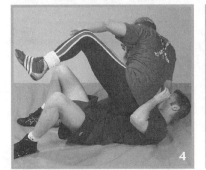

Erik Paulson is trapped in his opponent's open guard (1). The opponent tries to sweep Erik (2), and get him out of balance (3). As soon as Erik feels the pressure of the sweep, he grabs his opponent's left foot (4), moves his left leg to the inside (5), passes it over his opponent's right leg (6), and applies a finishing ankle lock (7).

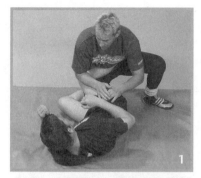

Erik Paulson is trapped inside his opponent's open guard (1). Erik pushes his opponent's chest to create space (2), and then under-hooks his right leg (3). As Erik rolls over him (4), in order to land on the other side (5), he applies a finishing ankle lock (6).

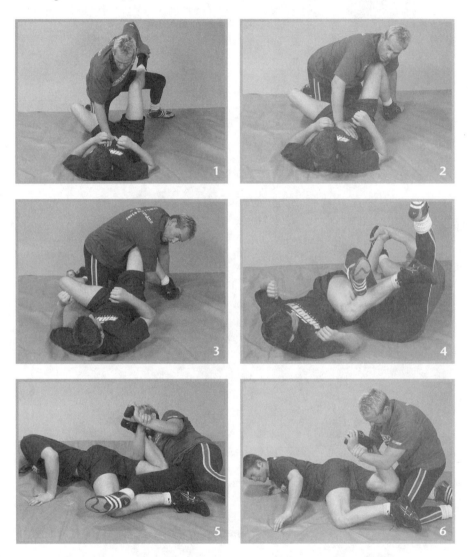

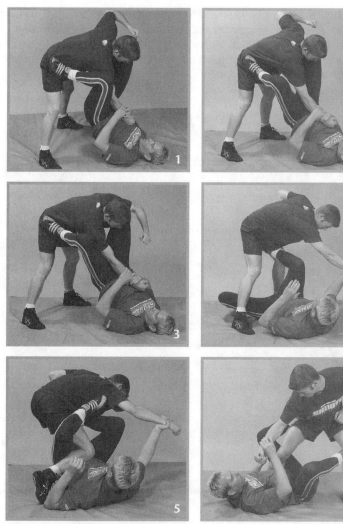

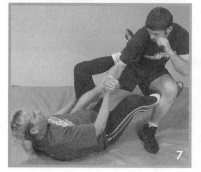

Erik Paulson faces an opponent (1), who is trying to hit him (2). Erik moves his hips up to create distance (3), and then drops his body down (4), placing his left leg between his opponent's legs. Erik then pushes with his right leg and passes his left over his opponent (5). Placing the hook on the left leg (6-sideview), Erik pushes with his left leg to unbalance his opponent (7), and than applies a finishing ankle lock (8).

Erik Paulson controls his opponent by placing his feet on the hips (1), and then slightly pushing forward (2). When his opponent tries to push back, Erik releases the hand grab (3), grabs both ankles simultaneously (4), inserts the hooks behind both knees (5), and brings him down (6). Erik immediately controls the opponent's left foot (7), moves his body sideways (8), and finishes with an ankle lock (9).

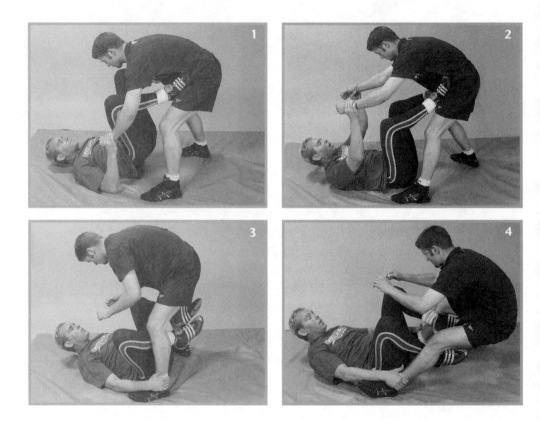

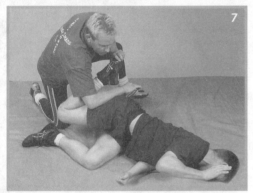

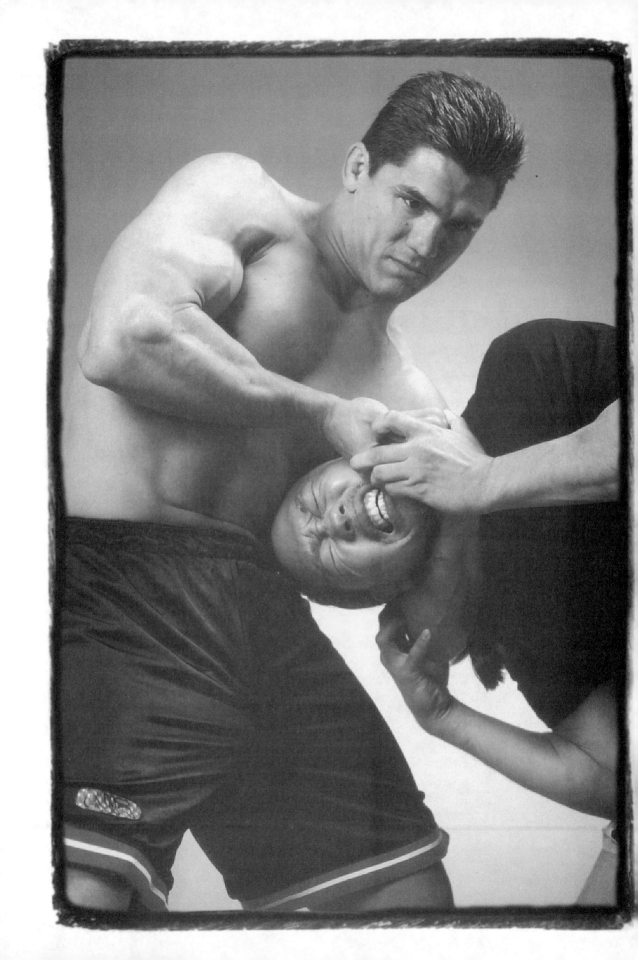

Frank Shamrock

The Icon of Submission Fighting

IN NHB AND SUBMISSION FIGHTING THERE IS NO OTHER MAN LIKE HIM. FRANK SHAMROCK IS AS CLOSE AS YOU CAN GET TO SUPERMAN. HIS PHYSIQUE COULD HAVE BEEN WORTH A SEVEN-FIGURE MODELING CONTRACT FOR CALVIN KLEIN, BUT THIS CALIFORNIA NATIVE TOOK A DIFFERENT PATH IN LIFE AND BECAME ONE OF THE GREATEST FIGHTERS IN THE HISTORY OF MARTIAL ARTS. AND HE CAN PROVE IT. HE IS HAPPY-GO-LUCKY AND EASY-GOING, BUT WHEN HE SETS HIS MIND TO SOMETHING, THE FRANK SHAMROCK YOU HANG OUT WITH DISAPPEARS AND HE BECOMES ONE OF THE MOST DETERMINED ATHLETES YOU CAN EVER FIND, REGARDLESS OF THE SPORT.

Q: Where did Frank Shamrock come from?
A: I was born on December 8, 1972, in Santa Monica, California. For over four years I lived there but then we moved to Redding, Northern California. We lived in an apartment building under a train trestle. They were very tough and very hard days in my life because I really felt confused about things, but I managed to not give up. Since I always wanted to be an athlete, that helped me to keep pushing my physical side. Being in foster homes is something than can make you feel very miserable and lonely if you don't find the best way to deal with the situation. To me, I guess it made me stronger day by day. It's hard to think how life could have been because the only data I have is what and where I was—so it's impossible to me to think "what if."

Q: What happened after that?
A: I went to a group home for over three years before Bob Shamrock adopted me. Growing up without a father figure is very hard because you don't have anyone to show you the right way things are done. As a result, you have to find out by yourself and this can get you in trouble. Bob definitely was not only very helpful but also very caring and loving. He has

"Entering competition was a natural progression for me. I was attracted to it because if you win, you win and if you lose, you are the only one to blame."

been a real role model for me, always helping and pushing me to do the things that I wanted to do in life.

Q: It was there that you met Ken Shamrock?
A: Yeah, Ken was ready to leave when I got there. In 1994, I was 22 and he asked me if I wanted to try to get in the Lion's Den. I liked the idea and I was hooked right away. I liked it because of the physical component of wrestling. Entering competition was a natural progression for me. I was attracted to it because if you win, you win and if you lose, you are the only one to blame. In team sports like football, baseball or basketball, you depend on you teammates and that idea didn't attract me at all. I always wanted to rely on myself. I really liked the training that was based on the knowledge Ken acquired during his training in Japan. We used to train five hours a day for five days a week. We used to do a lot of different exercises and I got hooked. I remember I had to do 500 free squats, sit-ups, push-ups and leg lifts and then fight Ken for another half an hour! Also other aspects such as self-discipline, dedication, and the respect for others were factors that made me feel comfortable in the training sessions.

Q: Fighters usually find no pleasure in teaching, but you really seem to enjoy it.
A: I have a real passion for teaching. I really love to teach; it makes me feel happy. The process of sharing something with someone and making

that person happy, is a great experience for me. It's not about money; it's about personal satisfaction.

Q: When preparing for a fight, do you follow any type of mental training?
A: I use a lot of meditation. This helps me to visualize my matches and mentally prepare to deal with the pressure of fighting. It helps me to be more focused so I can think about all the little details of the fight in a more precise way. The way I do it is similar to a chess game. I visualize everything that can happen and start building reactions to that. This way I formulate a certain plan and it's almost impossible to be caught by surprise. Before getting in there, I see everything that can happen in the ring. Many fighters only focus on the physical part of the game, but fighting is a very mental activity, it's a psychological game. This mental aspect affects the physical component of the equation to a very high extent. If you are a natural fighter then you don't need this component as much as any other athlete who just likes to fight. A natural fighter has that mentality within himself, anytime, anywhere. An athlete who fights needs to set up a certain type of mental environment that allows him to deal with that and be successful. I'm this kind of guy. I love to compete but I don't love to fight. I enjoy the competition aspect but not necessarily the fighting side of it. I know it's going to sound funny, but I'm not the kind of guy who has no problem punching people. So I really have to make an effort and visualize myself doing this. Violence is not a natural thing to me, so I have to work to be able to fight. Like I said, it's a mental thing.

"I visualize everything that can happen and start building reactions to that. This way I formulate a certain plan and it's almost impossible to be caught by surprise. Before getting in there, I see everything that can happen in the ring."

"Confidence is one of the most important mental components in a fighter. No confidence in yourself and you are done. You don't want to be unsure of your abilities because that is going to be a very heavy weight during the fight."

Q: What's your procedure to scout your opponent?
A: The formula is very personal. From a physical point of view I watch tapes of my opponent's fights, I think of him and I analyze his weak and strong points. My mental training goes parallel to the physical part but it's done mostly in private, when resting, in bed, walking, et cetera—mostly between my three-times-per-day training schedule.

Q: Winning is not always possible and defeat has always been part of the great champions in all combat sports. How do you deal with the two sides of the same coin?
A: I deal with victory better than with defeat! Kidding aside, winning definitely boots your confidence and desire to keep going. As everybody knows, confidence is one of the most important mental components in a fighter. No confidence in yourself and you are done. You don't want to be unsure of your abilities because that is going to be a very heavy weight during the fight. You want to be confident but not over-confident. That can be devastating for a fighter.

As far as losing, it's not that I like it, but I understand it's part of the game. For me, it's not a big deal if you know how to use that defeat to overcome your mistakes and work on your weak points. When you lose a

fight, don't blame anyone but yourself. Go back home and work harder than before. Do your homework so "they" won't have a reason to declare your opponent victorious. Sometimes, losing can be the best thing that can happen to you. It's tough to lose, but if you do lose, make sure it doesn't happen again. When I did lose, I felt bad about it but not depressed or anything like that. I used that experience to reinforce my desire to compete again and win. It's just a mental game.

Q: When you have a fight schedule, how long does it take for you to peak?
A: Usually it takes me six weeks to peak for a fight. Because I'm always training and I keep myself active, I really don't make any drastic changes in my life when I

"Because I'm always training and I keep myself active, when I start preparing for a fight I really don't make any drastic changes in my life. I just train more intensely and I put a lot of emphasis in my cardio routine."

start preparing for a fight. I just train more intensely and I put a lot of emphasis in my cardio routine. From the tactical and strategic point of view, I watch tapes of my opponent and try to see what kinds of things he does and what kinds of things he cannot do. I watch for his strong points and weak points so I can defend against the former and exploit the latter. Depending on whom I'm going to fight, I train with a fighter in that style so I can better deal with that particular method. When the fight is getting close, I try to relax as much as I can. I only feel a little nervous right before the fight, but I focus on my breathing and relaxation techniques as I replay in my mind all the things I've visualized for a week about the upcoming fight. Once I'm in the ring, it's like a déjà vu...I have

"Some people rely more on their strength and other base their plan simply on a technical component. I don't believe the theory that technique is only what you need. You need a certain amount of strength and sometimes strength can be the only way to escape from a difficult situation. So make sure you have it, just in case you need it."

been there before. I just have to make things happen the exact same way I visualized them.

Q: You are an example of physical fitness and fighting skills. How do you approach your training as far as the different components of strength, flexibility, endurance, et cetera?

A: Strength is important but you can always get around it with good technique. So you have to be careful. Strength is a physical component that makes you explosive and for your adversaries, a harder opponent to deal with. But technique is more important because in the end a good technique is what finishes a fight. The reason I say this is because technique is something that once you have it, you have it forever. Strength is something that comes and goes depending on your training and age. The good thing is that if you have both components, then you can win any fight. It's a perfect combination but a very hard one to achieve. Some people rely more on their strength, and others base their plan simply on a technical component. I don't believe the theory that technique is only what you need. You need a certain amount of strength and sometimes strength can be the only way to escape from a difficult situation. So make sure you have it, just in case you need it. I personally work with free weights to get the strength I need for my fights, but my routine changes often since I don't like to do the same program all the time. You have to understand not only the benefits of strength training but also the downfalls. If you lift heavy and don't stretch you are going to have some problems, because you'll get tight and slow.

Q: You have amazing flexibility for someone of your muscular size, how do you work this physical component in your routine?

A: Stretching and flexibility are essential for me. The more you work out, the more you train, the more stiff you get. With age, you don't get more flexible but more rusty. I like natural stretching exercises that I do before and after each one of my training sessions. If I have three training sessions per day, then I work on my flexibility six times a day. I don't like the sensation of not feeling flexible and loose all the time. I look at my stretching time as a moment to relax and feel in touch with my inner-self. I relax and breath properly so I can

"Conditioning is the most important thing you can do to your body. Knowing that you are a conditioned fighter will build confidence in your mind because you know you can perform the actions and pull the techniques off."

stretch those muscles naturally without bouncing up and down. Breathing is vital in all kind of elasticity and flexibility programs. This is one of the most important components in a professional fighter. All the great fighters, regardless of sport, are extremely flexible.

Q: What is most important?

A: If I have to decide what's the most important part of the physical training I'd have to say conditioning. If you are in better shape than your opponent, you can outlast the guy. If you are not in shape, then the game is over. You can't win. For me, conditioning is the most important thing you can do to your body. Knowing that you are a conditioned fighter will build confidence in your mind because you know you can perform the actions and pull the techniques off. I've personally developed a set of exercises that are sport-specific and that increase my speed and

"In martial arts in general, to maintain the vitality of your chosen art, you must put aside prejudices and inflexibility and be open to any innovation that would result in an improvement of what you are doing. I have a style that has no rules."

power. In martial arts, you need to train your body to do specific activities—on command and reflexively. It's only by repetitive training that your body can do those fighting motions. The cardiovascular training gives you that gas to reach the finishing line. You have the best submission technique when your body is in top condition. If you don't follow a good cardio program, you won't last very long in a fight. It's that easy.

Once your body gives up because of a lack of endurance, you can't think. If you can't think, there is no way you can fight a good fight and if you can't fight a good fight, then you can't win. I use different exercises and apparatus for my cardio workouts; from simply running, to stairmaster, stationary bike, treadmill, rowing machine and even rope jumping. I try to make it fun and enjoyable. My overall philosophy is very direct and simple; your game should be based on fitness. Period.

Q: How would you describe your style?
A: Considering the direction martial arts is going these days, you have to keep an open mind to absorb things that are useful and helpful for what you are doing. In order to improve, you have to get rid of all the prejudices you have from previous training and simply try to become more effective. My style is not a grappling method because I don't consider myself to be a grappler or a wrestler. My method is based on submission fighting. I can punch, kick, and fight on the ground. It is a complete approach to fighting and is not limited to groundwork. Many people have asked me why I don't participate in grappling events. Simply said, I don't train to score points like people do in judo, wrestling, or jiu-jitsu. My goal is not to grapple with an opponent for twenty minutes—I want to end a fight now. My style doesn't fit into grappling events. In order to compete in any of them I would have to change my fighting format and my training—it just isn't worth it to me. My background is submission wrestling

and in this method all positions are equal. No points are scored. When I fight, I don't roll with my opponent, I dominate him.

Q: As a professional fighter, how do you motivate yourself to stay on the right mental track all the time?
A: When you are a professional fighter you need to find different ways to keep yourself motivated. In the beginning, money and exposure may be the reason but after a while you need more than that. My secret is to take a lot of time off. This keeps me relaxed because I love to train and teach but without the pressure and stress of an upcoming fight. I have also realized that the people around you have a major influence on your state of mind and mood. That's why I really choose the people I hang out with. It is very difficult to stay motivated on your own. You really need a part-

"It's extremely important to have a partner you enjoy working with, someone you get along with. As a fighter, both winning and losing can be very motivational, it just depends how you approach victory and defeat."

ner, especially in submission wrestling. It's extremely important to have a partner you enjoy working with, someone you get along with. As a fighter, both winning and losing can be very motivational, it just depends how you approach victory and defeat.

When you stop competing and fighting then you need to find a reason to keep doing it as part of your daily life. The goal, the aim of a title fight, is not there so you have to re-evaluate your motives to train in martial arts and keep dragging your butt to the gym every single day. But I

"There are much more injuries in pro football than in NHB fights. All fighters are professionals and they are very well trained and conditioned. They are aware of what they are going to do and they know how to effectively deal with it."

love to train and teach so for me it's not a problem to stay motivated. Either I'm fighting or not.

Q: NHB and submission fighting have been the target of many campaigns by politicians due to the violence involved; what's your opinion about this?

A: Definitely NHB is a contact sport and athletes can get hurt but I don't think it's more violent than boxing, kickboxing, or even football. It is not a barbaric activity and it is not as dangerous as the critics say. There are much more injuries in pro football than in NHB fights. All fighters are professionals and they are very well trained and conditioned. They are aware of what they are going to do and they know how to effectively deal with it. Of course, there is always people who criticize any combat sport. If they attack and criticize point karate, how are they not going to criticize boxing? And if they criticize boxing, how are they not going to complain about kickboxing? And, of course, if kickboxing is described as "brutal," then submission fighting is even worse!

Unfortunately, all these comments come from people and critics who are not educated about martial arts, or they have some personal interest in preventing the sport from growing. It's going to take a while to educate these people about what we are doing. Politicians have been using our sport to get attention, and they have been saying a lot of nonsense about what we do and who we are. Of course a broken nose, or a swollen eye looks scary, but it comes with the territory and in football you can see much more dangerous injuries. On top of that, when you are a fighter you go out there knowing that you can get hit and you have been trained to deal with it. When you get hit in a football game with an elbow in the face or a guy tackling you and intentionally hitting your knee, that's a different game. You haven't trained for that...you don't expect that. It's not part of the game. In our sport we train to deal with it. We know what is ahead of us and we are prepared to take it.

Q: What about people who claim martial arts are not for fighting?
A: Martial arts offer many benefits but I'm a professional fighter so I think that those words come from people who don't want to fight. Traditional martial artists try to shy away from our sport because they normally don't fight very well. I make my living fighting, so it's my job. Of course, you can train in martial arts and have no need to fight. The simple training can bring you a lot of joy

"It's going to take a while to educate these people about what we are doing. Politicians have been using our sport to get attention and they have been saying a lot of nonsense about what we do and who we are."

and pleasure without getting involved in any type of combat. You can take from martial arts what is good for you. It all depends on what you want from it. That's your gig.

"Simple training can bring you a lot of joy and pleasure without getting involved in any type of combat. You can take from martial arts what is good for you. It all depends on what you want from it."

Q: What type of nutrition and diet do you follow, and how do you think it affects your performance?
A: The food you take is the fuel of your body. Your body will perform according to the type of food you put in it. To follow a demanding training schedule as a professional fighter, you need to know the right kind of food and how these nutrients affect your body. It's not only about having knowledge of the nutrients but also about when and how much of them you should eat. I eat over five small meals a day and try to stay away from high-fat foods. Basically I aim to have a balanced diet and I know how to "reward" myself with something enjoyable every now and then. I truly believe that if you have the right kind of food you don't need to rely on supplements. But I also understand that sometimes you can't get the

right food at the right time so these supplements can help to balance your nutritional intake to a certain extent.

Q: What does the future hold for you?
A: Nobody has a crystal ball and knows what the future holds. All I know for sure is that hard work, commitment, honor, and effort are the keys to success. Fighting has been an integral part of my life—but life is change and change is the only thing in the universe that you can really depend on. I haven't fought that much lately because I really need the motivation of a big fight to put me in the right state of mind to train hard. I don't see myself fighting at all ten years from now, but that's all part of life's natural progression.

There are many opportunities in front of me now, that I'm willing to explore. Fighting is one element of my life, but it is not the only one. As soon as something captures my attention the same as fighting did in the past, I'll put myself into it 100 percent—I'm certain I'll be successful. I love to teach and I love acting – so we'll see what happens when the right door opens.

I have left a lot of myself in the Octagon, and this includes not only years of training but also parts of my body which have been seriously injured! Maybe the time for me to heal is close. I have always been very natural and relaxed in my approach

"You can only be a fighter for so long and I've given it my heart, my money and my soul. And my body too, with so many injuries over all these years!"

to the things I've done in my life. That's the way I am and that's the way I'll be. I love to teach and I love to share what I have learned with other people. Teaching is something that I see myself doing for a long time; as far as the rest, only time will tell. The future looks good. ☼

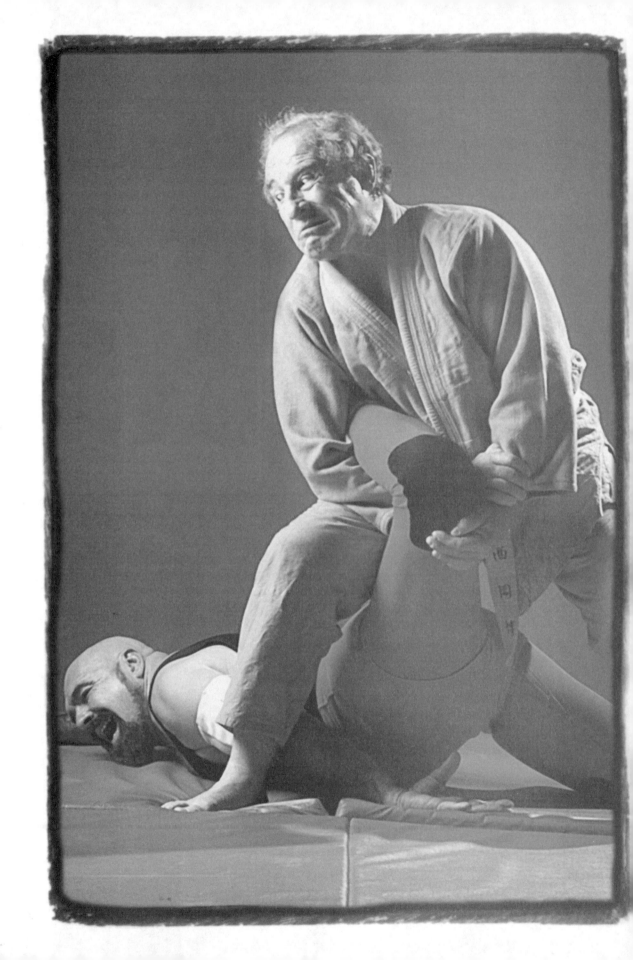

Gene LeBell

Jokes, Chokes, and Locks

WHETHER APPLYING ONE OF HIS NUMEROUS NECK CHOKES, OR REGALING YOU WITH ONE OF HIS NUMEROUS BAD JOKES OR STORIES, GENE LEBELL WILL ALWAYS FIND A WAY TO PUT YOU TO SLEEP. ONE OF MARTIAL ARTS GREATEST HEROES AND A LIVING TREASURE OF KNOWLEDGE AND LORE, "JUDO" GENE IS A COMPETITOR WHO HAS NEVER LACKED THE COURAGE TO BE HIMSELF, AND WHO, BY HIS LEADERSHIP, HAS ENRICHED AND ENCOURAGED THE MARTIAL ART OF GRAPPLING ALL AROUND THE WORLD.

LONG BEFORE THE GRAPPLING ARTS BECAME THE "IN" THING TO DO, GENE LEBELL WAS ALREADY A LIVING LEGEND. HIS SENSE OF HUMOR IS SECOND ONLY TO HIS GRAPPLING SKILLS—AND IF HE CAN CHOKE YOU IN ANY OF A HUNDRED OF DIFFERENT WAYS, HE CAN ALSO DRIVE YOU CRAZY WITH ANY ONE OF HIS THOUSAND ONE-LINERS.

LEBELL CAPTURED THE AAU HEAVYWEIGHT AND OPEN CLASS JUDO CHAMPIONSHIPS IN 1954 AND '55 AND THEN TURNED TO PROFESSIONAL WRESTLING, SEEING IT AS THE ONLY WAY A MARTIAL ARTIST OF THAT DAY COULD EARN A LIVING DOING WHAT HE LOVED. WHEN THE GREATEST BOXER OF ALL TIMES, MUHAMMAD ALI, AGREED TO FIGHT JAPANESE WRESTLER ANTONIO INOKI, ALI DEMANDED THAT GENE LEBELL REFEREE THE MATCH OR HE WOULDN'T FIGHT—WHAT A COMPLIMENT!

JUDO GENE SPENT TIME AND TRAINED WITH THE GREAT BRUCE LEE HIMSELF, AND TAUGHT THE GRAPPLING AND SUBMISSION ARTS TO MANY OF THE GREATEST AMERICAN KARATE FIGHTERS. ALL OF THEM HAVE NOTHING BUT COMPLIMENTS AND RESPECT FOR JUDO GENE LEBELL. LATER, HE WENT ON TO A CAREER AS A STUNT COORDINATOR IN HOLLYWOOD, BECOMING ONE OF THE MOST RESPECTED PROFESSIONALS IN THE BUSINESS.

AT 16, LEBELL FOUND HIMSELF IN THE GYM WITH SUGAR RAY ROBINSON. ROBINSON ASKED THE TEENAGER IF HE FELT LIKE SPARRING. EVER HUMBLE, GENE AGREED AND PROMISED NOT TO HURT THE WELTERWEIGHT CHAMPION. AFTER BEING HIT BY OVER 300 OF ROBINSON'S JABS, LEBELL TOLD SUGAR RAY TO COME BACK THE NEXT DAY IF HE WANTED ANOTHER BEATING. THIS IS GENE LEBELL, THE SELF-PROCLAIMED "BEST-LOOKING MAN" IN MARTIAL ARTS.

Q: When did you begin martial arts?
A: Nine o' clock yesterday morning, right after coffee.

"A lot of the finishing moves that I learned in catch wrestling are illegal in judo competition, but they are great for fighting and self-defense, so why not use them?"

Q: I've heard that it's very hard to have a serious conversation with you.
A: Well, this time I'm gonna behave myself, but if you tell anyone that I was nice to you don't be surprised if your house burns down.

Q: OK! I'll take my chances. Are you a traditionalist?
A: In some aspects I am, but I also believe in changing and adding things from other styles to your system. Also, I don't much like kata, which is not a very important part of judo. I liked judo very much, ever since I was a kid.

Q: Have you incorporated moves from other martial arts into your judo?
A: A lot of the finishing moves that I learned in catch wrestling are illegal in judo competition, but they are great for fighting and self-defense, so why not use them? I've also incorporated a lot of things from boxing, karate, savate, et cetera.

Q: Is it true that your mother was a boxing and wrestling promoter for the Olympic Auditorium in Los Angeles?
A: Yes, she was. That's the reason I began to wrestle when I was 7 years old. I also trained in jiu-jitsu, but it was not classical jiu-jitsu. It was more similar to what the Machado and Gracie brothers are doing these days.

"At first I used all the wrestling moves that I knew, so the judo instructors would kick me out of class for using those techniques. It was all the practical stuff—catch or submission wrestling— not Greco-Roman or freestyle. I used every single forbidden technique."

Q: When did you begin judo training?
A: It was a little bit later. At first I used all the wrestling moves that I knew, so the judo instructors would kick me out of class for using those techniques.

Q: What kind of wrestling are you talking about?
A: It was all the practical stuff—catch or submission wrestling—not Greco-Roman or freestyle. I used every single forbidden technique.

Q: What's your combat philosophy?
A: Use anything that helps you. Don't follow the rules, break them to win. In the street there are no rules! Fighting is not about how you play the

"You need to have a good base and then expand on it. It takes a high IQ and an open mind. Look at guys like Benny Urquidez, Joe Lewis, and Bill Wallace—they added boxing and grappling to their karate in order to improve as martial artists. They are very well-rounded now."

game—the only thing that counts is who's standing at the end.

Q: Do you believe that every system has something to offer?
A: Pretty much, but it depends a lot on what you're looking for. My system is about fighting—even dirty fighting if you have to. Many of the old systems were effective back then because nobody knew about them. Times have changed and every street fighter knows how to deal with a front kick or a reverse punch, so the old stuff doesn't work anymore. Therefore, you'd better change and adapt. You have to keep an open mind because you're never too old to be a student again.

Q: You knew Bruce Lee and even worked out with him, right?
A: Yes. He was a great guy—very powerful and talented. I showed him the importance of learning grappling and being able to defend yourself in a ground situation. He really liked having that option, but his own personal preference was to stay out of that range. I don't think he felt very comfortable on the ground.

Q: What is your system comprised of?
A: Grappling is just a word for me because I use boxing, karate, savate, jiu-jitsu, wrestling, aikido, sambo, tire iron, engine, transmission, et cetera. You need to have a good base and then expand on it. It takes a high IQ and an open mind. Look at guys like Benny Urquidez, Joe Lewis, and Bill Wallace—they added boxing and grappling to their karate in order to improve as martial artists. They are very well-rounded now.

Q: You mentioned that don't play other people's games. What do you mean by that?

A: First, every style has certain weaknesses, and every fighter has different weaknesses. You have to find out what they are and then use them to your advantage. For instance, if you're fighting a boxer you know his system has no defense below the waist, so you tackle him to the ground or kick low to the legs. This way you play your game, not his.

Q: Do you think a grappler has advantages over a striker?

A: I think so—but of course I'm a grappler. If the striker does not know anything else and neither does the grappler, I think the grappler can take the striker to the ground much easier than the striker can make the grappler stand up on his feet all the time. But a fight really comes down to people, not styles.

"If the striker does not know anything else and neither does the grappler, I think the grappler can take the striker to the ground much easier than the striker can make the grappler stand up on his feet all the time. But a fight really comes down to people, not styles."

Q: You talk about dirty fighting. Why?

A: Because when you trying to survive you can't play around. That's not sport, that's survival. Pictures this, you're 5'7" and Ken Shamrock is coming at you. What kind of technique are you going to use?

Q: I don't understand.

A: He has such a size advantage that you can't try to arm-lock him or punch him in the face because you won't get anything but a broken hand. So to survive you have to fight dirty. You have attack the eyes or the groin. That's your only way out. And no one can resist being poked really hard in

"The physical techniques have to be second nature. In a real fight your techniques have to come out instinctively, and you have to repeat then in practice until they are recorded in your nervous system."

the eye because the nerves are really close to the brain.

Q: What's the key to improving in martial arts?
A: Try to practice as much as you can because the more you train the better you'll be. The physical techniques have to be second nature. In a real fight your techniques have to come out instinctively, and you have to repeat then in practice until they are recorded in your nervous system. It takes years for the physical techniques to become second nature but there's no other way. Sparring is very important because it gives you the right timing for the techniques—and the golden rule is conditioning.

Q: Just being in shape?
A: The reason Bruce Lee was so good was because he was in great shape. He could do things other people knew just as well, but they physically couldn't perform them.

"I don't do any weight training but I am not against it. Just remember that a martial artist should not train as a bodybuilder. It should be used as a supplement to your training. Lots of reps with moderate weights will give you better results."

Q: Do you recommend weight training?
A: I don't do any but I am not against it. If it is done the right way, I am all for it. Just remember that a martial artist should not train as a bodybuilder and it should not replace his martial arts training. It should be used as a supplement to your training. Doing low reps with heavy weights is not good for the martial artist. Lots of reps with moderate weights will give you better results.

Q: Do you think traditional martial arts have something to offer in modern times?
A: Yes, and there are three reasons why. They can build confidence and that's very important in the long run. Secondly, they build character and

"In self-defense you want to be on your opponent's back so he has no weapons to attack you with."

third, they are effective if you know when and how to use their techniques. So the answer is definitely yes.

Q: What is the difference between teaching sport and self-defense techniques?
A: Certain techniques can be used in both scenarios, but the attitude has to be different because your life is in the line of fire. Therefore, you need to know those dirty tricks. I mentioned before that are not allowed in sport competitions. In self-defense you want to be on your opponent's back so he has no weapons to attack you with.

Q: You like to talk about Joe Lewis, Chuck Norris, Benny Urquidez, and Bill Wallace. Why is that?
A: Because they are great champions on their own right. They are humble and all of them understand two important points in martial arts—the first is that learning grappling techniques is important…

Q: And the second?
A: Something that you too will realize one day—that I am the best-looking guy in martial arts.

Q: Where did you learn to box?
A: I grew up at the Main Street Gym in Los Angeles. Being there all the time, I had chances to box a lot of champions.

Q: You founded the Gene LeBell Grappling World. Why?
A: It's just a loose collection of martial artists whose goal is to bring people together. There are great teachers and martial artist out there that are working with me. If you don't like Gene LeBell's stuff you can always learn

sambo and jiu-jitsu from Gokor Chivichyan, judo from Hayward Nishioka, Brazilian jiu-jitsu from the Machado brothers, karate from Benny Urquidez, et cetera. Not a bad line-up, eh?

Q: You have a special training center, don't you?
A: I like to teach at my dojo, up in the mountains. I only teach advanced students who have ability. I really like to learn new techniques from talented martial artists, but these techniques have to work under combative fighting.

Q: What advice would you give to any martial artist?
A: Be ready for everything. Don't challenge people. Make friends and then be there when they need you. Don't keep secrets. Teach what you know because that's what people appreciate the most—honesty. I don't believe that a teacher should hold back techniques. Why take secrets to your grave? When you die you live on through your students. ○

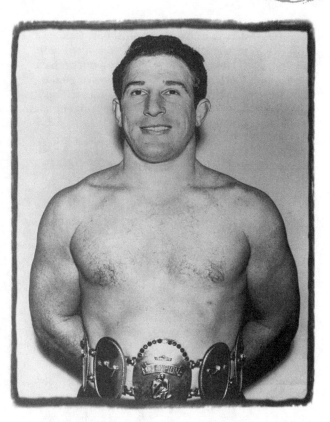

"Be ready for everything. Don't challenge people. Make friends and then be there when they need you. Don't keep secrets."

Gene LeBell faces an attacker (1). As soon as his opponent shoots for the takedown (2), Gene under-hooks both arms (3), and applies forward pressure (4). He then turns sideways to gain a better attack angle (5), grabs his right wrist with his left hand (6), and applies a finishing neck crank (7).

Gene LeBell avoids an attacker's punch (1), moves-in quickly (2), and positions himself on his opponent's back (3). He then brings his right arm to the aggressor's face (4), pulls down (5), and applies a finishing neck crank (6).

Masters Techniques

Gene LeBell faces Gokor Chivichyan (1). Gokor's kick is blocked by Gene (2), who grabs his leg (3), pushes forward (4), ducks under Gokor (5), and lifts him into the air (6). Gene then spins around (7), drops Gokor violently on the ground (8), controls the arm (9), and applies a finishing arm-lock (10).

Gene LeBell avoids an attacker's kick (1), stays close enough to go under it (2), then grabs the foot of the supporting leg (3). Bringing the attacker to the ground (4), Gene controls the right leg (5), and achieves final control (6).

Gerson Sanginitto

Generation X-cellent

WHEN THE ART OF BRAZILIAN JIU-JITSU TOOK THE WORLD IN EARLY 90's, THE TWO MOST SIGNIFICANT FAMILIES TO SPREAD THE ART AND SERVE AS A SOURCE OF WORLDWIDE KNOWLEDGE WERE THE GRACIES AND THE MACHADOS. A DECADE AFTER ROYCE GRACIE WON THE FIRST UFC, HOWEVER, A SECOND GENERATION OF CAPABLE INSTRUCTORS HAS TAKEN ON THE RESPONSIBILITY OF SHARING AND UPDATING THE TECHNICAL ASPECTS OF THE ART. MANY THINGS HAVE CHANGED IN BRAZILIAN JIU-JITSU, DUE TO THE HIGHLY CHARGED COMPETITION ATMOSPHERE, AND NEW TECHNICAL DEVELOPMENTS HAVE MADE SOME OF THE TECHNIQUES USED AS RECENTLY AS 10 YEARS AGO OBSOLETE!

GERSON SANGINITTO IS ONE OF THE SECOND GENERATION OF BRAZILIAN JIU-JITSU INSTRUCTORS, AND HAS BEEN TEACHING IN THE UNITED STATES FOR OVER FIVE YEARS. HIS KNOWLEDGE OF THE GRAPPLING ARTS IS NOT JUST LIMITED TO THE COVETED RANK OF *FAIXA PRETA* (BLACK BELT) IN BRAZILIAN JIU-JITSU, BUT ALSO HOLDS A BLACK BELT IN JAPANESE JUDO. THIS IS A COMBINATION THAT MANY TOP BRAZILIAN FIGHTERS AND INSTRUCTORS CONSIDER EXCEPTIONAL, DUE TO THE DIFFERENT EMPHASIS THE TWO ARTS PUT ONTO THROWING TECHNIQUES (JUDO) AND GROUND TECHNIQUES (BRAZILIAN JIU-JITSU).

A DIRECT STUDENT OF THE PRESIDENT OF THE BRAZILIAN JIU-JITSU FEDERATION, CARLOS GRACIE JR., SANGINITTO HAS SHARED MANY HOURS OF TRAINING WITH SOME OF THE TOP-NAMES OF JIU-JITSU, INCLUDING BOTH RIGAN MACHADO AND RENZO GRACIE. IN MANY WAYS, IT IS SAFE TO SAY THAT THE FUTURE OF THE BRAZILIAN ART IS IN THE HANDS OF THIS NEW GENERATION OF YOUNG TEACHERS WHO STILL HAVE THE PASSION AND DRIVE TO TEACH A FIRST-DAY WHITE BELT WITH THE SAME MOTIVATION THEY HAVE WHEN THEY IMPART KNOWLEDGE TO A CLASS FULL OF BROWN BELTS.

Q: How long have you been practicing martial arts?
A: I started in 1973 and I haven't stopped since. I haven't specifically trained in any other styles than grappling. I started judo first, and then began jiu-jitsu in 1984. As far as other martial arts systems like kung-fu, taekwondo, and karate, I never trained steadily, although through friends I have been exposed to them. My teacher is Carlos Gracie Jr. but there are also many people who have taught me a lot about jiu-jitsu. These include

"I guess the main reason why I was fast at learning jiu-jitsu was because of my judo training. I really think that my previous training in judo helped me a lot in my jiu-jitsu evolution."

Paulo Cesar Mulatinho, Rigan Machado, Renzo Gracie and Antonio Rodrigues.

Q: Have you ever had to use jiu-jitsu in a real fight?

A: Back in the 80's, in my early 20's, a friend of mine invited me to go to Ipanema to visit a karate academy and learn some of their moves. At first, we were only exchanging techniques in a friendly manner. But when it came to free training, things changed a little. I started to train with one of the instructors. He surprised me and came after me and really wanted to beat me up. I was thinking that this was going to be just an easy practice of the punches and kick I had just learned. But instead, the guy came at me right away and surprised me and gave me a fat lip. After his punch I went after him to tap him out. I was not trying to punch him back, but I was enraged and wanted to prove that my technique was more effective than his. So I went for a double leg, took him down, mounted him, and then all of a sudden changed my mind and started to punch the guy in the face! I kept going until my friends finally made me stop. I guess that was my first vale tudo and the end of my karate training!

Q: Were you a natural at jiu-jitsu?

A: I don't know if I would say it that strongly, but I did learn the movements very easily. I remember that when I got my blue belt, I became an instructor for beginners because I always had a certain skill for teaching. It was probably because I always liked to teach, and I truly enjoy doing it. I guess the main reason why I was fast at learning jiu-jitsu was because of my judo training. I really think that my previous training in judo helped me a lot in my jiu-jitsu evolution. I was very comfortable with the idea of grabbing an opponent and grappling them on the ground. My transition to jiu-jitsu was very smooth and easy. Of course, there were aspects that were more difficult to absorb, but the idea of the grappling game was already in my body.

Q: Do you like vale tudo events such as UFC and Pride?

A: It's great exposure for jiu-jitsu fighters and for jiu-jitsu itself—these events demonstrate the effectiveness of Brazilian jiu-jitsu. Groundwork was something that nobody knew before the UFC. Royce Gracie opened doors for a lot of people because he showed martial artists from other styles how much it helped to have a knowledge of grappling. In general, I believe that all mixed martial arts events are positive. They bring publicity to all the martial arts and they help the sport of grappling to be recognized and to grow. When it comes to the athletes themselves, they acquire the added bonus of personal recognition and a little extra income. Fighters who participate in these events have to be extremely dedicated professionals. It is a job that requires hard training and full concentration. Besides building inner strength, the athletes learn different styles so they can understand and defend themselves against all attacks. So I feel MMA helps the technical aspects of all martial arts to improve.

Q: Do you think that jiu-jitsu in America has caught up with jiu-jitsu in Brazil?

A: American students are definitely improving, but they are not quite there yet. Jiu-jitsu has been a mainstream martial art in Brazil since the early 80's and has been practiced since the early 20's. Also, the number of practitioners is a lot higher and the number of competitions is incredible—there are events every weekend. However, now there are many top Brazilian instructors living in the US and they have American students who have a natural ability for the art. I'd say that pretty soon the Americans are going to get even with Brazil. But for now, Brazil is still number one.

Q: Do you feel that you have more to learn?

A: Definitely! A big part of jiu-jitsu is learning something every day—especially since jiu-jitsu is a growing and evolving art. It is in constant development. This is true not only in techniques, but also in regard to new strategies and tactics to use against different opponents. Skillful and creative fighters are always creating new positions and improving the game. So, we are always learning and implementing our knowledge with each other. As a practitioner and as a instructor, my schedules are different. As a practitioner, I use more time to building my physical conditioning, while as an instructor I have to dedicate time to planning out the best strategy for teaching a class. It is important that my students fully understand the principles of the art and consequently keep improving their game, endurance, and confidence. That takes planning on my part.

Q: What are the major changes in jiu-jitsu since you began training?
A: Brazilian jiu-jitsu has evolved a lot since the early '80s. Initially, BJJ was made up of just the Gracie family and their friends. Nowadays, the media has shown the world how great this martial art is. It started as a small community, but it has now become one of the greatest martial arts in the world. All this has happened without breaking or changing its principles, which proves its strength and effectiveness. A few years ago, the art of jiu-jitsu was more aggressive than it is today. The rules have changed a lot, so all practitioners, including myself, had to adjust our game accordingly. My game had to become extremely strategic and aggressive, since now a single mistake can be lethal. The level of the game is so high that any little mistake can cause you to lose a match. In the old days, for instance, there was a huge difference between a purple belt and a brown belt. Nowadays, you see purple belts giving a real hard time to both brown and black belts! The purple belt may lose in the end, but they give the top guys a run for their money. I think this is good for the art and the sport, because it means the technical level is going up.

Q: With whom would you like to personally train?
A: I would like to train with Rickson Gracie—or at least get on the mat with him just to feel his technique. Carlos Gracie Jr. took us to his academy a few times, but I have never trained with him personally. Everyone is a little different in jiu-jitsu, so it is good to train with all the top people. The strength of jiu-jitsu is in its differences. A person should find the style that best fits their aptitude and their desire. It is very important for students to find a place where they feel comfortable. Only in the right environment, can the right learning and improvement occur. Even now, my passion for the art and for teaching is what keeps me going. It brings me great fulfillment to see my students successfully applying a technique that I taught.

Q: Do you think it is necessary to fight on the street in order to try out jiu-jitsu self-defense techniques?
A: Not really, because nowadays a fighter can have specific training in his own academy and also test his skills in no-holds-barred events. However, if someone has fought a lot in the streets, this person does learn what they are capable of and might have an advantage over a person that does not have such experience. These real situations teach you how to effectively deal with the adrenaline rush, which can work in your favor or against you.

Q: What's your opinion about mixing styles?
A: I think it is good to know more than one style. The goal of an athlete should be to become a complete fighter. However, a person should specialize in one style and enhance his skill with some training in other styles. Brazilian jiu-jitsu requires great dedication and steady training. I don't believe that a student should jump from art to art, because in the end they won't achieve full proficiency in any style.

Q: Has Brazilian jiu-jitsu been of personal benefit to you?
A: It brings me great joy and has brought me many new friends. I feel like I'm a part of a big family. It brings discipline, confidence, and attitude. Also, the challenge of competition helps to keep me fresh and excited about the sport. A successful competitor in Brazilian jiu-jitsu has discipline, dedication, persistence, and passion for what they do. Natural ability is the start, and these qualities will keep you in the game. But you have to work hard. I guess these qualities are common not only in Brazilian jiu-jitsu, but in any serious competitor from any legitimate sport. It takes these qualities to become a good competitor.

"A big part of jiu-jitsu is learning something every day—especially since jiu-jitsu is a growing and evolving art. It is in constant development."

Q: Is supplementary training important?
A: After grappling students have committed themselves to BJJ, they can complement their skills with other types of training. In particular, cardiovascular conditioning is crucial for the jiu-jitsu athlete. Weight training and stretching are also effective tools that will greatly help a fighter. But I always stress the fact that nothing replaces time on the mat. Technique is the main thing everyone needs to develop and that only comes from mat time. Hours spent pumping iron won't improve your jiu-jitsu if your technique is not good. Focus on technique first and then later move to supplementary aspects to enhance your technical skills.

Q: What are your plans for the future?
A: I want to keep teaching for as long as I can. ↻

Masters Techniques

Gerson pushes his opponent's shoulder (1), moves his hip to the left and brings his knee out (2), then spins his back and throws his leg over his opponent's shoulder (3). He then holds the opponent's belt, locks the omoplata, and starts to sit up (4), adjusting the lock by pulling his left leg back (5). He then finishes the submission by moving his body forward (6).

Gerson holds his opponent's right cuff (1). Without letting go of the cuff, he brings his opponent's arm behind his head (2), and traps the arm by holding the opposite collar (3). He then pushes his opponent's shoulder and frees his knee (4), and moves his hip towards the arm he is attacking (5). Gerson's opponent defends the arm lock by pulling his elbow out (6), so Gerson holds his opponent's pants with his right hand, throws his left leg over the shoulder and moves his hip towards the opposite side of the arm, submitting him with the bent arm-lock (7).

105

Gerson's opponent plants both hands on the ground (1). Gerson attacks his opponent's left arm and controls it (2). He simultaneously moves his hip towards the arm, plants his left foot on the opponent's hip, and makes his opponent lose his base (3). He then brings his right knee on top of his opponent's shoulder and starts to pressure the arm (4). He completes the submission by squeezing his knees together and by lifting his head (5).

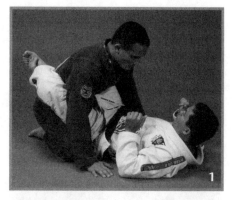

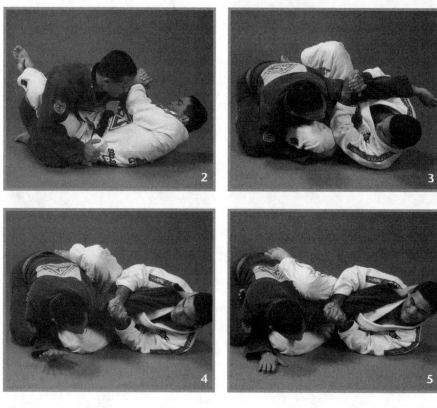

Gerson stands holding his opponent's legs (1). He brings his right knee between them and places his left arm under the leg (2). He then twists and brings his right knee over the opponent's leg (3), and keeps rotating and holding his opponent's leg in order to keep it straight (4). Gerson then falls on his back with the trapped leg and lifts his hip for the submission (5).

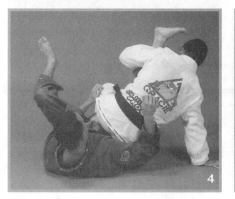

Gerson is inside his opponent's half-guard, holding his collar and arm (1). He passes his left leg over his opponent's head (2), reaches the other side and traps his opponent's leg (3). He then starts to fall back, keeping his opponent's leg trapped (4), and completes the submission by pulling the leg down and lifting the hip (5).

Gerson is on his knees with his opponent attacking his back (1). He grabs his opponent's left leg, which is between his legs (2). He then rolls over his right shoulder, making his opponent lose his balance (3), and finishes the roll by trapping his opponent's leg (4). Gerson keeps the pressure on the leg, and submits his opponent by hugging the foot under the arm pit and lifting the hip (5).

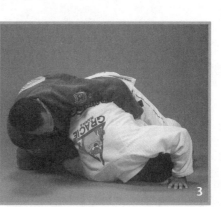

Gerson is in control from his opponent's side (1). He attacks his opponent's collar by bringing the thumbs inside (2), and bringing his left arm under his opponent's shoulder (3). He then grabs his opponent's collar with his left hand (4), and finishes the choke by squeezing and bringing the elbows together (5).

Gerson holds his opponent's elbows (1). He pushes with both elbows and starts to climb the guard (2). Bringing both legs on top of his opponent's shoulder, he locks the feet (3), and applies a double arm-bar by holding the wrists and lifting his hips (4).

Gerson is in control from his opponent's side (1). His opponent tries to open space by pushing Gerson's face (2). Gerson brings his knee over his opponent's stomach (3), and applies the arm bar by putting pressure on his opponent's elbow (4).

111

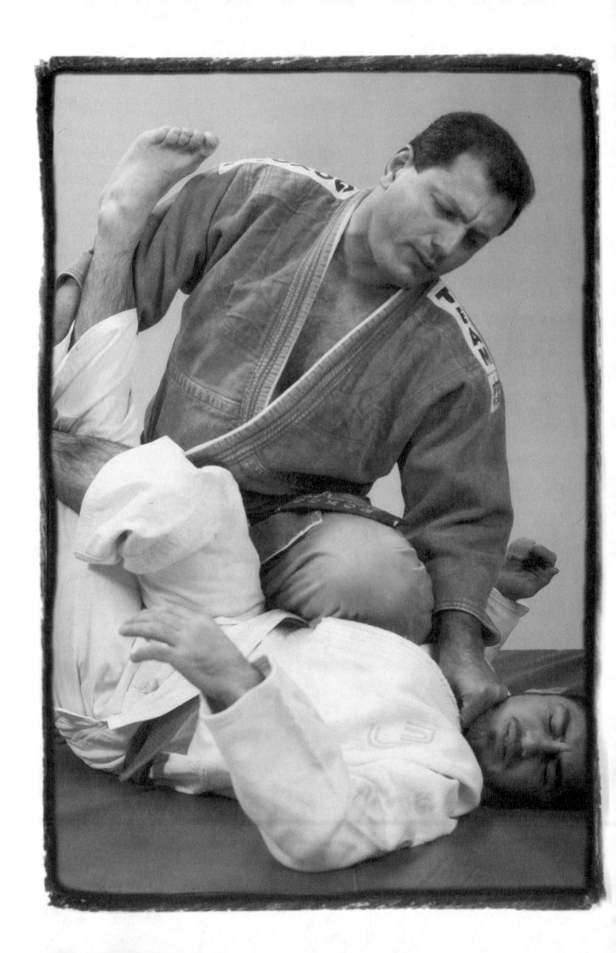

Gokor Chivichyan

Master of a Thousand Submissions

BORN IN ARMENIA, A REPUBLIC OF THE FORMER SOVIET UNION, GOKOR CHIVICHYAN GOT INVOLVED IN THE RUSSIAN GRAPPLING ART OF SAMBO AT AGE 5. HE LATER TOOK-UP JUDO AND HASN'T STOPPED TRAINING SINCE. AFTER YEARS OF COMPETITION AND A SUCCESSFUL WINNING CAREER, HE DECIDED TO ENTER IN THE WORLD GAMES AND U.S. OPEN WHERE HE TOOK FIRST PLACE. HE WAS PREPARED TO COMPETE IN THE OLYMPICS BUT DUE TO POLITICS ANOTHER FIGHTER WAS CHOSEN TO PARTICIPATE. IN 1981, GOKOR CHIVICHYAN DECIDED TO MOVE TO THE UNITED STATES. SINCE HIS ARRIVAL, HE HAS BEEN A LEADING NAME IN SPREADING THE GRAPPLING ARTS ALL ACROSS THE COUNTRY. AS A TRAINER, HE SHARED HIS KNOWLEDGE WITH MANY TOP JUDO, SAMBO, JIU JITSU AND NO-HOLDS-BARRED (NHB) FIGHTERS OVER THE YEARS. HIS STUDENTS ARE GENERALLY REGARDED AS SOME OF THE MOST TECHNICAL GRAPPLERS IN THE WORLD.

AFTER SEVERAL YEARS IN THE WEST, HE JOINED FORCES WITH THE ULTIMATE GRAPPLER IN THE BUSINESS—THE LEGENDARY "JUDO" GENE LEBELL. TOGETHER, THEY RUN THE WORLD GRAPPLING FEDERATION, ONE OF THE MOST SUCCESSFUL MARTIAL ARTS AND GRAPPLING ORGANIZATIONS ANYWHERE. LOOKING BACK ON HIS YOUTH, GOKOR ADMITS THAT HIS OWN RECKLESS ACTIONS CAUSED MANY PERSONAL AND FAMILY PROBLEMS THAT HE HAD TO DEAL WITH—BUT THANKS TO HIS DEDICATION TO THE MARTIAL ARTS HIS LIFE TOOK A DIFFERENT DIRECTION. "CHANGING YOUR LIFE AROUND IS A MATTER OF SETTING GOALS AND THEN FIGHTING FOR THEM," GOKOR SAYS. "MARTIAL ARTS, LIKE LIFE ITSELF, ARE AN EVERYDAY CHALLENGE THAT WE HAVE TO FACE AND OVERCOME AGAIN AND AGAIN. IT'S STRICTLY UP TO US IF WE ARE GOING TO FIGHT OR GIVE UP."

Q: How long have you been practicing martial arts?
A: I started when I was 5 years old. A sambo champion saw me and came to my house to take me to train. Two years later, I started to compete and sometimes I won and sometimes I lost. When I turned 9, I began to count my fights as victories only. I began to winning tournaments. Later on I became involved with what is called "khok," which is a form of bare-knuckle combat. It's an Armenian fighting method. You can punch, kick and do everything. This combat method interested the Russians and they

*"My main instructor was Gagik Dabagyan,
but after many years of training in martial arts
I had the opportunity to learn from many other
great teachers. They all left their mark in me,
not only technically but also as human being."*

asked the Armenians to teach them.

Q: How many styles have you trained in?
A: I started with sambo wrestling in 1968 in Armenia. A few years later I began to train in judo. It was natural after having a foundation in submission grappling. I didn't know what judo was, but it was very familiar with ground work and so I gave it a try. I also studied boxing because I realized that it would be a great complement to my previous training as far as knowing how to fight a striker. Boxing helped me a lot and opened my eyes as far as understanding what a properly-trained fighter can do with his hands. I guess I was right in my research instincts, because today nearly every no-holds-barred fighter studies boxing.

My main instructor was Gagik Dabagyan, but after many years of training in martial arts I had the opportunity to learn from many other great teachers. They all left their mark in me, not only technically but also as human being. Some of them may not teach you much from a technical point of view, but their attitude and spirit is the best you will ever find. Therefore, they have a strong influence on you. I believe that people are a product of many influences, and not simply the result of the teachings of one instructor.

Q: Were you aggressive in your early years?
A: When I was young I was always looking for trouble and getting into a lot of fights. Thank God, I decided to train in martial arts and stick to it.

Spending most of my time in the dojo changed my life for the better or I could have gotten into serious trouble and ended up in jail. I remember that in the beginning my kicks weren't very effective and I didn't use them much. Then the other guys started to kick harder and harder and my legs began to hurt more and more. I decided to take serious kicking lessons and I went to a friend of mine who was a Thai champion. He taught me muay Thai and my kicking changed completely.

Another person who really changed me was Gene LeBell. At the time I met him, I thought that with my submission arsenal I could beat everybody. I met him and showed him how we trained in Armenia. We shared some thoughts and finally said, "What you are doing is good, but I'll teach you how to fight like a man!" Needless to say, I found out that I was missing something! I never enjoyed the martial arts as much as I did after I met Gene LeBell. He makes working-out fun because he is always joking and that relaxes you so you can learn more. I adopted a lot of his teaching philosophy and use it into my own classes. I get a kick out of making students feel good. The more relaxed the atmosphere is, the more a student can learn

"I never enjoyed the martial arts as much as I did after I met Gene LeBell. He makes working-out fun because he is always joking and that relaxes you so you can learn more. I adopted a lot of his teaching philosophy and use it into my own classes."

Q: Did the movements come easily to you?
A: I believe that everybody—regardless of their natural talent—has to work hard to obtain a high level in any physical activity. Having natural talent doesn't mean anything if you don't back it up with dedication and hours of hard work. Only this will bring results and allow you to reach your full potential. Once you put thousands of hours into training and you look

115

"As an instructor I make sure everything I teach works on the mat and the street. I don't teach things that can get my students hurt because they are useless and ineffective under real circumstances. I want my student to be able to defend themselves and also to compete under many different rules."

back, you can always say, "It wasn't that hard." But the truth is that it was very hard and you went through many ups and downs to be where you are today. The only way to become a champion is to put in many hours of hard training without holding anything back. There is no other way, no shortcuts.

Q: How has your personal fighting system developed over the years?

A: Times change and you have to change with them. The training methods are different, the techniques are constantly evolving, and new movements are being created all the time. You need to find a way to adapt to the ever-changing flow of things. Therefore, you can't get stagnant and stick with the same methods that you used 20 years ago because they won't work. As an instructor I make sure everything I teach works on the mat and the street. I don't teach things that can get my students hurt because they are useless and ineffective under real circumstances. I want my students to be able to defend themselves and also to compete under many different rules. My students can kick, punch and grapple. If we are doing judo, they will put on a gi and play under judo rules. If we do sambo, they will get their shorts and play by sambo rules. If I tell them that we are going to compete in jiu-jitsu, then they will do it. Our fighting system is well-rounded and allows the students to fight under different rules.

Q: Do you think there are still pure systems of martial arts or do people tend to combine styles and cross-train?

A: My life and training has been strongly influenced by one of the greatest grapplers in history—Gene LeBell. Gene's training and fighting method is a combination of several elements—judo, wrestling, boxing,

and karate—and he is an eclectic martial artist. His idea is to study as many arts as you can and try to find common threads that allow you to put everything together. Once you have a strong foundation and a deep knowledge of your own capabilities—strong and weak points—then you can choose the movements and tactics that are best for you as individual. As instructor, you have to give your students a wide variety of possibilities. Many of them may not be the one you'd use personally, but you have to teach those to the students because they may fit them. Your personal training as an instructor is totally different from the goals you may have as a fighter. In some aspects, I dare say that they are opposites. What you need and want as a fighter is not necessarily what you need and want as an instructor.

"As instructor, you have to give your students a wide variety of possibilities. Many of them may not be the one you'd use personally, but you have to teach those to the students because they may fit them. Your personal training as an instructor is totally different from the goals you may have as a fighter."

Q: What is your opinion of no-holds-barred events?

A: It proves who is the best on a given night. It is a very demanding sport and only qualified people should enter. Unless the technical skill is really good, it resembles any other kind of combat sport—one night one fighter can win, the next maybe the other one will be victorious. Even if you are better than your opponent, your opponent may have a great day and you a miserable one. So you end up losing and he ends up winning—or vice versa. An important point about fighting professionally is that you have to prepare for it and put all your time and dedication into it. I advocate for full contact in punches and kicks but I also understand that this is not suitable for everybody. It is also good to have tournaments and championships that allow students to compete under more controlled sets of rules that prevents unnecessary injuries.

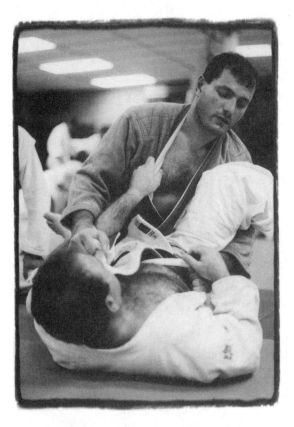

"You never stop learning until you die. As I said before, if you stop studying and researching new techniques and tactics, you are going to be in trouble because the art is progressing very fast. You have to keep moving forward to be able to stay on top."

Q: What tactics work best in NHB?
A: The first thing you need to do is to develop a game plan. Once you have that and all your basics are covered, you need to spot your opponent's weakness and exploit it. If he is a kickboxer then his weak point will be groundwork, and the opposite is true if he happens to be a grappler. You always attack or counterattack his weakness. Even within the limitations of a particular martial arts style, you'll find that your adversary has weak areas that you should work on. If he is a grappler maybe he is better on the top that from the guard. So you have to look for that.

Obviously it is easier for a grappler to fight against a boxer—he can't defend himself from the waist down. Nowadays, fighters are all very well-rounded and they know how to punch, kick, and fight on the ground, so taking advantage of the other fighter's weakness is more a matter of training for what the fighter specifically does, rather than a particular set of techniques.

Q: Do you feel that you still have further to go in your studies?
A: You never stop learning until you die. As I said before, if you stop studying and researching new techniques and tactics, you are going to be in trouble because the art is progressing very fast. You have to keep moving forward to be able to stay on top. The martial arts in America have improved so much that you don't really need to leave the country to learn. The best instructors are in America so why not take advantage of that? We all need to keep learning and driving the grappling arts forward.

Q: What are the major changes in grappling since you began training?

A: Everything! Today there are more books, videos, the Internet, et cetera. This has brought a huge amount of information to practitioners. They can search and find details about the arts they practice that were unheard 20 years ago. On the Internet everybody has a voice and that can bring a lot of good information to the readers—but also a lot of bad information. One thing I do not like is people attacking other people without even knowing them. Unfortunately, there is a lot of hate out there and many people have the wrong attitude toward other human beings. These people never show up at your school so you can perform on them what Gene LeBell calls "attitude adjustment." They hide behind a screen name and never come straight to your face and tell you what they think about—mainly because they don't even know you! So I try to not make these people part of my life.

Q: With whom would you like to train whom you have not?

A: I'd love to have trained with all the great teachers of all martial arts styles. I

"Don't settle with what one single instructor tells you at the first school you visit. Analyze what they teach, look at the students, and question the main instructor so you can find what is best for you. Don't be afraid to ask. This is the only way you'll be able to find what it really works for you and makes you happy."

know it sounds weird but it's true. There is so much knowledge out there to be absorbed, and I enjoy the idea of training with all good teachers of martial arts. But don't get me wrong, I'm not only talking about the techniques, a good teacher teaches you the right attitude and spirit as well.

Q: What would you say to someone who is interested in learning grappling?

A: Go to different schools and see which one is best for you. Don't settle with what one single instructor tells you at the first school you visit. Analyze what they teach, look at the students, and question the main

"Fighting in the street is a lose-lose situation. Even if you win, there is a big loss in who you are. A true martial artist should be above all these childish ego games. If you are good at something and it is second nature—like walking—you will be all right if one day you have to defend yourself. If you need to get into fights to prove anything, then you need to re-evaluate who you."

instructor so you can find what is best for you. Don't be afraid to ask. This is the only way you'll be able to find what it really works for you and makes you happy. Don't forget that in order to get better you need to enjoy what you are doing. If you don't like the style you're practicing, you won't go very far—you'll get bored, tired, and your motivation will fly out the window.

Q: What keeps you motivated after all these years?
A: I truly love the martial arts, so for me to keep training and teaching does not equire a big effort. I'm blessed because I am doing what I love, so I consider myself a lucky person. I meet a lot of nice people, and many have become my personal friends who I share my life with them. I guess you need motivation when you perform a task you don't enjoy, but when you love what you do and you have fun at it, then motivation is easy. Martial arts are a great way of life. They give me a peace of mind that helps to balance the rest of my life.

Q: Do you think it is necessary to do NHB fighting to achieve good street-fighting skills?
A: You are talking about two different things. Competition is a sport and not a real fight. Of course, if you are a professional fighter you are going to have a great advantage on the street. But my advice is not to be silly and get into fights simply to find out if the techniques you learn in the school work. Fighting in the street is a lose-lose situation. Even if you win, there is a big loss in who you are. A true martial artist should be above all these childish ego games. If you are good at something and it is second nature—like walking—you will be all right if one day you have to defend

yourself. Many streetfights happen because both people are terribly insecure and have something to prove to themselves. If you need to get into fights to prove anything, then you need to re-evaluate who you are and what you are doing in martial arts—because there is something wrong with you.

Q: Do you think grappling is the ultimate self-defense art?
A: Not really. Due to the UFC, people tend to believe that grappling is the final answer to all fighting questions and the grappling knowledge comes only from the Gracie Family. Neither one of these statements is true. Grappling is great but there are situations when you just don't want to grapple. For instance, if you are attacked by two individuals it's dumb to take one guy to the floor and grapple with him because the other will attack your back. It is true that a good throw can knock your opponent out, but against multiple attackers you'd better rely on punches and kicks. As far as popularizing the grappling arts, the Gracies opened the eyes of many people and they deserve a lot of credit for that. But the grappling arts didn't come from them—there were many different grappling methods before the UFC and the Gracie family came into the picture.

"Grappling is great but there are situations when you just don't want to grapple. For instance, if you are attacked by two individuals it's dumb to take one guy to the floor and grapple with him because the other will attack your back."

Q: What's your opinion about mixing styles? Can it be beneficial?
A: I don't think that one art nullifies the effectiveness of the other. But it is true that you can't mix apples and oranges. The mixture needs to have a structure and a method that can be used as a foundation to integrate the rest of the styles that you train in. Sooner or later, you'll realize that you enjoy fighting at a certain distance and that you don't like other distances as much. For instance, you may enjoy close-quarter range so you'll put more time into grappling. This will be your foundation. Then you can study different grappling methods in order to make your preference

stronger and more complete. Later, you can train in kickboxing to develop your punches and kicks, but you need to know how to incorporate this new element. The kickboxing aspect will complement your core grappling. You may not want to become a kickboxer, but knowing how to use elements of kickboxing will make you a more complete fighter. If you don't know how to integrate—and please note that I say integrate and not add—you will nullify the effectiveness of any art. Just learn, learn, learn everything and use what you do best.

"The number one priority should be your cardiovascular conditioning. If you don't have good wind, it won't matter how good technically you are because you won't be able to execute your moves. This is Fighting 101—cardiovascular endurance."

Q: What about supplementary training?
A: The number one priority should be your cardiovascular conditioning. If you don't have good wind, it won't matter how good technically you are because you won't be able to execute your moves. This is Fighting 101—cardiovascular endurance. Muscle conditioning is next. You need to work your muscles because they are responsible for performing physical action and movement. You need a fair amount of strength these days to be a winner. Technical skill isn't enough. Accept the fact that weight and strength training has to be one of your priorities. Finally, speed needs to be worked on. It doesn't matter how strong you are—if you move too slow you won't hit anybody. Speed and strength go hand-in-hand—one has to work for the other and visa versa. Of course, all these supplementary aspects of your training should come into the picture once you have a good technical foundation. Technique is the first thing to develop, and if you have a limited amount of workout time then that should be your priority. Any additional time can be spent on supplementary training.

Q: What are your thoughts on the future of NHB?

A: The first thing that needs to happen is to get the rules straight—there are too many rules variations from one event to another. This confuses the fighters and coaches. Basketball has one set of rules, football the same, and NHB should have only one set, too. Next is to increase the purses for the fighters. A professional fighter spends weeks training and then gets offered a small amount of money for entering an event—that's not right. Another important thing is to get TV to show the events so people can be educated about the sport and the rules. Once they understand what they are seeing they will enjoy it. And finally, since we are talking about a sport, we need to limit certain techniques that can damage fighters and destroy their careers. We need to protect the fighters because in the end the fighters are the ones who make the shows. They deserve the protection.

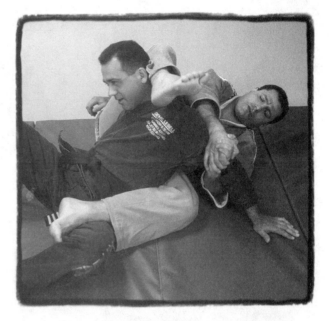

"Don't talk bad about anyone. Train hard and focus on your own training and life. Criticism only brings bad things, and if you spend time looking and worrying about what other people do, you won't be using that time to improve yourself. If a man shows you something, give him credit. Always give credit where credit is due."

Q: Do you have any general advice for grapplers?

A: Don't talk bad about anyone. Train hard and focus on your own training and life. Criticism only brings bad things, and if you spend time looking and worrying about what other people do, you won't be using that time to improve yourself. It's also extremely important give credit to the teachers you learn from. If a man shows you something, give him credit—even if it is only one single technique. Always give credit where credit is due. ↻

Helio Gracie

Brazilian Jiu-Jitsu's Greatest Champion

FROM A SICKLY CHILD TO A FEARED JIU-JITSU CHAMPION TAKING ON ALLCOMERS, HELIO GRACIE'S BELIEF IN HIMSELF AND HIS SYSTEM OF FIGHTING ENABLED HIM TO TURN HIS LIFE AROUND AND NOT ONLY HELP HIMSELF, BUT ALSO HELP OTHERS.

HELIO GRACIE, THE FATHER OF THE GRACIE JIU-JITSU SYSTEM, WAS BORN THE YOUNGEST OF FIVE BROTHERS ON OCTOBER 1, 1913 IN THE BRAZILIAN CITY OF BELEM, IN THE STATE OF PARA. A SICKLY CHILD, HELIO SUFFERED FROM AN INEXPLICABLE WEAKNESS THAT RESULTED IN SEVERE FAINTING SPELLS. DUE TO THIS PROBLEM, HE WAS FORBIDDEN FROM ENGAGING ANY KIND OF PHYSICAL ACTIVITY. BY WATCHING HIS OLDER BROTHER, CARLOS, TEACH EVERY DAY, HELIO MEMORIZED EVERY SINGLE MOVE SHOWN AT THE CLASS. ONE DAY, WHEN CARLOS MISSED CLASS, HELIO HAD THE OPPORTUNITY TO TEACH ONE OF HIS STUDENTS. THE MAN WAS SO IMPRESSED WITH HELIO'S TEACHING SKILLS THAT HE ASKED CARLOS TO LET HIM KEEP TRAINING UNDER THE "YOUNG GUY." THE REST, AS THEY SAY, IS HISTORY.

HELIO GRACIE MODIFIED THE JAPANESE VERSION OF JIU-JITSU, CHALLENGED OTHER FIGHTERS AND NEVER HESITATED TO STEP ONTO THE MAT AND PUT HIS SYSTEM TO THE TEST. THIS WAS THE BEGINNING OF THE FAMOUS "GRACIE CHALLENGE," WHICH PUT THEIR GRAPPLING STYLE OF COMBAT TO THE TEST AGAINST ALL FIGHTERS FROM THE STRIKING ARTS. IT WASN'T UNTIL HIS SON, RORION, CREATED THE ULTIMATE FIGHTING CHAMPIONSHIP THAT THE GRACIE METHOD OF JIU-JITSU BECAME KNOWN AROUND THE WORLD. SON ROYCE GRACIE SHOCKED THE MARTIAL ARTS WORLD BY WINNING THE UFC THREE TIMES, AND ANOTHER SON, RICKSON GRACIE, A LEGEND IN HIS OWN RIGHT, WENT TO JAPAN TO REPEAT HISTORY AND DEFEATED JAPAN'S BEST MARTIAL ARTISTS USING THE TECHNIQUES HIS FATHER DEVELOPED.

BY FIGHTING ALL-COMERS, AND STANDING UP FOR WHAT HE BELIEVED, HELIO EARNED A REPUTATION AS A MAN OF HONOR, SKILL, AND BRAVERY THAT ENDURES TO THIS DAY.

Q: How did you start your jiu-jitsu training?

A: My older brother Carlos learned the art its Japanese version, from a Japanese immigrant named Esai Maeda, who taught him the art out of respect for my father, Gastao Gracie, who had helped him get established.

Maeda was a fighter who had studied judo, sumo, and several forms of wrestling. A little bit later, my brother Carlos began to formally teach. I watched the classes but I wasn't allowed to participate due to my physical condition. I used to sit there every single day, memorizing all the moves in my mind. One day, Carlos was late for a private class, so I just walked up and told the student I'd teach him that day.

Q: What happened afterwards?
A: Carlos came and said to the student, "OK, let's get started." But the man said that I had already taught him. He said that he was very happy with me and he would like to have me as instructor from that day on. That man turned out to be the President of the Bank of Brazil!

"I wasn't allowed to participate due to my physical condition. I used to sit there every single day, memorizing all the moves in my mind. One day, Carlos was late for a private class, so I just walked up and told the student I'd teach him that day."

Q: Why weren't you allowed to teach at first?
A: As a child I was always sick and very small for my age. When I attended school I used to experience fainting spells. I guess that I was very allergic to the school! The school forbade me from engaging in any kind of physical activity because the family doctor said that I was a physically deprived child.

Q: Did they find the problem?
A: Yes, they found out that I had a problem in my nervous system. Pretty much everyone in my family suffers from this, but I had it the worst. This is why my brother Carlos developed the Gracie Diet.

*"I lacked the physical power to make some techniques really work,
so I began to adapt what I had seen to my own physical
limitations. It was something very instinctive."*

Q: How were your days at the school?
A: I didn't attend very much and I wasn't a good student. I was smaller
that the other kids and I had a real smart mouth, so I used to get in trouble very often.

Q: When did you start to modify the techniques?
A: Well, it was not that I intentionally wanted to change anything. I
lacked the physical power to make some techniques really work, so I
began to adapt what I had seen to my own physical limitations. It was
something very instinctive.

Q: So you didn't change for the sake of change?
A: No, I had to make things work for me. Sometimes I'd find myself in a
situation, using the technique the way it was taught to my brother,

"I always say that when you can handle a physical situation you are more confident. When you are more confident and secure, you become much more tolerant of others because you don't need to prove yourself."

Carlos, by the Japanese teacher. But I couldn't get it to work because the classical techniques would require a lot of strength. So I had to find a way to make it work using leverage, not muscle strength.

Q: When did you begin to think about improving the whole system?
A: Pretty soon, I realized that what I was doing was something that anybody could do. The techniques that I was developing would work for anyone, not just for me. At that point I decided to devote my life to jiu-jitsu.

Q: Did your health improve?
A: Yes, very much. I guess the correct diet and the right exercise made me healthier. But also, and this is very important, I began to get rid off the mental complexes that I had as a weak child. I was not insecure anymore and I became more confident and outgoing as I began teaching and helping other people to improve.

Q: Do you think martial arts training can change people's lives?
A: Sure it can! I always say that when you can handle a physical situation you are more confident. When you are more confident and secure, you become much more tolerant of others because you don't need to prove yourself. It's like if you win the lottery—you don't have to worry about money anymore so you're happier. If you know how to defend yourself

*"The Gracie Challenge was a way of improving our system and letting
the people see how good the techniques were. It put us in constant
difficulty and we had to develop new techniques and strategies
to deal with other systems. It never was a personal thing."*

properly you don't have to worry about being victimized. It clears your
mind to concentrate on other things.

Q: Isn't this a direct contradiction of the famous Gracie Challenge?
A: No, because the Gracie Challenge was a way of improving our system
and letting the people see how good the techniques were. It was not a
personal thing or an ego trip. If you really look at it from the right perspective, the challenge was very much for ourselves because it put us in
constant difficulty and we had to develop new techniques and strategies
to deal with other systems. It never was a personal thing.

Grappling Masters

"In Japan, they have a tradition that the top guy doesn't fight challengers unless they defeat his best student. So I had to fight Kato, who was Kimura's top student and 40 pounds heavier than me."

Q: You challenged the great boxers, Joe Louis and Primo Carnera, correct?
A: Yes. I wanted to prove the effectiveness of the system. I personally had nothing against them. They were just big men and big names and I was sure that I could take them.

Q: Didn't you once fight for three hours and forty-five minutes straight?
A: Yes, they were going to enter it in the *Guiness Book of World Records*, but they finally decided against it because they felt it would push people into fighting to beat the record.

Q: How did you became so famous in Japan?
A: I don't know. Maybe because of my many fights in Brazil.

Q: How did you come to fight Kimura?
A: Kimura was considered "the toughest man who ever lived," at that time. He heard about me and decided that he wanted to fight me. I said, "Fine, let's go." In Japan, they have a tradition that the top guy doesn't fight challengers unless they defeat his best student. So I had to fight Kato, who was Kimura's top student and 40 pounds heavier than me.

Q: What happened?
A: I defeated Kato. I choked him into unconsciousness. All the Japanese were shocked because no foreigner had ever defeated a Japanese jiu-jitsu champion before. So that gave me the chance to fight Kimura.

"Kimura was so sure about his victory that he said if I lasted for more than three minutes, I would be considered the victor. And I did."

Q: Was he good?
A: Yes, he was very good. In fact I never felt I could win because he was over 80 pounds heavier than me and greatly skilled.

Q: Why did you fight him then?
A: Because I always enjoyed fighting against the odds. Kimura was so sure about his victory that he said if I lasted for more than three minutes, I would be considered the victor. And I did. I lasted for 13 minutes and I was still fighting when my brother Carlos threw in the towel because he was afraid that the arm-lock Kimura had would shatter my arm.

Q: What did Kimura say afterwards?
A: He was so impressed that he invited me to Japan to teach at his academy. But I kindly refused. I was very honored but I couldn't leave my family and go.

"I'm so very proud of my sons. Rorion worked very hard in the United States to promote jiu-jitsu. Of course, Royce and Rickson also did a great job and they have great reputations as fighters and teachers."

Q: What is your teaching and martial arts philosophy?

A: I firmly believe in helping people. That's why I departed from tradition, because I wanted to find better and easier ways of doing things. I've seen a lot of instructors throwing the students when in fact the students are paying for throwing the instructor. No one learns being thrown!

Q: Do you teach women?

A: Yes I do. Women are more concerned about self-defense and don't train to fight as men do. But even that is changing now.

Q: Are you happy with the great popularity of Gracie jiu-jitsu these days?

A: Yes I am. I'm so very proud of my sons. Rorion worked very hard in the United States to promote jiu-jitsu. Of course, Royce and Rickson also did a great job and they have great reputations as fighters and teachers.

Q: Is it true that you wear a blue belt?

A: Yes, this is out of protest for all the so-called Gracie jiu-jitsu and Brazilian jiu-jitsu masters. Everybody is a black belt or a master in jiu-jitsu these days. But there is a big difference in the way my system is taught in the Torrance Academy and the way others teach their own version of jiu-jitsu. That's why we registered Gracie jiu-jitsu name. The way, the art and the values I developed during my whole life as Gracie jiu-jitsu can be taught correctly. Other people might have the arm lock or the choke and that's fine. Anyone can train the way they like but I only endorse the teachings at the Torrance Academy and legitimate affiliated schools.

Q: Do you still teach?
A: Yes, a little. I know my sons are spreading the art around the world and I'm very happy that my work is appreciated by those who want to keep the knowledge alive for the future generations. If you teach it the right way, Gracie jiu-jitsu can make you a better person and make you happier with yourself.

Q: Many modern fighters have as many NHB fights in one or two years as you did in your whole life. Do you feel no-holds-barred fighting has taken on a different meaning today?
A: I didn't have that many vale tudo fights but definitely the

"My sons are spreading the art around the world and I'm very happy that my work is appreciated by those who want to keep the knowledge alive for the future generations."

things are different today. When I fought I did it for a cause and for a reason. The reason was to prove the efficiency of the method of jiu-jitsu that I was developing. I never did for money. Today, fighters do it simply for money, that's their only objective and goal. It's understandable that when the reason why a person is doing something changes, the whole picture changes too. Fighters today are truly professionals, there is a whole industry that allows a lot of people make a lot of money fighting in NHB. As far as that is concerned we cannot compare my times with the current ones.

Q: When you fought, was your strategy to remain on the bottom, tire your opponent, and then submit him?
A: Absolutely not. My strategy never was to remain on the bottom and tire

"My strategy never was to remain on the bottom and tire my opponent. That's something that I had to do for obvious reasons. It was a consequence, not my way of fighting. I have always fought bigger and stronger opponents, some of them simply grabbed my gi and put me on the ground."

my opponent. That's something that I had to do for obvious reasons. It was a consequence, not my way of fighting. I have always fought bigger and stronger opponents, some of them simply grabbed my gi and put me on the ground. Because of my light bodyweight I always ended up on the bottom, but that didn't happened because I wanted to fight from that position! No way. What I wanted was to mount the guy and submit him from there but the weight difference always made that difficult to me so the most of the time I was having the guy on my guard. When you are on the ground the bigger opponent always will use the bodyweight advantage to stay on the top. It's a natural thing but once again no, remain on the bottom was never my strategy, it was the result of circumstances and never my goal. I couldn't choose. Fortunately, when I found myself on the bottom the technical resources I had in jiu-jitsu allowed me to become victorious.

Q: Do you feel that modern fighters have figured out how to beat the guard?
A: Let me tell you something about the guard and how people are using it today. It is not that the new fighter totally figured out how to pass the guard—which it is partially true because they have began to learn jiu-jitsu to do that. The problem is not in the guard, the problem lies with the fighters whom don't know how to properly use the guard. If you are not fully capable of using the guard, then it doesn't take a great fighter to pass the guard, but this doesn't mean the guard is not good anymore or you shouldn't use it because people now know how to pass it. The guard is like Michael Schumacher's F-1 car; if you drive it I'm sure you won't win a Grand Prix, but if he does it, he will. The problem it is not the car is not

good—you are the problem because you are not good enough driving the car. If you don't know how to properly use the guard, people are going to pass it, but that's not the guard's fault, it's your fault. And that's what is happening today.

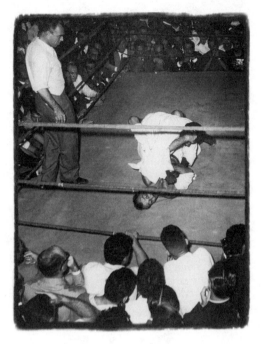

"The guard is like Michael Schumacher's F-1 car; if you drive it I'm sure you won't win a Grand Prix, but if he does it, he will. The problem it is not the car is not good— you are the problem because you are not good enough driving the car."

Q: If you were in your fighting prime of 30 years old, how do you feel you would do against the top NHB fighters today and what would be your strategy against them?
A: I'm sure that I would find a lot of difficulties mainly because my body weight—but I had this problem when I was younger anyway. Fighters nowadays are extremely big—some of them due not to natural foods, that's obvious. Technique-wise, since everyone is learning jiu-jitsu, it would make it more difficult but I have yet to see a fighter with a technical level that could defeat me. The only way you can beat a top jiu-jitsu fighter is with jiu-jitsu. The way I developed the jiu-jitsu techniques make the art almost an impenetrable fortress. The fighters nowadays use a lot of strength and force when they fight. I never used those because I have always fought bigger and stronger opponents. It could have been suicidal to do it. My strategy was always based on technique, not strength. That's why I could fight for 3 hours and 45 minutes. Nobody can fight that long if all he uses is pure force.

Q: Do you feel that the gi is an advantage or disadvantage in a no-holds-barred fight?
A: Although it could be advantageous for our opponents, I believe that jiu-jitsu should be represented by a fighter wearing a gi.

"I can't compensate a lack of technique with strength if I don't have it. I have to make sure I do the technique 100 percent perfect. Then, I don't need all this muscle. In modern jiu-jitsu competitions, fighters are using force and pure strength to compensate for the lack of polished technique. And that is not good."

Q: Do you think the jiu-jitsu techniques that are taught and used today are more effective than the techniques taught and used 60 years ago?

A: The new "modified" techniques are not better than the old techniques. What is an "old" technique? This is ridiculous! The problem lies in that modern practitioners are stronger than in the past—they don't really need to polish their technique to make a basic technique work because they compensate with brute force. For instance, you can apply a choking technique and apply the technique wrong, but if you are 220 pounds and you have arms like a bodybuilder, you are going to choke the guy out, no matter what. But it doesn't mean you are doing the technique right. If I use the incorrect way of doing it—like the bodybuilder did—I won't be able to apply it effectively. Why? Because I don't have the force to apply a movement that is being performed technically wrong. I can't compensate a lack of technique with strength if I don't have it. I have to make sure I do the technique 100 percent perfect. Then I don't need all this muscle. In modern jiu-jitsu competitions, fighters are using force and pure strength to compensate for the lack of polished technique. And that is not good. Maybe you'll be able to win some tournaments with the modern and inconsistent rules but this approach is a shortcut that will take you nowhere.

Q: What is your opinion of all the modern competitors talking about "new" and "modified" techniques?

A: When a fighter is not competent using the basic and fundamental techniques, he always tries to compensate and create new things to cope with that. Then they criticize the basics describing them as "old." This is a nonsense affirmation. Modern boxers are using the same boxing techniques that Joe Louis did. The overall approach to boxing training has changed but they still doing the jab, cross, hook and uppercut. It's that simple. Once you have a good and strong technical arsenal and game plan, all you need is to be able to apply them at will. To be able of funtionalize what you have. That's what your dedication and training should be focused on, and not trying to create new things that are simply a reflection of your lack of skill in jiu-jitsu basics. All these new and modified techniques do no more than try to reinvent the wheel. They are simply a modification of principles and concepts already established in the basic techniques. Nothing new. The funny thing is that some these "new" techniques can only be applied against a less skilled opponent— no way you'll be able to apply them against a good fighter. Having to use and develop "modi-

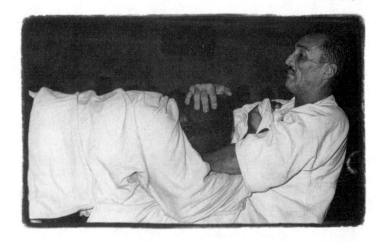

"All these new and modified techniques do no more than try to reinvent the wheel. They are simply a modification of principles and concepts already established in the basic techniques. Nothing new. The funny thing is that some these "new" techniques can only be applied against a less skilled opponent."

fied" and "new" technique to beat a less-skilled opponent doesn't say much about you as a jiu-jitsu fighter and practitioner.

Q: What is the major risk for a jiu-jitsu fighter in a NHB fight?
A: The difference is that the jiu-jitsu fighter has the risk of being punched and knocked out. That's why I have always covered myself to avoid being knocked out. If my opponent didn't knocked me out, then everything was going to be alright. A victory through a knockout is what I call an "accidental victory." Not a victory based on technique and strategy. Anyone can get knocked out with one accidental punch but it doesn't mean the opponent is better and more technical than you.

Q: You're generally acknowledged as the originator of the modern Gracie jiu-jitsu style. Excluding yourself, rank the top jiu-jitsu exponents, technique-wise, in the Gracie family?
A: Definitely my sons. They are the ones I have spent more time with and you can see that in their technique. I haven't dedicated myself that much to my nephews, cousins, et cetera, so I can say that my sons are the more

"At the time Rickson was representing the family in the fights in Brazil, it's true that he was without a doubt the best fighter in the family. Now there are other members that are coming close, but at that time he was the absolute champion of the family."

technical exponents in the Gracie family. Even today my sons have their own lives and I don't spend much time with them. The exception to this is Rorion and his sons Ryron, Rener and Ralek with whom I spend a lot of my time and personally train and guide them every time I am in California or they go to Brazil. These are the only people in the family that currently I personally train and supervise these days.

Q: Rickson is regarded as the number-one fighter in the Gracie family. What are his qualities as a fighter?
A: At the time Rickson was representing the family in the fights in Brazil, it's true that he was without a doubt the best fighter in the family. Now there are other members who are coming close, but at that time he was the absolute champion in the family. His qualities as a fighter are many and he was gifted with a great and strong body. This makes everything easier. Then he has always been very dedicated to jiu-jitsu, and last but not least he has the right mentality and temperament to be a fighter. You put everything together and that's Rickson Gracie.

Q: Outside of the Gracie family members, which modern fighters do you feel have good jiu-jitsu technique, and that you like to watch?
A: I don't really watch many fights. I'm sure there are many good fighters out there but I'm not interested in watching other people fight.

Q: Many people recommend doing yoga as a great complement to jiu-jitsu, what do you think?

A: Yoga is a good activity regardless if you do jiu-jitsu or not. I never did, I never needed it. Sure it can be good for your body, but all I needed were the specific drills and exercises I developed for jiu-jitsu.

Q: When you started teaching martial arts, did you think that Gracie jiu-jitsu, a style that you developed and made famous in Rio de Janeiro, would ever become as popular all over the world as it is now?

A: No. I never practiced jiu-jitsu with popularity and money goals in mind. I never cared about it. My only objective was to make the art better and make myself better to better protect myself, then pass it on to my sons and students. My goal in teaching was always to teach my students to be able to defeat me, because when they got better, they pushed me harder and I had to get better too. I never taught in the wrong way or hid things from my students. The popularity the art has today is due to my son Rorion. He is the person who really made the name of Gracie jiu-jitsu well-known around the world. Very few people knew

"The popularity the art has today, it is due to my son Rorion. He is the person who really made the name of Gracie jiu-jitsu well-known around the world. Very few people knew my jiu-jitsu and my name before Rorion came to America and created the UFC."

my jiu-jitsu and my name before Rorion came to America and created the UFC. After that a whole business was developed for all Brazilians to come to the United States and other countries around the world, open schools, teach jiu-jitsu and to start organizing NHB events and make a lot of money. Now, it is a new ball game but when I was teaching and fighting I never had money in mind. Never crossed my mind.

Q: What is the difference between Gracie jiu-jitsu and Brazilian jiu-jitsu?

A: My brother Carlos introduced me to the jiu-jitsu he learned from Esai Maeda. As I modified and perfected those techniques a Brazilian style of jiu-jitsu was born. We never changed the name. It remained simply jiu-jitsu. When my son Rorion came to America in the 70's he decided to pay tribute to the teaching method I developed and started calling it Gracie jiu-jitsu to differentiate it from the Japanese method of jiu-jitsu that some

"Competition rules and time limits of today are ridiculous and change everything. Today the competitions are built on a commercial basis. The goal of jiu-jitsu is to win, not to play silly games to win a match. That's not jiu-jitsu. Unfortunately, that is what it is right now."

people in the United States had heard about during the war. Through his dedication and great business sense, Rorion made Gracie jiu-jitsu the most popular martial art in the world today. So directly or indirectly, everyone that practices Brazilian jiu-jitsu is using the moves I have developed, some with better techniques than others. What surprises me, it is that some members of the Gracie family and individuals that really know that both styles are the same, prefer to call it "Brazilian jiu-jitsu." Credit should be given where credit is due. If what I have developed is internationally known as Gracie jiu-jistu, that is what it should be called. There is no other way around it.

Q: If you could change anything about modern Brazilian jiu-jitsu competitions today, what would it be?

A: The rules. Competition rules and time limits of today are ridiculous and change everything. Today the competitions are built on a commercial basis. The goal of jiu-jitsu is to win, not to play silly games to win a match. That's not jiu-jitsu. Unfortunately, that is what it is right now. I have created a new set of rules and regulations to make jiu-jitsu competitions more real and less manipulative. You are there to win by submission, not by playing and trying to stall a fight without doing anything, letting the time pass, and win without having done anything at all. A jiu-jitsu fighter must enter in a competition to win, not to compete. Today people fight in competitions to not lose, and that's embarrassing for the art.

Q: When you fought you did it for a cause. Today fighters and even members of the Gracie family do it for money. How do you feel about it and how do you think it affects the mental state when you fight for honor or fight for money?

A: There are a lot of things that money can buy, but let me tell you that it won't buy courage and passion. You can fight hard for money but there always will be a limit—a line you won't trespass simply for money. When you fight for honor or because your life is at stake, you can do things that you'll never do for money—you can endure punishment that no money will make you to. There are a lot of crazy things a professional fighter will do for big sums of money, but when you fight for other reasons bigger than money, you can do and endure things you can't even imagine. Today people simply fight for money, not because they are brave and want to prove something to the rest of the world. They simply do it for money, and there are things money can't buy and there are things no money in the world will make a person do. There are limitations to everything, even for what money can do in people's behavior. Money doesn't encourage an individual to evolve and improve as a fighter either.

Q: What would be your final message to all practitioners of jiu-jitsu around the world?

A: To be honest, grateful and true human beings. I would like to remind them to always give credit where credit is due. We all have our own lives but it doesn't mean we have to negate our roots and not recognize those who opened the doors for us. Today the art is well known all over the world, and many Brazilian instructors are making their living thanks to what my son Rorion did here in the United States. He opened the doors for everybody. I would like to see people recognize that and then go on with their lives and business as usual. The worse thing in life is to not be grateful. Technique-wise, I would tell them to stick to the basics and train hard to make the basics work against any type of opponent and under any kind of situation. Don't waste time with new "technical fantasies" that will take you nowhere. Stick to the basics. ○

Masters Techniques

An attacker approaches from behind (1), and reaches to grab Professor Helio Gracie (2). As soon as he feels the hand on his hip, Professor Helio grabs the aggressor's hand (3), passes his right arm over to grab his

own left wrist *(4)*, and turns around *(5)*. Professor Helio then applies pressure *(6)*, and simultaneously pushes downward *(7)*, submitting his opponent on the ground with a shoulder lock *(8)*.

Jean Jacques Machado

Conquering Doubt

IT WOULD HAVE BEEN EASY FOR JEAN JACQUES MACHADO TO GIVE INTO FEAR. BORN WITHOUT FINGERS ON HIS LEFT HAND, MACHADO SEEMED FOREVER FATED TO SIT ON THE SIDELINES AND WATCH HIS ATHLETIC BROTHERS RISE TO SPORTS STARDOM. BUT MACHADO HAD NO QUIT IN HIM AND REFUSED TO LISTEN TO THOSE WHO SAID THAT IT WAS TOO DANGEROUS FOR HIM TO COMPETE. SUPPORTED BY PARENTS WHO TAUGHT HIM THAT HE HAD NO LIMITS, AND ENCOURAGED BY BROTHERS WHO TAUGHT HIM TO NEVER BACK DOWN FROM A CHALLENGE, JEAN JACQUES SOON REALIZED THAT HE HAD ATHLETIC GIFTS THAT A MERE HANDICAP COULD NEVER STOP AND A FIGHTING SPIRIT THAT FEAR COULD NEVER CONQUER. COMPETING IN JIU-JITSU, THIS "SPECIAL" CHILD WAS SOON TURNING HEADS AND WINNING TROPHIES WITH HIS ATTACKING, TAKE-NO-PRISONERS STYLE OF SUBMISSION FIGHTING.

UNDER THE TUTELAGE OF THE LEGENDARY CARLOS GRACIE JR., HIS TECHNICAL PROWESS BECAME BREATHTAKING. ABSORBING EVERY SINGLE DETAIL OF THE ART OF JIU-JITSU, JEAN JACQUES LEARNED HOW TO DECIPHER EVERY SUBTLE SIGN HIS OPPONENTS GAVE, AND TO USE HIS MIND TO MORE THAN MAKE UP FOR ANY PHYSICAL DEFICIENCY. HIS ATTITUDE OF "NO LIMITS, NO FEAR" SPREAD TO HIS PERSONAL LIFE AS WELL, AND JEAN JACQUES GAINED A REPUTATION AS A TRUE GENTLEMAN AND A WORLDWIDE AMBASSADOR FOR THE SPORT. HIS TECHNICAL MASTERY WAS IN FULL FORCE WHEN, IN THE 1999 ABU DHABI SUBMISSION WRESTLING WORLD CHAMPIONSHIPS IN THE UNITED ARAB EMIRATES, MACHADO FACED FOUR OF THE TOUGHEST FIGHTERS ON PLANET EARTH AND SUBMITTED THEM ALL INCLUDING SAKURAI AND UNO—THE ONLY TIME THAT FEAT HAS EVER BEEN ACCOMPLISHED.

A FIERCE COMPETITOR ON THE MAT, BUT A COMPASSIONATE AND SUPPORTIVE TEACHER OFF, MACHADO HAS USED HIS LIFE LESSONS TO TRANSFORM HIMSELF INTO A COMPLETE INDIVIDUAL IN AN INCOMPLETE BODY. AN INSPIRATION AND A ROLE MODEL AS A FIGHTER, TEACHER, AND DEVOTED FAMILY MAN, JEAN JACQUES MACHADO IS TRULY AN INTERNATIONAL EMISSARY FOR ALL THE GRAPPLING ARTS.

"When you say jiu-jitsu you have to link it to the Gracie family. I think that everyone today that knows Brazilian jiu-jitsu learned it, directly or indirectly, from a member of the Gracie family. Everyone should be grateful to them for that."

Q: How did you get started in jiu-jitsu?
A: Carlos Gracie Jr. was our teacher from the beginning. When you say jiu-jitsu you have to link it to the Gracie family. That's the family that started our jiu-jitsu style and we're just one part of that clan. I think that everyone today that knows Brazilian jiu-jitsu learned it, directly or indirectly, from a member of the Gracie family. Everyone should be grateful to them for that. I also learned a lot from my older brothers. Since they have been training for so long, even when I was just starting, they always taught me new techniques and corrected my positions—I learned a lot from being the youngest. Even today I'm still learning; every time I train with my brothers I feel I learn something new. When I have questions it's always good to have more than one head thinking about the movement. You get more answers than you can come up with yourself.

Q: Did you ever think that you weren't going to be as good as your brothers?
A: No, I never had that thought. My coach, my cousins in the Gracie family, and my brothers, never said anything like that—I never had any time to think like that. I was always very athletic and I really liked to do sports. Sometimes, though, a normal sport for someone else would be a dangerous sport for me. For example, I used to play hockey where you have to use your hands all the time. You can hurt your hands or your fingers very easily. I remember my parents being very worried, but they didn't want to tell me that I couldn't do it. They didn't want me to get it in my head that there was something other kids could do, that I couldn't. But still you wonder and sometimes feel a little bad. I remember one time that I felt very bad and my brother John said to my parents, "I want to be like Jean Jacques and cut off my fingers, too, so I can be good like him." So when

you hear something like that it makes you feel good about life, not just about jiu-jitsu.

Q: Explain the ranking system in jiu-jitsu.

A: In Brazilian jiu-jitsu we have four belts: blue, purple, brown and black. I have to say that there's not a huge difference between the blue and purple; nor is there a huge difference between brown and black. The purple belt knows a little bit more than the blue as far as the amount of techniques, but the real difference is based on his experience and the ability to apply these techniques. The purple belt can apply all the moves while wrestling. The blue belt is someone who has already developed some sort of "game" idea, but the purple belt is someone who has a better application of the game. From purple belt to brown belt is a big step. The brown belt has to know a lot more

"In jiu-jitsu, submission is the only thing I ever go for. It is the reward for the art. No matter where I am I'm looking for the finishing move. I learned this way and I feel that it is a very creative style."

physical techniques and have a higher level of understanding about the art. He needs what we call "body intelligence." A brown belt has some positions that are perfect; if he gets these positions, there's no escape for the opponent. He has to be able to do whatever he wants.

Q: What is your philosophy on submission fighting?

A: In jiu-jitsu, submission is the only thing I ever go for. It is the reward for the art. If you see a lot of the jiu-jitsu fighters, each one has their own style. Some guys like to fight from the bottom, some guys more from the top. But my style is that I just want to finish. No matter where I am, I'm looking for the finishing move. I learned this way and I feel that it is a very creative style. In order to get a good finish, of course, you should have some type of control of the other person. It doesn't have to be a physical

"I am always just focused on the particular fight that I have ahead of me. After the competition is over and everything has settled down a little, then I can have a nice time and relax a little. But I am always really focused on the event."

control. Control can also mean forcing the person into a position where you know how they're going to react.

If I try to get 20 submission attempts but I fail, I don't go and play the points game. Not being able to get the submission only makes me feel that I have to work more on my game. I give all the credit to that person who survives all my finishing attempts—the bottom line is that I didn't finish him so I deserve to lose. But I won't try to just get points. To me the only true proof of how good you are is to finish by submission. It is the true measure of the art.

Q: You do very good in no-gi tournaments like Abu Dhabi. Why?
A: I think Abu Dhabi is a great opportunity for any fighter to show how good they are. I've never seen a tournament that has so much money involved and so many great athletes from all kinds of styles: no-holds-barred, wrestling, judo, jiu-jitsu, shooto and even sumo I think. If you see the names of the people that fought over there it's really the best of the best. I saw it as a great opportunity to try my jiu-jitsu against other jiu-jitsu guys, or some wrestlers, or just any style. I was looking for that challenge and I think I had success. I proved my point that the Machado style of jiu-jitsu is very good.

Q: Do you do any kind of mental training before a fight?
A: Well, competing is extremely important for me, so I don't feel like talking much. I am always just focused on the particular fight that I have ahead of me. I am there to fight and to compete. After the competition is over and everything has settled down a little, then I can have a nice time and relax a little. But I am always really focused on the event.

Jean Jacques
Machado

Q: Do you fight on instinct and reaction or do you have a set plan?

A: I think that you have your game by the time you get to fight. After training so much, your body and mind develop their own reactions. When you train grappling, which I have been doing all my life, you pretty much feel all the reactions that are possible in a given situation. Because when you are training with students there will be some beginners, some intermediate, and some advanced ones that will all react differently to a move you apply. Then, your body pretty much absorbs and learns what to do when somebody reacts this way. So when you train a lot, after a while you don't

"When you train grappling, which I have been doing all my life, you pretty much feel all the reactions that are possible in a given situation. Then your body pretty much absorbs and learns what to do when somebody reacts this way. That's the way I look for perfection in a technique. The more automatic I am, that's what I'm looking for. If I have to think, then I don't know the move."

have to think anymore; your body just reacts. It's the same as if you touch your finger to something hot. You're not going to think, you're just going to pull your arm back. That's the way I look for perfection in a technique. The more automatic I am, that's what I'm looking for. If I have to think, then I don't know the move.

Q: Is your attacking style very popular?

A: My fighting style is well-known by everybody in jiu-jitsu—I'm always looking for a finish. Even if I don't win the match, they will know that they almost lost to me by submission. The lucky guys who escape from that don't want to face me again because they know how close to the cliff they were. Because I was away from competition since my brothers and I came to America, and it was hard to return to Brazil for the big tournaments because of the distance, I think maybe some people forgot how hard I try to finish a match by submission. A lot of them came up to me afterwards and said, "Man, I haven't seen that in a long time. It was great. Just like the old days."

"Martial arts, and especially jiu-jitsu, is like water: it fits in every shape and in every body. It doesn't matter how big or small you are, or what kind of physical problems that you have. You're just going to have to adjust the jiu-jitsu to you, not adjust yourself to the jiu-jitsu."

Q: So you don't get that much satisfaction just winning by points?

A: Not really (laughs). As I said before each fighter is different. Some are more aggressive and some more defensive. Each one has his own way of thinking. If you have a jiu-jitsu class with each of my brothers, teaching the same position, they'll show you a different angle that ends in the same submission. But each has a different way to apply the action or the movement. So I think I'm very aggressive in submission and I think that my brothers are like that too and are very submission oriented.

Q: You train with everyone straight-up, yet you have no fingers on your left hand.

A: The way my parents raised me was to tell me that I could do anything I wanted. That's the way I still think. And for a lot of people they're not used to thinking like that. For myself, for example, I don't have four fingers on my left hand, but I was born like that. And I had to learn how to deal with it. Martial arts, and especially jiu-jitsu, is like water: it fits in every shape and in every body. It doesn't matter how big or small you are, or what kind of physical problems that you have. You're just going to have to adjust the jiu-jitsu to you, not adjust yourself to the jiu-jitsu. And that's what happened with me—I do movements that a person with a normal left hand doesn't do, because that's the way that jiu-jitsu fits me. I have developed jiu-jitsu to fit my touch. And I don't see any other person who trains jiu-jitsu that does it with the same type of problem that I have. I see it as a challenge and it empowers me and stimulates me to do better.

Q: How about when you were growing up?

A: I think I surprised a lot of people. Here I have pretty much no left hand, and most people in jiu-jitsu use both their hands to grab and to hold, but I did very well. I was always rated number one, or close to number one, in my weight class. So I tell my own students, "Look, if I can do it, you can do it." Success is in your spirit—it's a very spiritual thing. You really have to believe in yourself. And I think that if you really believe in yourself, you can do anything you want. No doubt about it.

Q: What is jiu-jitsu like in Brazil in comparison to Abu Dhabi?

A: The rules in Abu Dhabi are very different than Brazilian jiu-jitsu rules. In Brazil, every month the rules change a little bit, because the promoters are trying to make the matches more exciting. Sometimes the changes work well, sometimes they don't. I went back to train a while ago and saw that they were really trying to win by using the rules to only score points. And that really surprised me. I was only playing for submission like I had always done, but the other guys were just looking to get control of a position and then hold it to just score some points. I would say they weren't doing bad. They were playing by the rules and that is why there are rules. But like I said, each fighter has their own style. There are a lot of great champions in Brazil, but each one of them chooses a little different direction to apply their game. So it is different from here, but there isn't all that much more submission attempts there, either. The art of the submission is being a little lost everywhere, I think.

Then we have the vale tudo format. There are many jiu-jitsu fighters that try vale tudo as an extension of what they are already doing. They

"Success is in your spirit—it's a very spiritual thing. You really have to believe in yourself. And I think that if you really believe in yourself, you can do anything you want. No doubt about it."

"Everyone has the common direction to show the world the Brazilian jiu-jitsu style. I think that each member of the family has a mission to pass along the style. It doesn't matter if the direction of each family member is different. You know, different people, different choices!"

find there is no more room for them to grow inside jiu-jitsu and they take the game to a different level. Some fighters are great in jiu-jitsu but are not good in vale tudo—others are great in vale tudo but not good in sport jiu-jitsu.

Q: Do you think that all the different branches of the Gracie family are as close as they were before coming to the U.S.?
A: I believe so. I believe everyone has the common direction to show the world the Brazilian jiu-jitsu style. That's what the family is doing now. Each member is going their own way by doing challenges, by competing in sport, or by going no-holds-barred. By having a lot of students and giving a lot of seminars everyone is spreading the art of jiu-jitsu. I think that each member of the family has a mission to pass along the style. It doesn't matter if the direction of each family member is different. I think it's good, actually, because there are a lot of different types of people that wouldn't be drawn to just one thing. You know, different people, different choices!

Q: The Machado name has really grown worldwide. What do you think is the main reason for that?
A: People know the link of our family with the Gracie family and that means quality in the art. Our jiu-jitsu came from the Gracie family, and we are happy to admit that we're proud of it. I learned from Carlos Gracie Jr. and he was not just my coach but also my cousin. We have the same blood. So with that knowledge we gained, we used it to make friends. We have lots of students that we treat like family, also. I think it counts a lot with them. I believe that's how martial arts should be used—to make friends, and bring people together, and grow inside. Our goal in the Machado schools is not just to see the students become better fighters,

but for them to become better persons as well to accept the challenge of life, to grow in life, to be a better father, to be a better friend, and to be better in their work. And we use the jiu-jitsu as a support for that. And I believe that most of our students feel that way and they like it. So we just keep making more and more friends as we teach more. I consider all my students in America to be part of my family. I'm very close to all my students. And that is the most important part of the martial arts to me.

Q: How do you train outside of jiu-jitsu?
A: I lift weights three times a week. I also do cardio every day. When I'm at the gym I use the machines. I go for an hour-and-a-half without stopping a half hour on each machine. I do the bike first, then I do the rowing, and then I end up with the stairclimber, sometimes I do the climber. I even do step aerobics. I train at Gold's Gym and they have everything there. It is the best place in the world to train. All of the gyms they have are so good. It is very important to understand that today being good in jiu-jitsu is not enough anymore. Years ago if a bigger and stronger guy didn't know jiu-jitsu it was easy to defeat him. Today the big and strong guys know jiu-jitsu so if you are not in top physical conditioning you are going to be in hot water! You need a complete package that involves cardiovascular training, weight training, jiu-jitsu training and proper nutrition. If you lack of one of these elements, it is going to be very hard for you to become a world-class jiu-jitsu athlete.

Q: Do you have plans to build-up sport jiu-jitsu in the United States?
A: Absolutely. If you go to any school of Brazilian jiu-jitsu you will find only a small percentage of people who actually fight vale tudo. Most of them do jiu-jitsu for health or exercise or self-defense or sportive reasons. So most people don't have an outlet to try what they know unless they enter a sport contest. In sport, also, there is not the same intensity and anger that you can get in vale tudo. You're not trying to hurt your opponent, as is the case in vale tudo, but you're trying to submit him or out point him. So this gives students a less intense outlet for what they practice. I think the potential for jiu-jitsu is much greater overall, in terms of actual competitors, than for vale tudo. We have just scratched the surface and my brothers and I are really concentrating on having a lot of tournaments that people can go to, and compete in, and have fun. We're very excited about it. ◯

Jean Jacques Machado faces Brazilian jiu-jitsu black belt Richard Norton, fighting from the open guard (1). Throwing Richard's legs to the side (2), Jean Jacques traps Richard's legs with his chest (3). Barrel-rolling forward (4), Jean Jacques takes the top position (5), and settles into side-control (6).

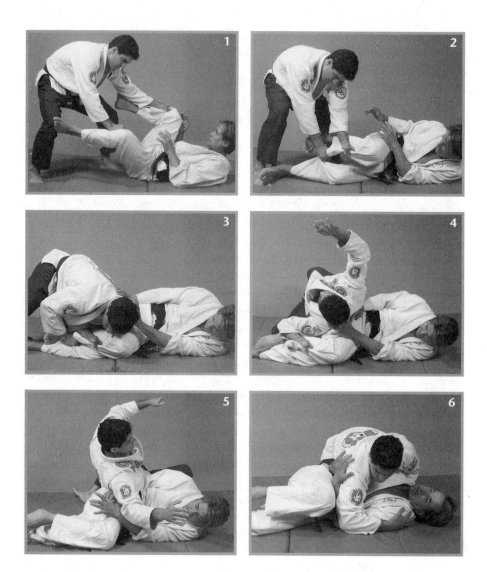

Jean Jacques
Machado

*Richad Norton keeps Jean Jacques Machado at bay with his feet on the hips (1).
Jean Jacques splits the legs by putting his knees onto Richard's thighs (2), and
then traps Richard's leg with his shin, while maintaining arm control via the gi (3).
Sliding over Richard's leg (4), Machado pulls his arm up to create space (5), then
settles into side control (6).*

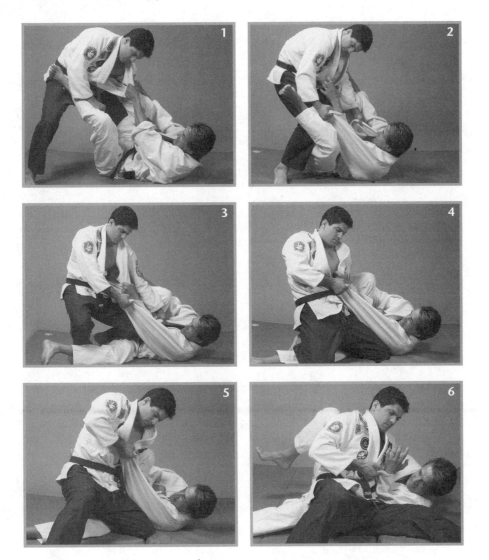

155

Masters Techniques

Richard Norton has Jean Jacques Machado in his guard (1). Richard starts to attempt a "raspada" (2), but Jean Jacques places his left hand between his legs to prevent the technique (3). Jean Jacques then brings his body down and pushes Richard's left arm with his right arm (4), moves his body to the side (5), passes to the right side (6), and gains side-control (7).

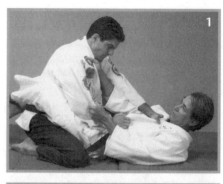

Jean Jacques Machado tries to pass Richard Norton's open guard (1). Machado grabs Richard's belt from behind (2), pulls up to make him roll (3), and makes Richard's head face him (4). Jean Jacques then moves to Richard's back (5), sits on the floor and inserts the hooks (6), and him finishes with a rear choke (7).

Masters Techniques

Richard Norton fights Jean Jacques Machado's attempt to pass the guard (1). As Jean Jacques pushes forward (2), Richard places his hips right under Jean Jacques (3), and attempts to throw him (4). Although Jean Jacques is thrown in the air, he changes the direction of his body (5), and lands behind Norton's head (6). He then moves to the side (7), and achieves side control with his knee on Richard's stomach (8).

Jean Jacques Machado is in Richard Norton's guard (1). Jean Jacques moves his hips back to open Richard's guard (2), and grabs his left thigh with his right hand (3), pushing down to move his right knee over Richard's left leg (4), preventing him from using it to defend (5). Jean Jacques then under-hooks Norton's right leg (6), grabs Norton's left shoulder to support himself (7), and passes his right leg back (8). He then positions himself on Richard's other side (9), and achieves side-control (10).

Marco Ruas

The King of the Streets

KNOWN WORLDWIDE AS THE KING OF THE STREETS, MARCO RUAS HAS BEEN INVOLVED IN MARTIAL ARTS FOR MORE THAN THREE DECADES.

A NATIVE OF RIO DE JANEIRO, BRAZIL, WHO NOW MAKES HIS HOME IN SOUTHERN CALIFORNIA, MARCO RUAS IS GENERALLY ACKNOWLEDGED TO BE ONE OF THE TOP VALE TUDO FIGHTERS IN THE HISTORY OF THE SPORT. A FAMILIAR FACE TO ANYONE WHO FOLLOWS NO-HOLDS-BARRED FIGHTING, RUAS HAS GRACED THE COVERS OF THE TOP MARTIAL ARTS MAGAZINES AROUND THE WORLD. HE IS A FIGHTING STAR CONSIDERED BY MANY TO BE ONE OF THE MOST BALANCED FIGHTERS TO EVER COMPETE INSIDE THE OCTAGON, WITH EQUAL SKILLS STANDING UP AND ON THE GROUND.

A PAST WINNER OF THE UFC, WHERE HE HAD TO OVERCOME A BROKEN FINGER IN HIS RIGHT HAND THE DAY BEFORE HIS FIRST TITLE MATCH, RUAS HAS ALSO TAKEN THE TOP SPOT IN THE PRESTIGIOUS WORLD VALE TUDO CHAMPIONSHIPS SEVERAL TIMES. STARDOM HASN'T COME EASY, HOWEVER, AND RUAS HAS WORKED VERY HARD TO GET TO THE TOP. HE HOLDS A BLACK BELT IN SEVERAL DIFFERENT MARTIAL ARTS STYLES AND HAS COMBINED HIS FAVORITE ELEMENTS OF EACH TO CREATE HIS OWN SYSTEM CALLED RUAS VALE TUDO.

Q: When and why did you begin to practice martial arts?
A: I was about 13 or 14 years of age and I liked martial arts. I used to watch an American TV series called *Kung Fu*. At that time in Rio de Janeiro, where I was born, martial arts were not very popular, except for taekwondo, which was enjoying big success. While I did not learn the art until later, my talent for fighting developed before that. I have seven brothers and they picked on me all the time, so it was usual for me to fight against all of them every day. I had to stay awake to protect myself!

One day I began to really develop physically and they weren't the big guys anymore. Then things began to change. I started to beat them up all the time. I was hyperactive and I showed interest in martial arts, so my father took me to practice with one of my cousins, Vinicius Ruas, a judo instructor. I practiced only a few months then I switched to boxing, which my friends did, and joined the Flamengo Club, which was already very

"Punches and kicks are what I like the most, but I have also practiced jiu-jitsu, judo, and luta livre. I consider myself a complete fighter. I prefer the stand-up fight and think it is more beautiful; nevertheless, I also like to fight on the ground."

famous for its soccer team. In addition, I started practicing taekwondo with Korean master Woo Jae Lee. Being a very dedicated athlete, I soon started competing in boxing and became the Rio de Janeiro State champion. In tae kwondo, I eventually got my black belt. As years went by I continued learning other martial arts. I returned to judo, got my black belt, and also competed with big success.

I then practiced capoeira, a martial art created by Africans in Brazil during the time of slavery, for five years, and learned to fight very well in that style. However, I was not allowed to get the title of master. To be a master in capoeira, one must be an artist. You have to play musical instruments and sing songs as well as fight. But I only dedicated myself to fighting; I could not sing and did not learn the instruments. I guess my future was not in the music business!

Q: So you are predominantly a stand-up fighter and like to punch and kick?
A: Punches and kicks are what I like the most, but I have also practiced jiu-jitsu, judo, and *luta livre*, which is Hugo Duarte's no-gi style of submission fighting. I consider myself a complete fighter. I prefer the stand-up fight and think it is more beautiful; nevertheless, I also like to fight on the ground.

When I came to the United States to fight in the UFC they labeled me a grappler, when in fact I considered myself a stand-up fighter. I like to punch and kick.

Q: Is there any other style of martial art you have practiced?
A: For the past ten years I have dedicated myself to muay Thai or Thai boxing. Today, it is the style I like the most. It's a very efficient martial art. Before I moved to the U.S., I was teaching at my muay Thai school in Rio.

Q: Why are you known worldwide as The King of the Streets?

A: That is just my last name. Ruas means *streets* in Portuguese, the language we speak in Brazil. When I first came to the U.S. to fight in the UFC, my manager thought it would be a good idea to introduce me as "The King of Streets." This title has made some people erroneously think that I enjoy picking fights on the streets—which is not true at all.

Q: How did you get involved in vale tudo?

A: In 1984, jiu-jitsu was challenging all other martial arts in Rio de Janeiro to prove it was superior. The organizers invited me to fight in one of the weight categories. I was to fight a jiu-jitsu man called Pinduka, one of the most respected students of the Gracie family. At that time I was already familiar with ground techniques, but had never had the desire to participate to challenges. Because I had been asked to fight, and because I had experience in stand-up as well as ground fighting, I accepted it. The representatives of jiu-jitsu dominated the challenge and won the majority of the fights. My fight, however, was an exception. They were certain that the famous Pinduka was going to win easily but our fight ended up in a draw. He dominated on the ground, but was unable to finish me because I had enough knowledge to escape his locks. Moreover, I hit him a lot. While on the ground, I continuously attacked him with my elbows and fists. Jiu-jitsu fighters were not good at this at that time.

"For the past ten years I have dedicated myself to muay Thai or Thai boxing. Today, it is the style I like the most. It's a very efficient martial art. Before I moved to the U.S., I was teaching at my muay Thai school in Rio."

Because of this fight against Pinduka, I became very famous in Rio. This motivated me and I decided to dedicate myself to vale tudo. I began to emphasize training ground fighting. I started to lift weights and became much stronger. Many opportunities to fight vale tudo fights appeared and I took them. There were also challenges from jiu-jitsu fighters, all of which I accepted. However, because of sponsorship problems, the fights never happened. But that also increased my name in the Brazilian martial arts circle.

"The truth is that I have nothing against jiu-jitsu and have great friends who train jiu-jitsu. I respect this style of fighting, I practice it and I think it is very good and very efficient. What I didn't like was some jiu-jitsu practitioners saying that their style was superior to all others. This is not true."

Q: Is there any rivalry between you and the Brazilian jiu-jitsu fighters?

A: At one time, perhaps, but not now. Everyone pretty much trains everything now—especially in the United States. The truth is that I have nothing against jiu-jitsu and have great friends who train jiu-jitsu. I respect this style of fighting, I practice it and I think it is very good and very efficient. What I didn't like was some jiu-jitsu practitioners saying that their style was superior to all others. This is not true. In the past, people who only train karate, taekwondo, boxing, or any stand-up style would lose to jiu-jitsu fighters because they knew nothing about ground techniques. It is not smart to fight in an "anything-goes" match without knowing anything about ground styles. I like stand-up fighting but I also know how to fight on the ground. This is true for most top NHB fighters now. I believe I am more prepared for a vale tudo match than someone who only knows stand-up techniques and also more prepared than someone who only knows the ground. I have nothing against jiu-jitsu. How can I? I use it.

Q: How did you come to fight in the Ultimate Fighting Championship?

A: I was in Brazil dedicating myself to the training of vale tudo and Thai boxing, competing in muay Thai. Vale tudo existed only inside Brazil until the moment the Gracies launched the Ultimate Fighting Championship in the U.S. and Royce Gracie won the first one and was a big success. The UFC heard about me, and made me an offer. I accepted and fought in UFC VII and won. Everybody was impressed with my way of fighting because I fought on my feet and on the ground. I became famous worldwide all of a sudden. That's how my international career got started.

Q: In UFC VII, why did you say your style was Ruas Vale Tudo?
A: After having learned so many styles of fighting such as boxing, jiu-jitsu, tae kwondo, judo, and capoeira, I didn't think it was fair for me to participate to the UFC under the label of just one fighting art. In reality, my style is a mixture of many styles. That's why I said Ruas Vale Tudo. I wanted to prove that no style is better than another. If you really want to be a successful fighter you need a combination of different elements and systems. You have to incorporate techniques from different arts.

"In reality, my style is a mixture of many styles. That's why I said Ruas Vale Tudo. If you really want to be a successful fighter you need a combination of different elements and systems. You have to incorporate techniques from different arts."

Q: You fought at UFC VII with an injury in your right hand, correct?
A: Yes, I had a broken finger. Of course, I knew that the UFC was going to be a serious challenge but it became a major one when I broke the middle finger in my right hand the day before the event. The doctor told to forget about fighting and that I was not going to be able to use that hand at all. The pain in my hand kept me awake the night before. I didn't sleep or eat the day of the fight and my motivation and my spirit suffered. But I managed to overcome this obstacle and take home the prize.

Q: What do you think about Royce Gracie? He has been criticized for his fights against Takada and Sakuraba.
A: I think Royce has fought very well in all of his fights. He has done more than I expected from someone of his body size, fighting against people much stronger, and using rules that don't favor his style of fighting. He beat Takada, remember? A win is a win. How can you criticize that? And

"I think Royce has fought very well in all of his fights. He has done more than I expected from someone of his body size, fighting against people much stronger, and using rules that don't favor his style of fighting. He is a classic jiu-jitsu man who gets his opponents down, tires them, and then submits them. His victories helped Brazilian martial artists to be respected and allowed us to show the world our techniques."

against Sakuraba, they stood them up after each round. Royce is not a round-based fighter. He is a classic jiu-jitsu man who gets his opponents down, tires them, and then submits them. Doesn't anyone remember his fight against Severn? That was Royce Gracie at his best. I think that if Royce would have gotten rules that favored him, that the results of the Sakuraba fight could have been a lot different. He got it really tough and he is held to a higher standard than anyone else. Royce opened very big doors for other Brazilian fighters, including myself. His victories helped Brazilian martial artists to be respected and allowed us to show the world our techniques. I'm not personal friends with Royce Gracie, but I respect all his accomplishments. I haven't forgotten what he did for Brazil and for the sport.

Q: What advice would you give to the fighters who want to participate in NHB?
A: I think one must be a complete fighter and know how to punch, kick, and fight on the ground. If one just know one of these skills, forget it! The level today is very good and is getting even better fast. The fighter of the future will be a cross-training one—a complete fighter on the ground and standing up. Even jiu-jitsu fighters who started this kind of competition, are practicing stand-up today. It is getting more and more difficult for them since the stand-up fighters are learning ground techniques. One must be a complete fighter.

Q: What do you think of Americans in vale tudo?
A: I am very impressed with the commitment Americans are showing and with the number interested in cross-training and learning Brazilian tech-

niques. It's incredible. I believe that Americans will dominate this style of fighting for several reasons. First, the best Brazilian athletes are here in the U.S. teaching vale tudo. Second, Americans have strong bodies, are very dedicated, and show up for practice in big numbers. Another good point is that Americans are used to the idea of cross-training. Other countries have this idea of being "loyal" to the first martial art ones practices, and not trying anything else.

Q: You seem to have basically settled in the United States.
A: Well, I have been here for many years and I really like it. I already have my green card and even though I love Rio and miss it, I need to stay here for my teaching and fighting career. In the beginning it was very difficult and I wasn't adapting very well, but now I have many friends and I'm very happy here with my family. Nevertheless, I don't know if I can be here forever—to stay away from the beaches of Rio is a very hard thing to do!

"The level today is very good and is getting even better fast. The fighter of the future will be a cross-training one—a complete fighter on the ground and standing up."

Q: Is there any difference between the vale tudo practiced in Brazil and in the U.S.?
A: In the beginning the two were very close, but now there is a lot of difference. The main one is that more and more rules and restrictions are being imposed in the U.S. I understand that's the only way for these types of competitions to take place. On the other hand, however, realism is being taken away from the fight itself. Here, if a fighter is bleeding even a little bit, the referee stops the match. In Brazil, the referee would never do that; bleeding is not a reason to terminate a fight. There, the fight gets stopped only if one of the fighters is in no condition to continue. Sometimes a fighter takes two or three punches to the face, bleeds a lot, but does not give up. Also, U.S. fights are limited in time. In Brazil, some fights have no time limit while others have long rounds of 10, 20, or even 30 minutes each.

167

"In the beginning it was very difficult and I wasn't adapting very well, but now I have many friends and I'm very happy here with my family. To stay away from the beaches of Rio is a very hard thing to do!"

Q: In the last few years you have focused more on training fighters than on fighting yourself. Are you retired?

A: Not at all. I had a very serious injury that kept me from competing. So I took time off from fighting, got an operation, and had a long period of rehabilitation. The funny thing about being off is that I taught so much that I feel it really improved my fighting game as far as my strategy and my mental approach. As you mature and grow you realize that fighting has a lot of mental aspects that you didn't know about when you were younger. So if anything, I feel like I am a better fighter now than when I won the UFC.

Q: How do you train?

A: I usually divide my daily training into two sections—one in the morning and the other in the afternoon—for a total of about six hours per day. In the morning I generally practice punches, kicks, hit various bags, do boxing training, and practice positions on the ground. In the afternoon I do the actual fighting part and spar stand-up as well as ground fighting. I also do other things because I am more of an athlete than just a fighter. I do weightlifting, running, and swimming. I train almost every day at a regular, sustainable pace, which I increase when a fight is getting close. I also like to stretch, usually before my morning practice.

Q: Do you feel variety is the key to avoid training burn-out?

A: I do. For instance, I love to swim. Swimming is a very important part of my training program. It's a great cardiovascular workout and relaxes the muscles and doesn't put any stress in your joints, which is a plus. I do it three times a week. I also add some punches and kicks underwater, which builds my muscle endurance. Weight training is something that I do once in a while. I have been gifted with a strong natural body so I don't need to use weights that much. I do a lot of strength calisthenics using my own body weight, though. I want sustainable strength not explosive one-time power, so my strength training centers around that. I understand, though, that for other fighters a weight training program might be necessary to increase their muscle mass. In NHB you need a certain amount of body weight and muscle mass to be successful.

Q: Do you follow a special diet?

A: No. I eat all kinds of food, even red meat. Of course, I avoid excesses fat and sugar but I don't deprive myself of anything. I train a lot and I train hard, so my body absorbs it all. I basically listen to what my body tells me. For the most part I eat a lot of vegetables, fruit, rice, and beans as a source of carbohydrates and lean meat for protein.

"As you mature and grow you realize that fighting has a lot of mental aspects that you didn't know about when you were younger. So if anything, I feel like I am a better fighter now than when I won the UFC."

Q: How have you stayed so motivated for so long?

A: I believe that your own spirituality as an individual has a lot to do with the motivation you need to gain success in life. I'm not necessarily talking from a religious point of view—I have strong faith in myself and in my spirit. This boosts my confidence in everything I do in life. I always set goals and then work to accomplish them. I have been doing this since I was a kid. Every goal is a project that I have to finish. I take one step at a time and pace myself properly to reach the finish line. I always want to excel in anything I do. But I don't get locked into any particular outcome. You have to be flexible enough to change your goals if circumstances change. Life often takes different directions that you have no control over, and your goals should adapt to your current situation and environment. "Realistic" is the key word here—set realistic goals and then focus on them. Being focused is a very important part of achieving anything. Part of being focused is staying relaxed. Even before a fight I focus on my breathing and try to stay calm. This is the only way you can keep yourself focused and motivated for long periods of time. ○

169

Mark Kerr

The Human Yardstick

HE EXEMPLIFIES EVERY PHYSICAL ATTRIBUTE ANY TOP ATHLETE WANTS. WITH POWER, SPEED, REFLEXES, STRENGTH AND AN UNBELIEVABLE SENSE OF CONTROL OVER HIS OPPONENT'S ACTIONS, MARK KERR DISPLAYS ALL THE TRAITS OF A TRUE WORLD CHAMPION WRESTLER AND A GREAT SUBMISSION FIGHTER. AFTER HIS PHENOMENAL REIGN IN THE WORLD OF WRESTLING, KERR DECIDED TO MOVE INTO THE MMA ARENA AND SUBMISSION FIGHTING. NOT SURPRISINGLY, HE TOOK THE MAJOR EVENTS AND BECAME THE "MAN TO BEAT" IN EVERY EVENT HE DECIDED TO PARTICIPATE IN. WITH A STRONG SUBMISSION WRESTLING FOUNDATION, KERR HAS TRAINED IN SEVERAL OTHER STYLES INCLUDING MUAY THAI AND BRAZILIAN JIU-JITSU. CONCEIVING THE FUTURE FIGHTER MORE LIKE A DECATHLETE, THIS ICON OF THE FIGHTING ARTS IS PLEASED TO BE THE HUMAN YARDSTICK AGAINST WHICH ALL MMA FIGHTERS ARE MEASURED.

Q: Would you please tell us a little bit about your wrestling background. What are some of your most memorable accomplishments?
A: I won three national freestyle collegiate titles, a U.S. world cup, a European championship, and I was an alternate on the U.S. Olympic team.

Q: How do you feel being one of the most admired fighters in Brazil, which is really the home of NHB? Does it surprise you?
A: I'll give you an example. I was standing in line in Rio, at a theater, to get tickets to a show there. And there was a gentleman standing in front of me with his wife. We stood there for about five minutes and then he turned around and asked, "Do you know Mark Kerr?" So I just smiled and laughed and said, "I'm Mark Kerr," without knowing that he was totally yanking my chain. He and his wife knew who I was and were both flabbergasted that I was standing in line behind them. We had about an hour-long conversation. They have a 15-year-old son who is very much into jiu-jitsu, and they were telling me things about my own fame that I didn't really know. So it is something I just don't think about, I guess, but I definitely like.

"A lot of fighters, once they reach the top of the rung, are afraid to fight. Others go ahead and prove themselves as good athletes and fighters like Royce Gracie. I give him a lot of credit."

Q: Why do you feel you've supplanted other native Brazilians as that country's favorite fighter?

A: It's what I said before. You can sit back and claim that you're the best, and sit on your laurels and some people will accept that. But I think the true fans, the ones that follow the fighters and the fights, really respect someone who isn't afraid to put themselves on the line and isn't afraid to lose. I guess it's a fear of failure, the reason people don't go out and try. If you let that control you, then you'll never compete.

Q: Why did you compete in events like Abu Dhabi that really aren't your specialty?

A: For a couple of reasons. One is that I'm not afraid to show up for a match or to compete anywhere. A lot of fighters, once they reach the top of the rung, are afraid to fight. Others go ahead and prove themselves as good athletes and fighters like Royce Gracie. For him to go compete against Wallid in Brazil in a straight jiu-jitsu match, I give him a lot of credit. I don't know of a lot of no-holds-barred fighters, who are used to punching and kicking, that would take that kind of a match.

Q: Given the fact that you have a legitimate, verifiable wrestling record, does that give you less fear of getting a blemish on it?

A: Yes, because the only people who are going to be considered the best, and who will stand the test of time, are those people who go out and fight everywhere and get a real record. I mean, respect won't be given to those guys who get 400 mythical dojo training victories against unknown opponents and then count them as wins. I mean, honestly, I have a 1000 wins if you count those. I hate to sound cynical but there is more truth in that than anything else. If you're supposedly the best fighter in the world, you have to go out there and compete against the best to prove it. I just can't sit back and semi-retire and be happy with myself. If you're considered the best, you have to prove it.

Q: Where do you rate a submission event against wrestling and no-holds-barred?
A: A submission event such as ADCC is a hard event. It's not easy. It's not something you can take lightly. I mean, only the top submission fighters in the world fight in those. Unfortunately, between NHB and submission, there isn't a clear crossover where someone who is great in submission is great in MMA. For example you may be a great submission fighter but just an ok no-holds-barred fighter. There are quite a few

"Unfortunately, between MMA and submission, there isn't a clear crossover, where someone who is great in submission is great in NHB. They are totally and completely different ball games."

examples of people who actually have a better artistry for submission than they do for NHB. They are totally and completely different ball games.

Q: What would you like to see different in MMA?
A: More respect. Look at jiu-jitsu. If you look around you'll see the jiu-jitsu practitioners have the infrastructure, and the clubs that compete, and the tradition. Probably the tradition more than anything is what drives them. You go to Brazil and jiu-jitsu is a legitimate sporting event, covered by the regular press. It's not like in the U.S. where it's treated like a freak show or a carnival sideshow or whatever. People know the fighters there, and they give them respect.

It's the same in Japan, too. There are a lot of legitimate events there. There's some worked fights too, which is not bad as long as it is advertised as such. I just don't like it when a fight is presented as real and then ends up being a work. And it's hard to tell. A lot of the works there are done very well. So you don't really know sometimes. And this opens some people up for criticism that they probably don't deserve. But it goes the other way, too. Some fighters get too much credit. But look, I don't necessarily criticize the fighters that take those fights, either. It's tough to earn a living and you have to do what's best for you and your family, so it's a personal decision. It's too bad the real events in the U.S. don't pay like the WWE or

173

"It's tough to earn a living and you have to do what's best for you and your family, so it's a personal decision. It's too bad the real events in the U.S. don't pay like the WWE or the WCW do."

the WCW do. Why else do you see legitimate fighters like Ken Shamrock and Dan Severn get into that? You'll probably see more fighters go that route, too.

In the United States the promoters need to give fighters the respect they deserve. You look at what some events pay fighters and it's a joke. You just can't make a living fighting in the United States. And it's not only the money. The promoters don't respect the fighters, either. Remember at my situation in the UFC. They were trying to wear me down. I have a stack of documents at my house, that I spent sixty grand on...and that was only because I have friends who are lawyers that did it at a discount. It could have easily cost me twice that. So after a while it became a matter of principle to me. I wasn't going to give in. Then, in the end, after all that, they just dropped the case and said I could fight if I wanted to...like they could have stopped me, you know?

And it's not just me, by the way. Look at Frank Shamrock. They gave him less money to fight after he became the champion. They probably told him the same thing they told me, "Don't look at this as a way to make money, look at it as a way to get fame and become well known." Yeah, right. Somebody is making money and it isn't the fighter, that's for sure. So that's the type of respect I'm talking about that the fighters don't get here. Basic respect as human beings.

Q: Why do you think that fighters who are considered the best don't really fight against the best opponents out there?
A: I guess some people are afraid to lose or they know they would lose if they face these opponents. Personally, I'm not afraid to lose. If I go out there tomorrow and lose in the tournament there's always the next day, and the next day. The world isn't going to end. I think in order to have any legitimacy as a fighter, and I keep saying this over and over again, you have to be willing to go out there and let it all hang out. I think if I come

out here and have the will to compete and walk away the victor or walk away the loser, there is always another day. In wrestling or boxing to be considered the best, you have to fight the best. If you don't, then it just a fantasy created and maintained by your fans and supporters. You're only the best if you fight against the best. Ali could have never been considered the best in boxing without fighting Foreman, Frazier, or Sonny Liston. He never rested on his laurels to make money. He put himself to the test all the time, against the best. That's what Olympic wrestlers always do. You get my point here, don't you? Period.

"I guess some people are afraid to lose or they know they would lose if the face these best opponents. I think in order to have any legitimacy as a fighter, and I keep saying this over and over again, you have to be willing to go out there and let it all hang out."

Q: For while it was said that Royce and Rickson Gracie would fight you. What happened?
A: It has been just a lot of rumors. You can't pay the bills from rumors and if I tried to pay bills from the rumors of them fighting me, I'd be broke now.

Q: Were you surprised that Royce got beat so quickly by Wallid?
A: No. Wallid is good. He's used to competing in those types of matches and Royce isn't. You put them in a closed room, with no one around, and maybe the match turns out different. But you have to be able to perform when it counts. It's like when I was in college, there were guys who would just dominate in practice, but then when we got in a tournament they would just fall apart.

Q: You have an amazing physique, was it built by using weights? Would you give us some information on how you use weight training for improving your skills?
A: Of course weight training is part of my training program but not as much as people think. Strength is a necessary factor in fighting. My weight training is mainly for conditioning so I usually pump iron three days per week and keep my reps high (15-25), thus no heavy weights and the series

"When you are stronger than your opponent you can get away from many situations and balance your lack of technique. But technique just by itself is useless, you need a certain amount of strength to help."

moderate, four or five. Usually if I find myself three months away from a fight I lift heavier. As we get closer to the date, I push my lifting to the back seat, lifting two days in a row and one of complete rest. Then two weeks before the fight I don't lift at all. I focus on my fighting skills only. My main objective in the lifting room is trying to duplicate the kind of movement and intensity that I'll be facing when fighting a real opponent, otherwise, what's the use of it?

Q: So how important do you think strength is in the overall conditioning program of an MMA fighter?
A: There has been a belief spread mainly by the jiu-jitsu fighters that technique is more important than strength. Well, that's true to a certain extent. When you are stronger than your opponent you can get away from many situations and balance your lack of technique. But technique just by itself is useless, you need a certain amount of strength to help. Personally, and maybe due to the fact I already have the strength I need, I spent more time in the gym trying to improve my technique and conditioning than pumping iron. Strength without conditioning is useless. If you can put together technique, strength and cardiovascular conditioning, you are meant to do something important. It's like a tripod, you need the three legs together to constitute the real base to grow.

Of course, there are other two factors that I would like to mention here; one is flexibility and the other is the proper nutrition. With so much training your body gets stiff and tight so you need to do something to "open" it. That's why flexibility and stretching is also a major part of any pro-athlete, and not only because you may kick higher! A flexibility program will help you to be more relaxed, more supple and quicker. It also helps to get rid of a lot of toxins in your body.

Q: What about nutrition?

A: This is extremely important and unfortunately neglected by many top fighters. The food is the fuel of your body. There are many fallacies about nutrition these days and not every body responds in the same way to a certain kind of diet. Basically you need to find out what works for you, and to do so you need information. And I tell you that it takes effort to get the best information. You need to understand how your body recovers after a hard training session or competition and how you have to nourish it.

In MMA events I don't have any problem with my weight because I'm naturally big, but when I compete in wrestling I need to keep control on every pound. Then I really need to keep an eye on my caloric intake. I always play with what I call "hard" and "soft" meals. I use the term "hard" to describe solid food and "soft" for liquid of protein shakes. I combine these two to make the best nutrition program for myself.

"If you can put together technique, strength and cardiovascular conditioning, you are meant to do something important. It's like a tripod, you need the three legs together to constitute the real base to grow."

Q: What kind of cardiovascular training do you do?

A: Cardio is a very important aspect of the overall training. I do mostly running and swimming. But I've really layed off the weights and watched my diet. I'm really light compared to what I used to be. I look like a swimmer now. I've got a swimmer's build. But you have to be in shape. I mean, no one gets a true perspective on this, and realizes how difficult this is to learn and to do. You look at me from two years ago, to where I am now, and I think technically I'm better but it has taken a lot of work. For instance, I'm really getting better at submissions, but I don't think I'll ever have it perfected like the guys who have been doing it for a lifetime. I guess this is normal…the submission fighter won't be able to take a guy down the same way I do it.

Q: Are these the main attributes of a fighter?

A: Today's fighters are the gladiators of the past. This is the bottom line. We are here to compete but they were there to save their lives. I believe we need to maintain that gladiator mentality. Strength and conditioning are the cornerstones of a good fighter. Then your martial art technique. The NHB events proved you need to borrow from several methods and systems if you really want to be competitive out there. One single style won't make it. Kickboxers found themselves helpless on the ground once taken down by a wrestler or jiu-jitsu guy. Grapplers found themselves stopped with punches and kicks as proven by Maurice Smith. You need the complete package, even though you'll always have your preferences. I know sometimes it's difficult to find someone who wants to work with a fighter from a different style without having prejudices and certain preconceptions. You need to find that right person who knows how to take what you have and fill in the blanks in your arsenal. Personally, I always found that these people are those who have an actual ring experience. They are fighters and only a fighter can understand another fighter's internal struggle.

Q: How do you prepare to face a new opponent?

A: Well, I always considered intelligence to be one of the fighter's more important tools. In order to be a winner you need to have a game plan and in order to have a game plan you need to know your opponent. I do this by watching tapes of his previous fights. I spend a great deal of time analyzing all the moves and tactics that my opponent likes to use. This allows me to know the best way to capitalize on those strengths and weakness. As you can see this is not an easy project. It takes time and effort. Then I take one of my partners and have him do the same moves and techniques that my opponent does. This is definitely more than just knowing your adversary's main style. You may know he is a boxer but you don't know how he feints, reacts, moves or what kind of punches he likes to set up.

With time I have realized that the more prepared you are, the more confidence you have in yourself. This becomes a very important aspect of the fight.

Q: Have you ever felt fear?

A: We all have our fears, no matter how big or great a champion you are. The trick is knowing how to canabalize this fear and make it work for you. Fear is good, it makes you aware of things and not to think you're too good!

Kerr

Q: Do you think that MMA is a sport of the future?
A: Definitely. Martial arts have become combat sports, and MMA is a complete fighting sport. We go back to the old pankration ideals. A complete fighter needs to know how to use punches and kicks, how to grapple on the ground, how to take an adversary down to the canvas and control him at will. I always said that the future fighter is a decathlete. He can't be closed minded about styles or training methods. He needs to combine different styles and methods and find his own way to deliver techniques. He must find his own perfect combination of elements and techniques.

On the other hand, I think the fighters should be considered professional athletes and be respected as such. When I go out and fight, I'm prepared, I did my best. Then I deserve respect, because what I do I take very seriously.

"People get bigger, faster, stronger, and better. It's just natural evolution. I'd like people to look back at me and just say that I had a positive impact on the sport."

Q: Is there anyone you pattern yourself after?
A: It's kind of like a racecar, you know? You take the best parts and put them together in the best way you can. Bas Rutten has certainly had an effect on me, he's very intense. Marco Ruas is very good, Pedro Rizzo for his heart, Rob Kaman for his focus. What they have over me, besides Pedro, is that they have a lot of fighting experience. That kind of experience is something you can't teach. You can't learn it. You have to live it.

Q: How would you like to be remembered 10 years from now?
A: I don't think, realistically, that people will look back on me and say, "There was the best fighter ever." People get bigger, faster, stronger, and better. It's just natural evolution. You look at the Frank Giffords of the 60's and they just can't compete with the John Elways of the 90's. They just can't. But, if anything, I'd like people to look back at me and just say that I had a positive impact on the sport. ○

Matt Furey

The King of Catch

WITH THE REVOLUTION IN THE MARTIAL ARTS WORLD DURING THE LAST DECADE AND THE EXPLOSION OF DIFFERENT GRAPPLING METHODS, THE "LOST" WESTERN SYSTEMS BECAME THE OBJECT OF STUDY AND ANALYSIS BY MANY FIGHTERS LOOKING TO DEVELOP A WELL-ROUNDED STRUCTURE IN THEIR FIGHTING SYSTEMS.

NO STRANGER TO THIS WORLD OF FORGOTTEN FIGHTING ARTS, MATT FUREY WAS A PIONEER IN REVITALIZING AND GIVING EXPOSURE TO THE OVERLOOKED ART OF CATCH WRESTLING. HIMSELF A NCAA WRESTLING CHAMPION, FUREY WENT DEEP INTO THE TEACHINGS OF KARL GOTCH—WHOM HE STARTED TRAINING UNDER IN 1999—TO FIND A COMPLETE GRAPPLING METHOD.

WITH MANY YEARS OF EXPERIENCE IN SEVERAL MARTIAL ARTS SYSTEMS, AND A WORLD CHAMPION IN CHINESE GRAPPLING, THIS CUTTING-EDGE WRESTLER IS CONSIDERING ONE OF THE MOST KNOWLEDGEABLE INSTRUCTORS IN CATCH WRESTLING WORLDWIDE. HIS GOAL HAS ALWAYS BEEN TO PRESERVE AND PERPETUATE ALL THE KNOWLEDGE PASSED ONTO HIM BY HIS INSTRUCTORS. HE BEGAN HIS TRAINING AT THE AGE OF 8 AND WAS PERSON-ALLY COACHED BY MEN LIKE DAN GABLE AND J. ROBINSON IN HIS NCAA CHAMPIONSHIP YEARS. HE ALSO BECAME A WORLD CHAMPION IN *SHAOLIN SHUAI-CHIAO*, A FORM OF CHINESE GRAPPLING. IN 1997, IN BEIJING, HE BECAME THE FIRST WESTERNER TO EVER WIN A WORLD GRAPPLING TITLE IN CHINA.

"I SINCERELY BELIEVE THAT THE TECHNIQUES OF TRADITIONAL CATCH WRESTLING AS TAUGHT BY KARL GOTCH ARE, AT THE VERY LEAST EQUAL, IF NOT MORE REFINED, THAN TODAY'S MOST POPULAR GRAPPLING ARTS," SAYS FUREY. "AND THAT INCLUDES BRAZILIAN JIU-JITSU."

Q: How long have you been practicing the martial arts and who were your first teachers?

A: Well, being that I consider wrestling a martial art, I've been training around 31 years. In Asian martial arts, it has been 11 years. In wrestling I have learned freestyle, Greco-Roman, collegiate (amateur catch) and pro-fessional catch-as-catch-can. I had eight months of the Korean system named *kook sul won* before going into Chinese martial arts, where I have

*"When I was in the seventh grade,
I had to wear a headgear for the first time.
I ended up putting it on the wrong way and it
was cutting off my circulation. So there I was,
in the middle of a match, defending against
my opponent's leg attack, and I threw up
all over him. It was horrible."*

studied shuai-chiao, as well as various styles of tai chi, including *Yang*, *Wu*, and *Chen* styles. My first wrestling teacher was Denny Donnelly. Then it was Lorne Greenfield and Bill Kane in high school. In college, I had Olympic champions Dan Gable, Bruce Baumgartner and Olympian J. Robinson as coaches. I also had some superstars coach me like Mike DeAnna, Lanny Davidson, Mark Johnson, Chuck Yagla and many others. As for the Chinese martial arts, I trained first under Adam Hsu and Ted Mancuso. Then I learned shuai-chiao under Dr. Daniel Weng.

Q: Would you tell us some interesting stories of your early days?
A: When I was in the seventh grade, in a wrestling match in my hometown of Carroll, Iowa, I had to wear a headgear for the first time. The school had these really tight headgears and I couldn't fig-ure out how to put it on and no one showed me how. I ended up putting it on the wrong way and it was cutting off my circulation. So there I was, in the middle of a match, defending against my opponent's leg attack, and I threw up all over him. I guess it was my body's natural reaction to pre-vent me from passing out. It was horrible. They had to clean the mat and the puke off my opponent's leg. I told the coach I couldn't breathe, that the headgear was too tight. He looked at it and said, "Damn, you got it on wrong" He unsnapped it and what a relief. He put it on the right way and I finished the match without a problem.

Q: Were you a natural at wrestling?
A: I wish I could say "Yes" to that one. But the truth is that I had a very diffi-cult time in the beginning. Nothing flowed. Nothing came easy. And this was a good thing as it taught me the value of out-working my oppo-nents—of spending more time on the mat than they did. It taught me that

to set goals and achieve them. When I started training in Chinese martial arts, though, a shift took place. For some reason learning wrestling holds and such got a lot easier. Maybe the Chinese system opened up another part of my brain. I can't say for sure. But now, I learn things incredibly fast and can even stand back and view moves and techniques from a perspective that few people have.

Q: How has your personal fighting system developed over the years?

A: In my early days, back in high school, when I got into a number of street fights, I double-legged the guy, slammed him on the ground, then whacked him a few times. Once in high school, when I had a fight with the "toughest guy" on campus, in the school bathroom of all places, he kept pushing me. When he did this I timed his movement and bear hugged him to the ground. He turned to his knees and I put the legs in to control him. He kept telling me, "Let me get up and I'll kick your butt." Realizing he better be hurt badly before he got up, I grabbed his hair—he had a big bushy mane, and I slammed his head against the cement stall a few times. This got his attention pretty well. He flattened out and I twisted his head around to face me

"Much of what I was doing back then is still the right thing to do. But today I would add more elbows and knees on the feet as well as the ground. Even though I practice submission all the time, in a street fight I wouldn't rely on them."

and popped him in the nose. He bled all over like a stuck hog. We became good friends afterward—which often happens after two people vent their frustrations in a brawl.

Much of what I was doing back then is still the right thing to do. But today I would add more elbows and knees on the feet as well as the ground. Even though I practice submission all the time, in a street fight I wouldn't rely on them. Face it, locks and chokes are good on the feet but once you hit the ground you want to end things as quickly as possible, and this is usually done with palm strikes, elbows and knees.

"People tend to think that what we know today is more advanced than what the old-timers knew, but that's sort of like an 18-year-old who first discovers sex. He actually believes that he and his buddies learned something new. But he's wrong."

Q: With all the technical changes during the last couple of decades, do you think there is still a "pure" system of wrestling, jiu-jitsu, judo, et cetera?

A: I wouldn't use the word "pure," I would use the word "complete." This is what I mean—wrestling today is not what it used to be. Holds that were once legal are illegal—and lots of them. Holds that hurt are stopped midway through, due to what the referee calls "potentially dangerous" situations. The pro style of catch wrestling is coming back due to the work I've done, and it's a perfect example of how much has been either lost or watered down and flowed out of the knowledge base. *Judo* isn't what it used to be. Hate to say it, but the Olympics basically ruined real judo. And Brazilian jiu-jitsu is mostly a spin-off of old-school judo, but only the groundwork portion of it. There again, it is not a complete rendering of what the old school judokas really knew and taught. So much is built on protecting people from injury, which is fine, but it's not complete in terms of what once existed.

People tend to think that what we know today is more advanced than what the old-timers knew, but that's sort of like an 18-year-old who first discovers sex. He actually believes that he and his buddies learned something new. He's sure that his mom and dad don't know. But he's wrong. So I get a kick out of people who think the treasure is in the "modern" methods and "modern" technical improvements—new techniques that are simply a modification of the pure basics—and it's not—it's in what the old-timers did, in the basics. The same can be said of boxing. The old-time boxers were incredible in what they had to know to survive in the ring. In terms of tactics, dirty tricks, and what not, there's no comparison to what we see today.

Q: NHB events have destroyed the old idea of how "deadly" one punch can be. Do you think that these events are positive for overall martial arts or only for the fighters?

A: They may have "destroyed" the idea of the one deadly punch for a lot of people, but one good punch can still be deadly as hell. You need to consider that the money isn't good enough for a Mike Tyson to enter a mixed martial arts contest. How many of today's mixed martial artists could take just one of his punches? Assuming Tyson would take the fight because the money was good enough, how many mixed martial artists would have the guts to actually challenge him? If he were fighting in these events, based upon the number of combatants who like to stay on their feet and trade punches, I believe that 90 percent of Tyson's opponents would get knocked cold inside of 60 seconds. I think the events are positive for those interested in fighting. Those who are simply inter-

"Wrestlers were able to capitalize on the inherent weaknesses of the Brazilian jiu-jitsu system. Wrestlers would take them down and stay out of trouble long enough to ground and pound, or simply stall and win."

ested in the "martial arts" aren't really affected one way or the other. Little Johnny who goes to *tae kwondo* with his father isn't affected in the least by these events.

Q: Brazilian jiu-jitsu became extremely popular and the representatives of this method were head and shoulders above everybody else for a while. Then American wrestlers started to beat the jiu-jitsu practitioners. Why do you think that happened?

A: Wrestlers were able to capitalize on the inherent weaknesses of the Brazilian jiu-jitsu system. Wrestlers would take them down and stay out of trouble long enough to ground and pound, or simply stall and win. Now, amateur style wrestling has its weaknesses, too, but their strengths, many times but not always, can deal a heavy blow to Brazilian jiu-jitsu. As a

"The old-time professional style of catch wrestling that I learned from Karl Gotch is truly awesome. Is it more advanced than Brazilian jiu-jitsu? I would say that the arsenal contained in the system is much more complete and that the techniques themselves require less strength. But ultimately, it is each individual fighter that determines the outcome of a bout."

result, the smart Brazilians started learning wrestling so that they could advance. But I must emphasize that not all wrestlers have done well against Brazilian jiu-jitsu.

Q: From a technical point of view, is the Brazilian method advanced when compared to wrestling?
A: First of all, it depends on what Brazilian method you're talking about. For instance, in the early UFC, Royce Gracie was aggressive. Then he started to use passive tactics and he wasn't as successful as before. Then he fought Sakuraba in Japan and you could see some flaws in the approach he was taking, not only on the feet, but on the ground as well. On the other side, you look at other Brazilian jiu-jitsu fighters and they are more aggressive. Basically, it depends who you are talking about.

Second, you need to ask what style of wrestling. Freestyle and Greco-Roman and the collegiate style—which is amateur catch wrestling—are flawed because of the rules the athletes have been subjected to for their entire career. But the old-time professional style of catch wrestling that I learned from Karl Gotch is truly awesome. Is it more advanced than Brazilian jiu-jitsu? I would say that the arsenal contained in the system is much more complete and that the techniques themselves require less strength. But ultimately, it is each individual fighter that determines the outcome of a bout. Who gives a damn about which system is more advanced or not? The bottom line is who won.

Q: Do you think that martial arts in the West has caught up with the East as far as skill level?
A: That depends on how things are evaluated. I think the Shaolin monks of China are more skilled—but are they fighters? Or will they fight in a way that we can evaluate them and compare them to others? I think they

can fight and would be good at it, but they choose not to. So we can only speculate. Nowadays martial arts are both sport and art but for most people they are mostly sport.

Q: Is wrestling a sport or a Western martial art?
A: It's a sport and it's a worldwide form of a martial art. Every country on earth has its own style of wrestling. The strongest nations on earth have always been those with the best wrestlers. From Mongolia, to China, to Turkey, to Germany, to England, to the U.S., and so on. All these countries, historically, have had great wrestlers. And wrestling is and always has been used on the battlefield.

Q: Do you have any general advice you would care to pass onto grapplers in general?
A: Yes. Open your mind, investigate and look. The saddest sight in the martial arts are the people who are so completely sold on their art that they are deaf, dumb and blind for the rest of their lives. No one art contains all the answers. No one person has all the answers either. Look to others for guidance. Investigate what others have to teach. But

"Look to others for guidance. Investigate what others have to teach. But most importantly, take time to sit still, to concentrate, then hopefully to tune into and listen to that still voice within you that knows far more than you give it credit for. You always have to go on in your studies, to think otherwise would be foolish."

most importantly, take time to sit still, to concentrate, then hopefully to tune into and listen to that still voice within you that knows far more than you give it credit for. You always have to go on in your studies, to think otherwise would be foolish. Success is a journey, not a destination. Once you stop learning, or think you know it all, you're through.

Q: What do you consider to be the major changes in the world of martial arts since you began your training?
A: The desire for practitioners to become more complete and more well-rounded. Yes, there are some who still cling to their "one holier than thou art," but not the smart people. The smartest people learn as much of

"I am always thirsty and hungry to learn more. It's like I'm in this river that I never leave. I'm always swimming in it and don't feel comfortable if I'm not in the water. The bottom line is you have to dedicate yourself to becoming all that you can be. Practice religiously and devote yourself to the task."

everything as they can. It's like doing research for a book or a term paper. You don't just search for all the answers from one source, unless you want a poor grade. You study and learn from as many knowledge banks as you can; you scan the horizons and look things over, then spend time thinking before you make up your mind; you stand back and look at things the way an eagle would scan the terrain looking for the one animal he's going to feast on.

Q: Who would you like to have trained with that you have not?
A: That's an easy answer: Farmer Burns.

Q: What is it that keeps you motivated after all these years?
A: I wish I knew. All I can say is that I totally love wrestling, submission training, martial arts, and the like. I am always thirsty and hungry to learn more. It's like I'm in this river that I never leave. I'm always swimming in it and don't feel comfortable if I'm not in the water. And even when I do get out, I sit on the bank and stare at the water, and oftentimes that's when the best ideas come floating downstream. The bottom line is you have to dedicate yourself to becoming all that you can be. Practice religiously and devote yourself to the task. Learn to use your mind and to develop your mind. It's the best weapon you have.

Q: Do you think it is necessary to engage in free-fighting to achieve good fighting skills in self-defense?
A: It certainly helps. But is it necessary? It depends on who the person is. Some people, those who haven't been ruined by society, are connected to the human being's natural desire to survive—and they'll fight. Now, on

the other hand, you have the wimps. You would think that a person didn't need to learn free fighting to stand up for his or her life, but our culture is so saturated with many who don't let their kids do anything rough from the time they're kids. So is it any wonder that these same people will not fight to protect the only life they have? Doesn't surprise me.

Q: Do you have any particular mental preparation method that you use before a fight?
A: I follow a system of deep breathing exercises that simultaneously energize my body and rid it of anything stressful that may interfere with me giving my all.

Q: Do you see yourself practicing any other traditional martial arts in the future?
A: In the disciple-to-the-master sense, no. But learning from them, yes. If I see a teacher who has great body awareness and movement, I'm going to study him and see how I can fit it into what I do. That's what I did with kung-fu, even with tai chi. I learned to relax more—to flow more—to move more gracefully. And it benefited my wrestling a great deal.

Q: What's your opinion about mixing martial arts styles?
A: The more overall knowledge you have, the better. But I do believe it is important,

"The more overall knowledge you have, the better. But I do believe it is important, at least in the beginning, to fall in love with one form of combat and become excellent at it. That way you always have one thing, one bread-and-butter art that you can fall back on. This is good not only from a technical standpoint, but from a mental conditioning standpoint."

at least in the beginning, to fall in love with one form of combat and become excellent at it. That way you always have one thing, one bread-and-butter art that you can fall back on. This is good not only from a technical standpoint, but from a mental conditioning standpoint. When

you look in the mirror each day, if the person staring back is half-assed at everything he does, then how can he radiate confidence? But if he *knows* he's great at something, then he knows how he got that way—through focus and practice. Once you've done it in one field, what's to prevent you from branching out and becoming great in others as well? Nothing.

Q: What is the philosophical basis for your training?
A: To become all what I'm capable of becoming. Wrestling, martial arts, and so on are simply a metaphor for all forms of life. They give you the opportunity to expand your mental and physical horizons. They allow you to get into the *now* through practice. They help you reach levels of enlightenment that I don't believe you can attain without physical activity. The Taoists of China have always believed that the body must be trained in order for the mind to reach its fullest potential. That's what I believe, too.

"Wrestling, martial arts, and so on are simply a metaphor for all forms of life. They give you the opportunity to expand your mental and physical horizons. They allow you to get into the now *through practice. They help you reach levels of enlightenment that I don't believe you can attain without physical activity."*

Q: Do you have a particularly memorable experience that has remained with you as an inspiration for your training?
A: When I was training for the world championships in China, and running hill sprints, and picturing the result I wanted to create, and then I actually won the title. In this instance I can say that I one hundred percent absolutely believe that "thoughts are things." Any desire you have, so long as you can picture it in your mind and back it up with a burning desire, you can manufacture that result in reality. I've done it in every area of my life—but once again, the power of the mind became known to me while I was engaged in physical activity.

Q: After all these years of training and experience, could you explain the meaning of practicing?

A: To me, practice is an opportunity to know the *self*. When I practice, I am as much aware as what I am thinking as what I am doing. I stay conscious and live in the moment. I explore new terrain. I challenge any assumptions I may have about moves, exercises and so on. My mind is open to new possibilities and improvements—looking for new ways of looking at the same puzzle. I find my comfort zone, then I figure out ways to expand the boundaries of my comfort zone. In doing all of the above, you get to know yourself, your strengths and weaknesses and what you intend to do with each of them.

"When I practice, I am as much aware as what I am thinking as what I am doing. I stay conscious and live in the moment. My mind is open to new possibilities and improvements—looking for new ways of looking at the same puzzle. I find my comfort zone, then I figure out ways to expand the boundaries of my comfort zone."

Q: Could I ask you what you consider to be the most important qualities of a successful fighter?

A: The largest most powerful creatures to ever walk the earth, dinosaurs, were destroyed in a couple of weeks. The human being pales in comparison to the physical strength of the dinosaur. And so—although the learning of technique and the practice of conditioning are vitally important—the single most important quality of a successful fighter is his mind. Your mind and the thoughts you think are your supreme weapon.

Q: Would you give us an example of what would be a complete training program?

A: A complete training program begins with pre-determined goals. You begin with the end in mind and work backwards. While working backwards you decide upon a plan that will help you accomplish the goal. It will without a doubt have a strong base in physical conditioning. It will have submission wrestling and offense and defense—on the feet and on the ground. It will have striking, including punches, kicks, elbows and

"Fear is not a good thing. Courage and confidence, balanced with realistic training and preparation, are what you want to increase. When you feel fear you paralyze yourself—you hold yourself back. You give less than your all. The key thing is to know that you are in charge."

knees. And it will have time spent on a daily basis to do the most important thing of all—*think*.

Q: Have there been times when you felt fear in your training?
A: Early on in my career, yes, I did feel fear. Then you learn to master your fears and channel any and all nervous energy. You learn to transform it into positive energy. Fear is not a good thing. Courage and confidence, balanced with realistic training and preparation, are what you want to increase. When you feel fear you paralyze yourself—you hold yourself back. You give less than your all. The key thing is to know that *you* are in charge. Fear doesn't just happen to you. And so, when and if you experience it, breathe deeply, calm yourself down, and change the words and images you're putting into your head.

Q: What are your thoughts on the future of mixed martial arts?
A: I think it will continue to grow. I think more and more fighters will become more complete, more well-rounded. However, I don't think the general public will ever accept it in a big way. Although less gruesome than say boxing, appearance is everything. When a guy is on his back and you're mounted on him and you belt him a couple times and a cut is opened and the blow flows—even though the referee steps in and immediately stops the action—appearance-wise, for the average person in America, it looks awful. But if you see Evander Holyfield beat Mike Tyson so badly that Tyson is out on his feet but won't fall, we don't mind seeing him get hit a few more times. It doesn't appear as bad, yet it is much worse. You take

race car driving and a fatality. It's sad but the American people will never insist that we ban race car driving. The reason why is because we only see a car crash. That's all. We don't see the driver inside the car getting his neck snapped. We don't see the impact to his head. We don't see his insides rupture. Appearance is everything. If there were a camera inside the race car that showed the impact of the collision, the blood trickling, the bones snapping, the last gasp of air—well, then it would be a different story.

I probably should bite my tongue and not say this, but mixed martial arts would be greatly improved by eliminating the guard. It's the most boring thing ever introduced to fighting. No one other than a die-hard grappling practitioner wants to watch someone lie on his back and hold someone between his legs. In boxing when there is a clinch, the referee separates you and restarts you. Why? Because if he didn't the fans would be bored. They want to see a slugfest. The same is true on the ground. No one really wants to see the guard in a fight. They want to see movement, lots of action. Fans want to see submissions and knockouts. And if you can't give them that, give them a lot of action.

Karl Gotch

"I probably should bite my tongue and not say this, but mixed martial arts would be greatly improved by eliminating the guard. It's the most boring thing ever introduced to fighting. No one really wants to see the guard in a fight. They want to see movement, lots of action. Fans want to see submissions and knockouts."

Q: What are your plans for the future?
A: They fill a legal pad, so there's not sufficient space to answer that one. Besides, it's never a good idea to tell anyone about your plans. ↻

Masters Techniques

Matt Furey is controlling his opponent from the back (1). As Matt pulls the hand back (2), he rolls to the side and extends the arm (3), and then applies a double wrist-lock for the submission (4).

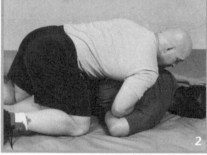

Trapped under his opponent (1), Matt Furey creates space by pressuring his opponent's nose (2). Matt then swings his leg in front of his opponent's face (3), and applies a finishing wrist-lock while trapping the head (4).

Matt Furey faces opponent Mark "The Bear" Smith (1). Mark shoots-in for the single-leg takedown (2), then pressures forward to upset Matt's balance (3). Stepping to the side to reduce Smith's attack angle (4), Furey hooks the arm (5), then forces Smith to the ground and applies a finishing arm-lock (6).

Matt Furey is trapped underneath his opponent's top mount (1). To escape, Matt traps the near arm and pushes on the far arm to unbalance his opponent (2). Rolling over while continuing to hold the arm extended (3), Matt goes on top for the reversal (4).

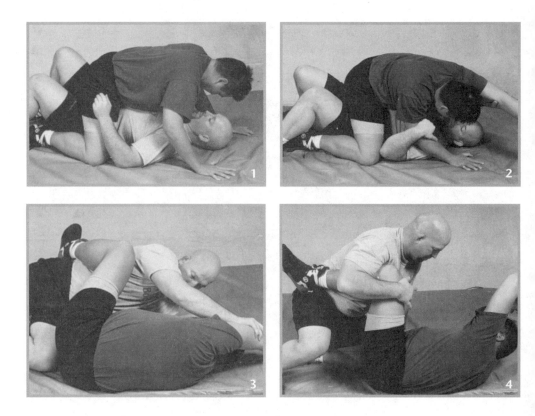

Matt Furey clinches with his opponent, Mark "The Bear" Smith (1). Matt suddenly drops down and puts his right leg between his opponent's legs (2). Matt then puts his left thigh behind his opponent's right knee to bring him down (3). Matt turns around (4), and applies a reverse leg lock for the finishing submission (5).

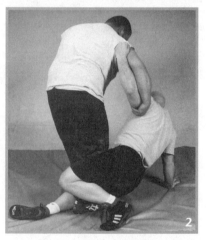

Oleg Taktarov

More than "15 Minutes"

BORN IN CAROV, RUSSIA, IN 1967, OLEG TAKTAROV DREAMED OF BECOMING A NUCLEAR SCIENTIST. SIDETRACKED BY HIS GIFTED ATHLETIC ABILITIES, HE WON EVERY POSSIBLE TOURNAMENT IN EUROPEAN SAMBO AND JIU-JITSU CIRCLES BETWEEN 1985 AND 1994. AFTER HIS APPEARANCE IN THE ULTIMATE FIGHTING CHAMPIONSHIP HE BECAME ONE OF THE MOST SOUGHT-AFTER FIGHTERS IN THE WORLD. TO MOST AMERICANS, HE IS THE MOST FAMOUS FIGHTER TO EVER COME FROM RUSSIA. NOT SATISFIED TO BE SIMPLY KNOWN AS A FIGHTER, HE BEGAN TO STUDY ACTING. HIS CO-STARRING ROLE IN THE BIG BUDGET HOLLYWOOD FILM *15 MINUTES* WITH ROBERT DENIRO SET A NEW DIRECTION IN HIS LIFE AND ESTABLISHED HIM AS MIXED MARTIAL ARTS FIRST TRUE CROSSOVER CELEBRITY.

TAKTAROV IS NOT ONLY A FIGHTER OF SUPERIOR ABILITY, HE IS ALSO ONE OF THE VERY BEST COACHES ANYONE COULD EVER HOPE TO TRAIN WITH. WITH MANY FIGHTS LEFT IN HIS HEART (AND PERHAPS A FEW IN HIS BODY) OLEG TAKTAROV HAS NOT RULED OUT ANYTHING IN HIS FUTURE. HE IS A ROLE MODEL NOT ONLY FOR NHB FIGHTERS, BUT FOR ANYONE WHO LOVES AND TRAINS GRAPPLING AND SUBMISSION. OLEG TAKTAROV IS TRULY A PIONEER OF MIXED MARTIAL ARTS AND REPRESENTS FAR MORE THAN WHAT HE EVER EXPECTED TO BE AND FAR LESS THAN WHAT HE WILL EVENTUALLY BECOME.

Q: How did you get started in martial arts?
A: I started in sambo when I was 10 years old. At that particular time the sambo training focused more on stand-up techniques—ground techniques were few in comparison to all the throws and stand-up fighting techniques.

Q: Did you feel comfortable with that?
A: Not really! I always felt very comfortable on the ground. I like to fight on the ground so when the instructor taught us groundwork I was extremely happy and lucky enough to be good at it. It was something natural to me. I attended the best fight training school in Russia, and they told me that if I did well in competition I would be allowed to go to the military and keep training there with better people. I decided to keep going and eventually, at

the age of 19, I started my judo training. Until then I practiced straight sambo.

Q: Why do you think sambo groundwork wasn't popular with your teacher?
A: I think it was a personal preference of that particular instructor. Sambo has a lot of groundwork but even at the time, in competition, the fighters didn't go to the ground much. They preferred to stay up and grapple on their feet. I guess it depends on the person and also has a lot to do with the sport regulations. I trained hard and decided to compete. Eventually, I won all the major titles and at age 23 I stopped competing. At that point I had won everything and had no worlds left to conquer.

"If you're really good you can play within the rules, but if you're not good then you find excuses to justify your mistakes and lack of skill and ability. I never blamed the rules for losing or winning a competition. Every fighter that steps into a ring knows the rules and has already agreed on them. So do your best and don't complain if you lose."

Q: How much influence do you think rules have in grappling?
A: The bottom line for me is that if you're really good you can play within the rules, but if you're not good then you will find excuses to justify your mistakes and lack of skill and ability. Of course, rules determine the limitations of the match but the rules are there for everyone to follow—me included. I never blamed the rules for losing or winning a competition. Every fighter that steps into a ring knows the rules and has already agreed on them. So do your best and don't complain if you lose—because if you win I'm pretty sure you won't say anything about the rules. However, if you're a sambo competitor who is used to sambo rules and you

decide to compete in judo, you may
have problems trying to adapt to that
particular type of competition.

Q: Would you give me an example?
A: In judo you can't spend too much
time on the ground, and in sambo
they do. When training for a competition, the sambo guys—and also the
Brazilian jiu-jitsu people these days—
spend more time training ground
techniques than stand-up or throwing. This doesn't mean that a good
judo fighter does not know much of
the *ne-waza*, not at all. It just means
that they may train more specifically
for one aspect than for the other.

**Q: Would you say that European
judo competition was highly influenced by Russian sambo techniques?**
A: It's true! All of a sudden the Russian
judo fighters began to win international competitions because they

*"All of a sudden the Russian judo fighters began
to win international competitions because they
adapted a lot of the sambo ground techniques.
They also modified many of the judo grips,
making everything more difficult for the
orthodox judo practitioner."*

adapted a lot of the sambo ground techniques. They also modified many of
the judo grips, making everything more difficult for the orthodox judo practitioner. The Georgians modified a great number of movements and their
approach has been always more physical than the practitioners of central
Russia. The people from Russia focused on groundwork more because of their
physical characteristics. The others, being bigger, practiced a rougher form of
stand-up grappling. The stand-up techniques are OK to show off, but the
ground is the best place to win if you are smaller than your opponent.

Q: Does it have something to do with the mentality and education?
A: Yes, it does. In Russia, showing off is not something nice—it's not appropriate. A well-mannered and educated person will never show off. It's the
worst you can do. Therefore, the Russian people never try to be showy or
cocky standing up. If they had to fight they did, but they could take you to

the ground and make you play their game.

Q: Did you cross-train in Russia?
A: Yes, I did open-style fighting. And in order to know more about other systems and at the same time improve my arsenal I had to cross-train. I did kickboxing and also studied other systems that fit into that particular competition approach. I improved my stand-up skills a lot and focused on techniques that helped me to understand a kickboxer's mentality and approach to fighting. Only if you know your opponent's game can you fight him and win. This type of training helped me to win the European title four times.

Q: Have you made any innovations to the styles you trained in?
A: Who hasn't? Everybody makes innovations to what they are practicing or teaching compared to what they learned in the past. Even all the great martial arts masters did. Who thinks Jigoro Kano, Gichin Funakoshi or Morihei Ueshiba taught exactly what was passed on to them by their teachers? They were very traditional in

"Everybody makes innovations to what they are practicing or teaching compared to what they learned in the past. Even all the great martial arts masters did. Who thinks Jigoro Kano, Gichin Funakoshi or Morihei Ueshiba taught exactly what was passed on to them by their teachers?"

the sense that they kept cultural values such as respect, moral and work ethics alive and didn't concentrate strictly on physical techniques. Innovations should be made based on realistic and functional experiences, otherwise they become a waste of time if what you want is a more practical fighting method. Of course, different people look for different things and that also determines the direction of their progress and evolution.

Q: In December 1994 you decided to move to the United States. Was your main reason to compete in the Ultimate Fighting Championship?

A: No, not at all! The reason I decided to move to America was because of movies, not because of the fighting! I was 27 years old and I had won my fifth big competition when I decided to stop competing. But almost right after the celebration I started to compete again. I knew that getting into the movies was going to take a while so fighting came along and I did it. I went to some Brazilian jiu-jitsu school to help them with leg locks, but some of the instructors were not very receptive to being shown leg locks. It was very interesting, to put it nicely.

"Innovations should be made based on realistic and functional experiences, otherwise they become a waste of time if what you want is a more practical fighting method."

Q: What was your first experience in the UFC like?

A: I was surprised, but it was a good experience. I was not used to fighting with no gloves or gi. After the first time I adapted and found ways to make my techniques work under those new circumstances. Then they didn't give me enough time to rest between the fights—time I should have had anyway—and I didn't feel very comfortable with the whole situation. After that I fought in several competitions, but honestly I have to say that my heart was not 100 percent there because all my motivation was focused on acting. I was fighting because it was convenient for me, not because I felt a need to do it. To fight professionally you have to put

"Mixed martial arts and NHB are new styles; and styles to me are like religions. There is always someone waiting around the block to make money with a new style. You have to find what is good for you and try to make it work."

yourself 100 percent into training and preparation. So if your mind is someplace else it's difficult.

Q: Are mixed martial arts and no-holds-barred the future of martial arts?

A: Mixed martial arts and NHB are new styles, and styles to me are like religions. There is always someone waiting around the block to make money with a new style. I definitely see that there is lots of room for this new approach—it's more complete for fighting than the old methods. You have to find what is good for you and try to make it work, but there is no ultimate style, because regulations direct the techniques and how they're used. For instance, if you allow gis you'll see a lot of arm locks and chokes because the gi gives you the versatility to manipulate your opponent arms and neck in effectively. If you allow pants you'll see more leg locks, because it is then easier to grab the legs. If you allow a gi, there will be less striking techniques because it is more difficult to punch when someone is grabbing your gi. So in some ways, the regulations determine the direction of the techniques and the evolution of the styles.

Q: Are these styles related to pure self-defense?

A: MMA and NHB methods are combat or fighting sports, not pure self-defense methods. Of course, if you train as a professional fighter you'd better know how to defend yourself! Self-defense is a completely different ball game. Self-defense is not a sport, it is simply survival.

Q: You've been practicing boxing lately, right?
A: Yes. I really like it and it's good for my acting career. It fits into the kind of movements needed for some acting roles. The other reason I'm training boxing is because I feel it's good for my body. My body has been used and molded as a grappler and I want to develop that finesse you see in boxers. Their body language is important to me. They seem very relaxed and ready to explode at the right moment. I really enjoy training Western boxing.

Q: What about the kicking aspects?
A: Kicking is good but I mostly focus on techniques I can use in the ring. Even in the movies you need three or four good techniques that look good on screen. And for fighting you don't want to do all that flashy-fancy stuff. The best kicking techniques for fighting are the Thai kicks. Keep them low and to the point!

"Cardiovascular training has always been the main focus of my training. Don't forget that even though I'm very strong for someone of my weight and size, I was not that strong compared to many of the people I fought. Cardiovascular endurance was the key to my victories."

Q: What's your personal training regimen when you fight?
A: Cardiovascular training has always been the main focus of my training. Don't forget that even though I'm very strong for someone of my weight and size, I was not that strong compared to many of the people I fought. Cardiovascular endurance was the key to my victories. I needed to be in much better shape and with a higher level of endurance than my opponents. When they ran out of gas, I was still going strong. That always

"My weight training is always important. Skill by itself is not enough. It boils down to the old game of scissors, rock, and paper. You have to be able to find the right counter for what your opponent is doing."

gave me an important edge and advantage.

My weight training is always important, especially if I'm going to fight in a weight division where power and strength rule. I remember that in Russia they thought that if you have technique, you'll be OK. And that's fine but if you already have the technique, why don't you just put some muscle into it? It will only improve your skill if you do the right training. Some people don't like the idea of weight training but believe me, it is necessary these days. Skill by itself is not enough. It boils down to the old game of scissors, rock, and paper. You have to be able to find the right counter for what your opponent is doing. Sometimes it's the rock, sometimes it's the scissors, and who knows when you'll need the paper! You have to be well-rounded in order to win. It's a combination of things that makes a fighter a champion these days.

No one using the orthodox original style of the method he practices will win the NHB events we have nowadays. You need a complete package, not only as far as physical conditioning is concerned but also the technical training. In the beginning, strikers were easily defeated by submission fighters. Then, all of a sudden the freestyle wrestlers were taking over and defeating the submission and Brazilian jiu-jitsu guys. Now, it's a combination of aspects that helps you to be on top. The timing and precision of the strikers, the explosiveness and strength of the wrestlers, and

the game plan and submissions of the jiu-jitsu fighters.

Q: How important is an open mind?
A: Extremely important. Sometimes it has more to do with being free from a strong influence rather that just being open minded. For instance, the Japanese were the first to incorporate leg locks because they were not under the influence of anyone. Even in a very traditional country in many aspects, they are pioneers and very progressive in the way they look at things. Their minds are always in the future. They take the best from everyone and create something. You have to give them credit for that.

Q: What kind of mental training do you do when preparing to fight?
A: Basically you have to set-up your mental structure and give priority to the fight. You have to isolate your training and preparation. Some people like to have a big group surrounding them before a fight, others prefer to be alone and to internalize what and why they are doing. It's a personal choice. Of course, when you have been fighting for so many years it becomes instinctive and reflexive. You

"The Japanese were the first to incorporate leg locks because they were not under the influence of anyone. Even in a very traditional country in many aspects, they are pioneers and very progressive in the way they look at things. Their minds are always in the future."

put yourself into a mental state that allows you to step into the ring and fight. Everything around you becomes a silent movie, you see but you don't hear. Believe me, the more attention you pay to the external factors surrounding a fight, the less focused you are the day of the fight. That's why the top professional boxers who have been doing this longer and for more money, are always isolated. They gather their energy and then give one big explosion the day of the fight. Their managers don't let them know much about what's going outside so they can focus on their goal—which is to win the fight and come out victorious.

"All fighters feel that fear inside, it is how they handle it that makes them winners or losers. It's not if you feel fear, but rather how you overcome it."

Q: Do you think fear is present in every fighter?

A: Where there is danger, fear is always present. There are some boxers who put on a funny show before the fight, but inside they are extremely focused. That may be their personal way of getting ready—to become cocky and arrogant so they can get into the required mental state to fight another person. All fighters feel that fear inside, it is how they handle it that makes them winners or losers. It would be like thinking Jackie Chan doesn't feel fear seconds before doing an extremely dangerous stunt. Of course he feels millions of butterflies in the stomach, but he goes and just does it. That is what makes him who he is—a living legend. Fighters are the same. It's not if you feel fear, but rather how you overcome it.

Q: What do you think could be improved at NHB events?

A: Well, to begin with we all have to understand that this is not a war. It is not a real fight. It is a sport and we fight to entertain people. We are entertainers who fight instead of telling jokes. Then we have to understand that promoters put on a show to make money. Finally, everybody has to understand and accept the fact that the fighters are the most important part of the event and should receive the respect they deserve. For their part, the fighters need to understand that the rules set-up by the promoters are meant to entertain the audience, since nobody wants to see two guys holding each other on the ground for 30 minutes. A lot of subtle things can be happening on the ground, but the audience won't understand and will get bored and stop watching the show. For instance, I don't like weight classes but I understand that it might be important for

the sport. I would like to see only three weight divisions: light, medium, and heavy. But I guess we all have to give up something we like in order to help the sport reach a higher level.

Q: Did your co-starring role in *15 Minutes* with Robert DeNiro change your life?

A: Yes, it did. It took my personal life into another dimension and opened a lot of doors for me in the movie business. After that role, I didn't have to prove myself as an actor anymore. As a fighter, every fight is a new movie where you have to prove yourself!

Q: Did martial arts change your life?

A: They did. Martial arts gave me a new direction in life. I had other goals, but my training helped me to focus on the aspects that were important. Don't get me wrong, I don't mean that martial arts will change your life if you have a basic lack of common sense because they won't. They are a great tool if you know how to use the different mental and philosophical aspects for self-improvement. Enrolling in a martial arts school was the best thing I ever did. ○

"Martial arts gave me a new direction in life. They are a great tool if you know how to use the different mental and philosophical aspects for self-improvement. Enrolling in a martial arts school was the best thing I ever did."

Masters Techniques

Oleg Taktarov is grabbed from behind by Matt Midyette (1). Immobilizing Matt's wrist (2), Oleg arches back and breaks the grip (3). Securely holding the left wrist, Oleg spins to the outside and traps Matt's shoulder (4). Under-hooking Matt's arm, Oleg grabs his own wrist (5), pivots to the inside (6), and then extends Matt's arm and locks the elbow for the submission (7).

Oleg Taktarov is put into a bear hug by an attacker (1).
Oleg moves his left leg backwards (2), and places himself
behind his opponent (3). Oleg then hits the attacker with
a elbow strike to the face (4), grabs his right leg and
shoulder (5), pulls him down to the ground (6), and
applies a finishing leg-lock (7).

An attacker tries to choke Oleg Taktarov from behind (1). Oleg grabs his opponent's left arm and applies a wrist lock (2), which allows him to extend the arm (3). Oleg then brings his legs between his opponent's arms (4), and applies a finishing arm-lock with his legs (5).

Oleg
Taktarov

Oleg Taktarov holds opponent Matt Midyette in his guard (1). Locking Matt's wrists inward, Oleg raises his legs on his Matt's back (2), bends his arm upward (3), inserts his hand under Matt's arm (4), pressures Matt's head (5), locks Matt's wrists together (6), and applies an elbow lock for the submission (7).

213

Masters Techniques

Oleg Taktarov is trapped inside his opponent's guard (1). Oleg moves his right leg over his opponent's body (2), grabs his right leg and spins around (3), and applies a finishing leg-lock by crossing his own legs over his opponent's right instep (4).

Oleg Taktarov has his opponent in his half-guard (1). Oleg moves to the right to avoid being choked (2), hooks his opponent's left ankle (3), and applies a finishing leg-lock (4).

*Oleg Taktarov is grappling with his
opponent from the north-south position
(1). Oleg hooks his opponent's right
arm (2), as he simultaneously grabs his
right leg (3). He then falls backwards
(4), and applies a finishing leg-lock (5).*

Relson Gracie

Passion and Art

AS A MEMBER OF THE WORLD FAMOUS GRACIE FAMILY, RELSON GRACIE LOVES SURFING, SOCCER AND, OF COURSE, JIU-JITSU. BUT BEHIND HIS RELAXED ATTITUDE AND HAPPY-GO-LUCKY SMILE IS A GREAT TECHNICAL KNOWLEDGE OF JIU-JITSU THAT GIVES HIM THE ABILITY TO CONTROL HIS OPPONENTS AND MAKE THEM TAP ON ALMOST A WHIM. BUT HE IS MORE THAN "JUST" A GREAT FIGHTER. HE IS A MASTER INSTRUCTOR WHO CAN TEACH A JIU-JITSU TECHNIQUE FOR ANY FIGHTING SITUATION IMAGINABLE. ORIGINALLY FROM RIO, HE MOVED TO HONOLULU AND OPENED A SCHOOL TO SHARE THE UNIQUE BRAZILIAN ART DEVELOPED BY HIS FATHER, HELIO GRACIE. RELSON GRACIE RECEIVES VISITS FROM STUDENTS WHO COME FROM ALL CORNERS OF THE WORLD. AFTER HE HAS TAUGHT THEM A NEW "JIU-JITSU TRICK," HE KINDLY SETS AN APPOINTMENT FOR HIS SUNDAY SOCCER GAME. AND IF YOU THINK RELSON IS INTENSE ON THE MAT, YOU'VE NEVER SEEN HIM ON A SOCCER FIELD! KEEP YOUR ELBOWS IN, YOUR CHIN DOWN AND PREPARE TO MEET RELSON GRACIE.

Q: How difficult has it been to popularize the system developed by your father?
A: It wasn't an easy task. The Gracie Challenge was created to put our system to the test and this is something very hard to keep up. During more than 70 years the different members of the Gracie family have been trying to prove that the jiu-jitsu method developed by the Gracies is a great and effective self-defense system. I understand that this is a little bit dangerous but we are talking here about martial arts, not dancing. The only way of proving an art effective is putting it to the test. Fortunately, during the last decade, martial artists from all styles and systems understood the importance of knowing how to deal with an opponent on the ground. They greatly accepted the grappling methods and the Gracie jiu-jitsu system. Some of them not only have incorporated some techniques into their repertoire but became full time jiu-jitsu practitioners as well. This situation brings a great rewarding feeling to the Gracie family—we had

"Fortunately, during the last decade, martial artists from all styles and systems understood the importance of knowing how to deal with an opponent on the ground. They greatly accepted the grappling methods and the Gracie jiu-jitsu system."

something important to share and we did. Fortunately, people accepted. The legacy is there to enjoy.

Q: What's your opinion of the UFC and other reality-based fighting events that revolutionized the world of martial arts?
A: I think today its format is very different than it used to be. The original concept and idea is lost. I believe that the UFC has been a very revealing experience for a lot of fighters and it has opened the eyes to a lot of martial artist about the efficiency of some self-defense method when confronting an uncooperative aggressor. For some reasons, completely political, the original idea of the UFC turned into a sport event. I may understand that PPV and politicians try to regulate the shows so more people can see them and more money can be made from it but when we started the whole things was not about PPV or bringing sport sponsor into the show, it was about proving a point, about making people realize some important thing about fighting and fighting has nothing to do with

"Punches and kicks are ok but the most of the fights end up on the ground. Down there it's impossible to use these punches and kicks with the same efficiency that being on a stand-up position; the leverage and body mechanics are very different."

sport. Basketball modified its format to fit TV, football also did and finally UFC did as well but not while the Gracie had a word on how to run the show.

Q: How would you define the essence of jiu-jitsu?
A: It's very difficult to describe the essence of a system on paper. Punches and kicks are OK but the most of the fights end up on the ground. Down there it's impossible to use these punches and kicks with the same efficiency that being on a stand-up position; the leverage and body mechanics are very different. On the ground the bigger guy is not always the one having the advantage. This was clearly proved by my brother Royce Gracie when he defeated bigger opponents at the Ultimate Fighting Championship. Understand the grappling aspect of a real fight is something very important for all martial artists.

219

Grappling Masters

"In a grappling situation you won't understand what's happening unless you have been educated about the grappling techniques. In jiu-jitsu a small movement of the hip may mean a lot but unfortunately the spectator won't realize the whole game until the physical action is over."

Q: Unfortunately, grappling is not very attractive for a television show when compared with boxing or kickboxing. Why is that?
A: The problem here is that in a grappling situation you won't understand what's happening unless you have been educated about the grappling techniques. In boxing, you see what's happening. In jiu-jitsu a small movement of the hip may mean a lot but unfortunately the spectator won't realize the whole game until the physical action is over. This is one of the reasons why the people controlling the sport are trying to change the format, in order to make it more appealing to the masses. And I understand their point of view but that is not what we are talking about. Grappling is much more subtle, requires an educated spectator to fully understand what the fighters are doing or trying to do. It's not something you can just sit down on the couch with a six pack (beer) and a pizza and you can appreciate. You can enjoy but definitely not understand what is going on there. You have to be educated to understand the subtleness of an expert grappler or jiu-jitsu practitioner—how he moves, what he does and why he is doing it.

Q: It has been said that strength is not necessary for using jiu-jitsu and many people disagree. What's your opinion about this?
A: I guess this concept has been misunderstood. The Brazilian jiu-jitsu practitioner uses leverage and body positioning above everything else. This is the only way of making the art work against bigger opponents. Therefore, the students are instructed to think about technique, not using brutal force to make the technique work. Of course, a certain amount of

strength is necessary but the efficiency of the techniques developed by my father don't require a great deal of muscle to make them work. As I said, there is a certain amount of force but never trade technique for strength. My father proved this theory for 65 years. If you use brutal strength to get your techniques, that's not jiu-jitsu. Using intelligence, leverage and body positioning—that is the key of the art.

Then you have another scenario: two fighters with equal skill and physical attributes. Then strength becomes an important factor. The technique may not require brutal force but because your opponent is as skilled as you are, then all the physical qualities will make the difference, and strength is not an exception.

"My father proved this theory for 65 years. If you use brutal strength to get your techniques, that's not jiu-jitsu. Using intelligence and body positioning—that is the key of the art."

Q: How do you feel now that everybody knows about Brazilian jiu-jitsu?
A: I am happy because the world has recognized my father's work. I don't mind teaching people the jiu-jitsu techniques and secrets. Why should I? I'm very happy sharing a great self-defense system with everybody who wants to learn it.

Q: What style can beat jiu-jitsu?
A: Only jiu-jitsu. The art shocked the world and some great wrestlers, to win over sport jiu-jitsu champions, had to study jiu-jitsu so...jiu-jitsu wins again. In order to win jiu-jitsu you have to study jiu-jitsu. It is clear... that to beat jiu-jitsu you have to analyze and study jiu-jitsu so in the very end, the victorious needs to know jiu-jitsu. We came up in a moment in time when everybody thought a punch or a kick was all they needed to

"People understand how important jiu-jitsu is and is a great feeling to see how many thousands of practitioners around the world have kindly embraced the art developed by my father."

defeat any kind of opponent. Don't get me wrong, it is not that you don't need to know how to punch and how to kick but everybody was lacking a complete understanding of a ground work and even more, they thought they could use all these punches and kicks on the ground and that nobody could ever take them down. Well, we proved things to be very different and brought light into the martial arts world.

Q: Do you consider yourself a modernist?
A: To be totally honest, I don't know how the term modernist or traditionalist applies to the martial arts. For instance...people like Gichin Funakoshi (karate), Jigoro Kano (judo) or Morihei Ueshiba (aikido) are considered traditionalists but if you read and look into their lives you'll find out they trained under different instructors and they did change a lot of the things they learned under their teachers. They modified, restructured and taught differently all the material they gathered throughout their lives. They were eclectic and pioneers (modernist), even more than many people nowadays. The difference is they kept the traditional values such as respect, ethics and morals. If you ask me if I am a tradition-

alist my answer would be "yes" because I kept all these important elements but if you consider to be a "traditionalist" to not evolve technically or modified things to make them better, then I'm a modernist. One thing doesn't exclude the other. It's a natural process and a necessary one if we want to improve what we are doing. It's that simple but unfortunately people love to fuss over it.

Q: After all these years of people wishing to learn the Brazilian jiu-jitsu "secrets," what's your perception of the art and its influence in the martial arts world?

A: As I said before I think a lot of people have been educated that in order to be a well-rounded martial artist you need to know and understand grappling. Now, our students like to practice jiu-jitsu just for jiu-jitsu sake. People understand how important jiu-jitsu is and it is a great feeling to see how many thousands of practitioners around the world have kindly embraced the art developed by my father. It makes me proud. As martial artist

"As martial artist we should look for quality and if someone is better in a certain fighting aspect there is nothing wrong with going to learn from that person. It's important to be humble and acknowledge that there are areas where you can improve."

we should look for quality and if someone is better in a certain fighting aspect there is nothing wrong with going to learn from that person. It's important to be humble and acknowledge that there are areas where you can improve. But to be a real martial artist is more than just training and fighting, many other mental components are involved. You have to be a martial artist 24 hours a day, live like one, think like one, be ready like one. This is the old Samurai attitude and it can be used in our times. For instance, I love to visualize attacks and reactions to those attacks. I like to

"I love to visualize attacks and reactions to those attacks. I like to train in a relaxed atmosphere so my motions become reflex, natural reactions, instinctive responses. This is the only way you can become one with your art, making your training melt with your human essence and inner self."

train in a relaxed atmosphere so my motions become reflex, natural reactions, instinctive responses. This is the only way you can become one with your art, making your training melt with your human essence and inner self.

Q: Why did you decide to move to Hawaii?

A: I lived in California for three years but my brother Rorion Gracie was already there so I thought that Hawaii, having its roots in Japan, would be a good place to live. The weather is very similar to Brazil and there's a lot of surfing, which I love! I don't think I could live anywhere else. I have everything I need and I enjoy all I have.

Q: What is your diet and personal training routine?

A: I follow the Gracie diet developed by my family. Once in a while I enjoy having something extra, but only here and there. I eat a lot of vegetables, fruits and try to keep my vitamins and minerals in the proper proportions. As far as my personal training, I like to think of myself as a technician with effective results. So my main focus in training is the technique and skill of jiu-jitsu. Of course you need other physical attributes to complement your basic skill, such as flexibility, strength, endurance, et cetera. Running, weight training, yoga, et cetera are good complementary methods that may enhance your jiu-jitsu. Just don't lose sight of your main goal.

"I think today its format now is very different than it used to be. The original concept and idea is lost. I believe that the UFC has been a very revealing experience for a lot of fighters and it has opened the eyes to a lot of martial artist about the efficiency of some self-defense method when confronting an uncooperative aggressor."

Q: What are you plans for the future?
A: I'm teaching here in Hawaii where I feel very happy. People come from all over the world for jiu-jitsu training! I have a good life here with my friends and my students. I relate to the Hawaiian environment and lifestyle so I feel like a fish in the sea! I hope to keep learning, improving and teaching my dedicated students all the knowledge that I gathered through my personal experiences in the arts. The instructor grows by his student's success. The better your students are, the better instructor and martial artist you will be.

Q: What do you do for relaxation?
A: What any Brazilian man can do to relax? Only one thing...play soccer! ☺

225

Masters Techniques

An attacker applies a headlock on Relson Gracie (1). Relson grabs the arm to prevent getting hit by a punch (2), and follows by grabbing his opponent and twisting his own body (3). This enables Relson to break free from the lock and apply a submission hold to his opponent's arm (4). Close-up (5).

An attacker applies a rear choke to Relson Gracie (1). Relson controls the elbow and places his right foot behind the leg (2), to unbalance him (3). Relson then takes him to the ground, where he applies a finishing arm-lock (4). Close-up (5).

226

Relson Gracie faces an opponent (1). The aggressor throws a punch to the face that Relson blocks with his left arm (2). Relson then hooks the attacking arm and gets close to the opponent (3), throws him to the ground (4), and finishes with an arm-lock (5).

Renato Magno

Living the Good Life

ORIGINALLY FROM SAO PAULO, BRAZIL, RENATO MAGNO BEGAN HIS MARTIAL ARTS TRAINING IN JUDO, BUT BRAZILIAN JIU-JITSU WAS WHAT TURNED HIS LIFE AROUND. LUCKY ENOUGH TO SPEND TIME AND TRAIN EXTENSIVELY WITH SEVERAL MEMBERS OF THE GRACIE FAMILY IN RIO DE JANEIRO, HE BECAME AN ACTIVE COMPETITOR WITH AN IMPRESSIVE LIST OF ACCOMPLISHMENTS. IN KEEPING WITH HIS REPUTATION OF A TOP JIU-JITSU MAN, HE DISPLAYS ALL THE TRAITS OF A TRUE MARTIAL ARTIST. OUT OF DEDICATION, HE SPENDS LONG HOURS ON THE MAT TRYING TO PASS ON THE KNOWLEDGE OF HIS BELOVED ART TO HIS NUMEROUS STUDENTS AT VARIOUS JIU-JITSU SCHOOLS IN SOUTHERN CALIFORNIA.

"NO QUESTION IS TOO INSIGNIFICANT TO ASK," SAYS MAGNO. "IF SOMEONE WANTS ME TO EXPLAIN A POSITION IT IS BECAUSE THEY DON'T UNDERSTAND IT. I'M GLAD TO HAVE THE KNOWLEDGE THAT ENABLES ME TO HELP SOMEONE. BEING AN INSTRUCTOR IS AS MUCH ABOUT HOW YOU RELATE, AS IT IS ABOUT HOW MUCH YOU KNOW. YOU CAN HAVE THE BEST TECHNIQUES IN THE WORLD, BUT IF YOU DON'T KNOW HOW TO GET YOUR POINT ACROSS THEN YOUR KNOWLEDGE IS WORTHLESS."

NO MATTER HOW REFINED HIS JIU-JITSU TECHNIQUES ARE, HOWEVER, MAGNO REC-OGNIZES THE NEED FOR VERSATILITY. "NO MODERN MARTIAL ART IS A COMPLETE SYSTEM IN ITSELF. IT'S VERY IMPORTANT FOR GRAPPLERS TO UNDERSTAND THE STRIKING ASPECTS OF COMBAT," HE SAYS. "IF YOU DON'T KNOW HOW TO DEFEND AGAINST STRIKES, SOME-ONE IS GOING TO HIT YOU AND KNOCK YOU OUT. BUT IF YOU KNOW HOW TO DEFEND AGAINST THEM, THEN YOU CAN TAKE A PERSON DOWN AND GRAPPLE." THIS REALISTIC APPROACH HAS CAUSED RENATO MAGNO TO BE WIDELY REGARDED AS ONE OF THE TOP BRAZILIAN JIU-JITSU INSTRUCTORS IN THE UNITED STATES.

Q: How did you begin your martial arts training?
A: In Sao Paulo, my father loved judo and he used to train several times a week. I wanted to do the same so I began going with him. My judo was with the Pinero club, one of the best in the city. Many competitors from there were selected to go to the Olympics, so the level was very high. I used to work out with Joan Gonzalvez and Fuscao, two great Brazilian judo instructors who taught me many techniques. After I began studying

"After I began studying jiu-jitsu, the combination of the two arts was very interesting. I used judo for the stand-up aspects of throws and takedowns, but on the ground my technique was pure Brazilian jiu-jitsu. I think they complemented each other very well—at least it worked for me."

jiu-jitsu, the combination of the two arts was very interesting. I used judo for the stand-up aspects of throws and takedowns, but on the ground my technique was pure Brazilian jiu-jitsu. I think they complemented each other very well—at least it worked for me. Judo is very effective in dealing with how to throw your opponent, and also how to control his balance and position while on the feet. Brazilian jiu-jitsu, of course, is the best art in the world for submissions.

Q: Why did you compete in judo and not jiu-jitsu?
A: Mainly because there weren't many jiu-jitsu competitions. So to improve my ground skills judo competition was the perfect place to start. I had many opportunities to compete and that increased my technical level. Of course, once my opponent was on the ground, I used jiu-jitsu all the way. Later on, jiu-jitsu competition began to grow and it was easier for me to compete there.

Q: When you moved to Rio de Janeiro, did you keep training jiu-jitsu?

A: I did, but there weren't many classes for kids. The jiu-jitsu training was more for adults than for kids. The training at that time under the Gracie family was very technical and very specific and detail oriented. For instance, when you learned a technique like the triangle, you were supposed to train that single technique for the whole month—changing the angle, the position, applying leverage in different ways, and paying attention to the little details that make the technique work. You spent weeks or even months working on that. By the end of the year you might know only 12 or 15 basic techniques but your knowledge and skill was so good that you could pull them off anytime almost at will. The transitions from one technique to the other were very smooth, and the control over the opponent's body was very important. The training was not competition oriented. It was very, very technical and we were not in any kind of rush to learn thousand of new movements to win a tournament. The basics were strongly emphasized and the technical level was very high.

"Personally, I had to work hard in order to get better at jiu-jitsu. I know some people are very natural and able to duplicate techniques very fast, but I had to work at it. I believe that it was good for me because it made me learn the value of hard work."

Q: Were you a natural at jiu-jitsu?

Personally, I had to work hard in order to get better at jiu-jitsu. I know some people are very natural and able to duplicate techniques very fast, but I had to work at it. I believe that it was good for me because it made me learn the value of hard work. Since those days, I always try to work positions that I don't feel comfortable using. I always try to improve on my weak points.

Q: Was the training more for self-defense or for competition?

A: There weren't many jiu-jitsu competitions so the focus was more on self-defense. The training was very quality-oriented and the sportive aspect was not fully developed. I don't even think too many of us were thinking about sport competition at all. A lot of the family members were

"The students who want to compete don't have time to spend an entire month polishing only one technique. There are new techniques all the time as a result of the tournaments. Competitors need to spend time catching-up with the new competition movements and can't spend hours and hours on the basics."

training there together: the Machado brothers, coached by Carlos Gracie Jr., Royler Gracie, Renzo Gracie, Ralph Gracie, Rillion Gracie and many other family members.

Q: There are competitions everywhere now. How has sport jiu-jitsu affected the art?

A: Now the whole thing is very different. The students who want to compete don't have time to spend an entire month polishing only one technique. There are new techniques all the time as a result of the tournaments. In some ways this is very good for the sport, but in other ways life in the fast lane is not all that. Competitors need to spend time catching-up with the new competition movements and can't spend hours and hours on the basics. It's very hard to find a good balance if the student's interest is in competition. The sophistication of the techniques is 100 percent superior to those in the past. There are new ways to hold the belt, better approaches to body controls, better entries and takedowns, et cetera. Unfortunately, some things have been lost along the way. That's the reason why it is more difficult to be a good teacher and a good competitor these days—you have to work twice as hard as in the past to get on top and stay on top.

Q: Are all jiu-jitsu instructors willing to change and adapt to the new techniques?

A: Regardless if your jiu-jitsu is more based on the old traditional techniques, or its focus is on modern competition, there is hardly ever an instructor who will not alter his methods to some extent. If he is convinced that an addition or change is more effective for a particular technique then he will replace it. In the end, the art of teaching is the sum total learned from theory and practice. But if you are not interested in sport competition then you have to train differently, maybe with a more traditional approach.

Q: Weren't you one of the first jiu-jitsu fighters to start training in boxing?

A: Yes, I was! I was living in Sao Paulo and I got interested in boxing, so I began to take classes. As time passed I became very good at it—or at least so I thought. I began to feel that boxing was the best art! Every time I went to Rio de Janeiro, I went to the Barra Gracie school. Carlos Gracie Jr., Renzo, Rigan and everybody else was there. I told them about box-

"Everybody knew I was into boxing. So they put me on the training mat to show my boxing skills, and I ended up on the ground and being choked-out every single time by several students. I was embarrassed in front of everybody!"

ing and they began to tease me over the whole thing. All of a sudden, everybody knew I was into boxing. So they put me on the training mat to show my boxing skills, and I ended up on the ground and being choked-out every single time by several students. I was embarrassed in front of everybody! From that on every time I went to visit Barra Gracie everybody would yell, "Watch out for Renato's boxing!" They all had a ball teasing me about it!

Q: Did you keep training in boxing?

A: I quit! At that time I was so frustrated with the whole experience that I decided to stop my boxing training—although, now I know as a fighter you need to know how to use your hands effectively. So I guess I was just ahead of my time and didn't realize it.

"These days, everything happens very fast and you need to be explosive and powerful on the ground—much more than in the past, simply because good mat technique is not enough in competition."

Q: Living in Sao Paulo, how did you train with the Gracie family in Rio?

A: It's a long distance from Sao Paulo to Rio de Janeiro—around seven or eight hours driving. My father used to drive to Rio and that's when I went to Barra Gracie. Fortunately, Renzo Gracie had a girlfriend in Sao Paulo so he was there all the time. That was perfect for me because he would come to my house and we would spend a lot of time together—not only training jiu-jitsu but also having fun.

Q: Haven't you been closely involved with the Machado brothers for many years?

A: Yes, I have. I still learn a great deal from them. It is interesting to note that each one has a different fighting style—Jean Jacques, Carlos, Rigan, John, and Roger have different strong points in their jiu-jitsu and I've had the great opportunity to learn specific information from each of them. I have also incorporated some other aspects like takedowns and controls from wrestling into my game. These days, everything happens very fast and you need to be explosive and powerful on the ground—much more than in the past, simply because good mat technique is not enough in competition. You need to be a very well-balanced competitor to make it into the top three. In the last few years, the technical level has risen enormously. The practitioners are more aware of other elements that make your jiu-jitsu better. The cardiovascular training, the nutrition, the stretching and flexibility aspects are really important these days and make a huge difference.

In the past we used to train straight jiu-jitsu—period. No weights and no concerns about cardiovascular training and endurance. We were not aware of the needs for specific training programs to gain strength and

cardio, and of the importance of
nutrition and rest in order to recover
from training. Don't forget that if
you don't sleep, your body doesn't
rest—and if you don't rest you can't
train hard. It's that simple; but unfortunately we didn't think about it in
the past.

Modern training methods is one
of the reasons why students are
improving so fast these days—they
know about all these elements. Even
if they combine them at a very basic
level, the overall result is far better
than what we had 20 years ago. In
some ways, you can't really compare
what we have now with what we
had in the early days. It's like basketball; you can't compare the NBA of
today with the NBA of 15 or 20 years
ago. It's still basketball, but all the
training around it is 100 percent better. Today, jiu-jitsu is all about having
a complete package.

*"Modern training methods is one of the reasons
why students are improving so fast these days—they
know about all these elements. Even if they combine
them at a very basic level, the overall result is far
better than what we had 20 years ago."*

Q: When is the appropriate time to incorporate other training elements into a student's routine?

A: Not as a beginner, that's for sure. Only when you have been training
jiu-jitsu for a while—maybe around one year when you have the basic
techniques down. But it should only be done if you have extra time. You
should start incorporating weight training, cardio, plyometrics, and flexibility training but always as a compliment to your jiu-jitsu and not as a
substitution. Running five miles a days, lifting weights for one hour, and
swimming for another hour won't improve your guard or mount position.
Don't get caught in the idea that because your body looks good after all
the weight training and running that you are good at jiu-jitsu. Jiu-jitsu is
about technique, not about the way you look.

"In sport jiu-jitsu, the techniques change and evolve all the time—a competitor needs to be updated constantly. Brazilian jiu-jitsu is not a very old art and there are millions of practitioners around the world already. It is one of the fastest growing sports."

Outside training also depends on the student's age and goals. For instance, if you are not interested in competing and just want to be in shape and enjoy the training, then you have to focus more on techniques, positions, and pure jiu-jitsu. If you do a jiu-jitsu workout three or four times a week, you'll be more than OK. That's because a jiu-jitsu workout gives you all the basic fitness elements with the calisthenics, strength, and stretching exercises you do in class. But if you are interested in competing and winning tournaments, then your supplementary training has to complement your jiu-jitsu. You'll need that extra edge that comes from running, swimming, stretching, and specific weight training routines. You need to know the latest technical improvements so you won't get caught by surprise in the half-guard game or by the new leg-locks.

In sport jiu-jitsu, the techniques change and evolve all the time—a competitor needs to be updated constantly. A regular student who trains jiu-jitsu for self-defense and for fun doesn't need to worry about all that. The principles and concepts of Brazilian jiu-jitsu cannot be changed. They are the same for everybody and standard throughout the world and every student learns them. The techniques, however, can be changed. Brazilian jiu-jitsu is not a very old art and there are millions of practitioners around the world already. It is one of the fastest growing sports.

Q: Is sport or self-defense training more popular?

A: In the United States, people are interested in competition but not as much as in Brazil. In Brazil, there are competitions every weekend, and this raises the technical level very fast. In America only a small amount of students want to compete. Therefore the way we teach the classes has to fit into that. The importance is about how to master the basics and not in learning a lot of competition techniques. It's in separate classes for those who want to compete, where you can focus on technical aspects more suitable for sport. Also, you have to understand that most students have day jobs and can't afford to get hurt in class because they won't be able to work the next day. Jiu-jitsu may be their passion but not the way they make their living. Therefore, as an instructor, you need to con-

"The importance is about how to master the basics and not in learning a lot of competition techniques. It's in separate classes for those who want to compete, where you can focus on technical aspects more suitable for sport."

trol and regulate the classes so the students know how much pressure to apply without hurting each other. It's stupid to try to fight against an arm bar when your classmate has the lock 70 percent completed. That's the reason I don't like to let beginners to train with beginners all the time. I like to mix the students so the higher belts can control the techniques and don't get involved in an ego contest. You need to know when you can't get out of a technique and when to let your partner finish the movement. If you develop a feeling for it, very soon you'll be able to feel the position and escape the lock just as your opponent begins to apply it. If you always try to use strength to resist a lock, then not only will you not learn anything but you'll get injured as well.

"The black belt is the essence of Brazilian jiu-jitsu. Although we have degrees within the black belt rank, the faixa preta *is the sign of the highest skill level in our art."*

Q: Why does it take so many years to get a black belt in Brazilian jiu-jitsu?

A: The black belt is the essence of Brazilian jiu-jitsu. It is not like some other arts where being a black belt has been watered down and doesn't mean anything anymore. Although we have degrees within the black belt rank, the *faixa preta* is the sign of the highest skill level in our art. Therefore, when a student reaches that rank he is pretty much on his own. There is not a lot of interest in getting the second or third degree black belt. It is simply not important to people. The first two belts in jiu-jitsu are the foundation for the rest and you have to spend time there. The blue and purple belts create a base for the student to grow. To a certain extent, a good purple belt knows almost every technique a black belt knows—he just lacks the time, fighting experience, and years of training and practice.

When you compare the jiu-jitsu belt ranking system to other martial arts, you'll notice that jiu-jitsu has only four belts (blue, purple, brown and black) while karate, for example, has six. So a Brazilian jiu-jitsu black belt is probably more equivalent to a second or third degree black in karate in terms of the time it takes to earn. So a BJJ black belt is better trained than black belts from other arts because it takes much longer to get.

On the other hand, there are undoubtedly BJJ who prevent or delay their students from getting their black belt because they're afraid of losing part of the business. Keeping a student in a belt rank too long is as unfair as giving out a belt too fast. In the very end, it boils down to the instructor's honesty. Nowadays, students train very hard and the time to achieve the black belt is shorter—not because of a lack of requirements but because people train harder and smarter than 20 years ago. There are exceptional people who achieve black belt rank in four or five years but these are very rare. They must train many hours a day, be physically gifted, and have a natural talent for jiu-jitsu. Their dedication to the art must be absolute.

"I have seen black belts who have won major championships who cannot properly explain the most basic techniques to a student. They are great as fighters and competitors but their ability to communicate is not adequate enough for them to teach properly. Effective teaching is the final responsibility of each instructor."

Q: Is a black belt automatically a good teacher?

A: A black belt can teach anyone he wants, of course, but it doesn't necessarily mean they know how to do it properly. I have seen black belts who have won major championships who cannot properly explain the most basic techniques to a student. They are great as fighters and competitors but their ability to communicate is not adequate enough for them to teach properly. On the other hand, I know purple belts who are not interested in competition, but yet who are extremely knowledgeable and can help a beginning student understand and apply almost any technique. They have the ability to transmit the essence of the art. In the future they will be the ones training the champions because they can pass the knowledge to future generations. Being a good fighter or competitor does not necessarily mean you'll be a good teacher. A good teacher will always know how to help the students recognize and deal with the important points of any technique. Effective teaching is the final responsibility of each instructor.

"When you are on the mat, you want to be relaxed physically and mentally. Your strong points should be your intelligence, your conditioning, and your ability to read your opponent. The essence of jiu-jitsu is to let the technique explode from within. You must use the art with feeling."

Q: What is the most important element in applying a jiu-jitsu technique in combat?

A: Relaxation is a big part of the game. Being relaxed is very important, especially when your opponent is in control. You want to be relaxed because that is the only way you'll eventually come out on top. When you are relaxed, good things just happen. Do not tense up or think too much because that is a waste of energy. When you are on the mat, you want to be relaxed physically and mentally. Your strong points should be your intelligence, your conditioning, and your ability to read your opponent. The essence of jiu-jitsu is to let the technique explode from within. You must use the art with feeling. It is vital to draw from all your physical and mental resources. To a true jiu-jitsu practitioner the words "try" and "impossible" do not exist—you simply execute a technique when the situation warrants it.

Q: What is the most important advice you can give a student?
A: Every time you train, do it with sincerity and heart. In all martial arts, sincerity is essential to building a credible technique, although many people can't see the relationship between sincerity and the actual physical movements of jiu-jitsu. You need to be serious and perseverant in your training, otherwise your training will have no value. You can't have the mindset that training is merely something to do to kill time. Don't go to the academy and merely go through the motions. Have a goal in mind every time you train—and train regularly.

Q: What have the martial arts meant to you?
A: The art of jiu-jitsu has given me everything I have in life. Jiu-

"You need to be serious and perseverant in your training, otherwise your training will have no value. You can't have the mindset that training is merely something to do to kill time."

jitsu keeps my body healthy and clean, relieves my mind of stress, and fills my life with goodness. If I live another thousand years, I'll spend them all studying the art of jiu-jitsu and living the good life in the company of family and friends. Life is good and I intend to live it to its fullest. ↻

Renato Magno is mounted on his opponent (1). He grabs the far elbow and lifts the arm upwards, while simultaneously grabbing the collar with his near hand (2). Controlling the elbow, he gives up the mount position to get better leverage and spins to the side (3). Releasing the elbow while keeping his opponent's body trapped with his leg (4), he grabs the collar and applies the finishing choke (5).

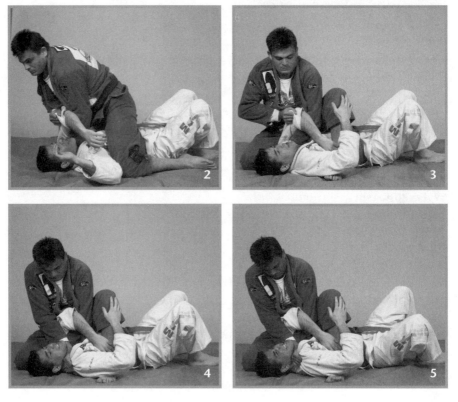

Facing an opponent on his knees, Renato Magno does an opposite-hand lapel grab (1). When his opponent leans forward to go for the takedown, Renato grabs the back of the gi with his free hand (2), and then crosses his arm and applies pressure to the neck for the finishing choke (3).

Renato Magno has his opponent immobilized with a tight side-control (1).
He raises up onto his knees (2), then jumps to the knee-on-stomach position (3).
He reaches down and straight grabs the collar (4), then spins to the north-south
position which causes his arms cross on the collar (5). He then leans forward and
applies pressure for the finishing choke (6).

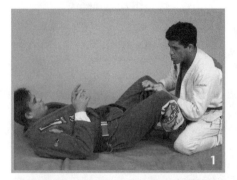

Renato Magno faces his opponent, who pushes forward with his hand to pass the guard (1). As soon as Renato feels the push, he moves backwards to create space (2), which makes his opponent push forward again. Renato then under-hooks the right arm (3), and grabs his left hand with his right hand (4). He moves his body to the side (5), positions himself for the submission (6), and applies a finishing shoulder-lock (7).

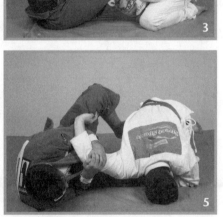

Rickson Gracie

The Brazilian Icon

RICKSON GRACIE HAS BEEN SAID TO HAVE THE MOST PERFECT TECHNIQUE OF ANY MEMBER OF THE LEGENDARY GRACIE FAMILY, CREATORS OF BRAZILIAN JIU-JITSU. RICKSON HAS DEDICATED HIS LIFE TO MARTIAL ARTS AND IS CONSIDERED BY MANY TO BE THE BEST FIGHTER ON THE PLANET.

HAVING LIVED IN CALIFORNIA FOR MANY YEARS, RICKSON IS THE FOUNDER OF THE RICKSON GRACIE JIU-JITSU ASSOCIATION WHICH HAS A LARGE FOLLOWING IN THE US, EUROPE, JAPAN AND BRAZIL. A GENUINE LEGEND, RICKSON HAS GAINED WORLDWIDE ACCLAIM FOR HIS LEADERSHIP IN SPREADING THE ART AND PHILOSOPHY OF JIU-JITSU. HE IS A MAN OF HONOR, TRADITION, HONESTY, AND KINDNESS. HE IS PROUD TO BE BOTH A FAMILY MAN AND A MODERN-DAY WARRIOR. RICKSON HAS WON SEVERAL OPEN VALE TUDO CHAMPIONSHIPS HELD IN JAPAN IN WHICH EXPERT FIGHTERS FROM ALL OVER THE WORLD, TRAINED IN A VARIETY OF MARTIAL ARTS STYLES, COMPETED. HE IS UNDEFEATED IN VALE TUDO, ENDING ALL FIGHTS VIA SUBMISSION OR CHOKE.

Q: How old were you when you began to train?
A: We all started when we were babies; not so much for the techniques or the discipline, but to start getting the feeling of the grip using the legs. My dad played with me even on the bed. When we started to actually get the movements, we already had the reflex and the conditioning to feel comfortable. I started competing at 6 years old, and since then I've been involved in the sport aspect of jiu-jitsu, just training and competing.

Q: Is it a tradition in your family that everyone learns jiu-jitsu?
A: Yes. Since we were born, we've been involved in jiu-jitsu. Jiu-jitsu offers a very special way for you to understand yourself. You can understand your limitations; you can improve your patience, sensitivity, coordination, and sportsmanship; you learn how to lose and how to win; and you learn how to be respectful. It's a very gentle way to learn. By doing this, you become a better person just by learning how to fight.

"Many people don't know that my specialty is free fighting. The goal is to be a well-rounded martial artist, especially when you are talking about real self-defense. An understanding of ground fighting will make you a better fighter and martial artist, that's all."

Q: How far did you go with your studies?
A: I did the college entry exam for Physical Education and I decided to stop because it wasn't what I wanted. It was there that I chose jiu-jitsu.

Q: When you promote jiu-jitsu are you insinuating that no other style or system has any value?
A: No, that would be foolish. Many people don't know that my specialty is free fighting. I punch, I kick and I fight very well on my feet and on the ground. The goal is to be a well-rounded martial artist, especially when you are talking about real self-defense. I only say, "Look at what we have to offer before you make any decisions about our system." An understanding of ground fighting will make you a better fighter and martial artist, that's all.

Q: What are the origins of the Gracie family?
A: The Gracie family came from Scotland and arrived in Brazil around 1900. The first generation that became involved in jiu-jitsu was my father, along with his brother Carlos Gracie. A Japanese named Maeda Koma, who had come to work in Brazil as a Japanese immigration representative, became very close to my grandfather, Gastao Gracie. As a gesture of friendship, he offered to teach jiu-jitsu to his children. Consequently, my Uncle Carlos began to learn jiu-jitsu around 1912. Since then he began to participate in the development of jiu-jitsu, adapting a lot more leverage and other techniques than those that had been already taught. He became the highest expression of jiu-jitsu in Brazil for a long time and was very well known worldwide. The next five generations represented jiu-jitsu and the

tradition of the family. This is what keeps us connected to the sport and to this life that we live.

Q: There are some differences in the family. What is the reason for this? Is it different techniques or just different applications?
A: The family is enormous. My father had nine children. My uncle had twenty-one children; the oldest is already over fifty. I have even lost count of the number of grandchildren and great-grandchildren in our family. It's evident that in a family so large, among the great many different types of people, some differences are going to appear, which is normal in any family. But on the other hand, a common union exists which refers to the sport. Everyone is interested in seeing jiu-jitsu grow because all of us are linked to it in one way or another.

Q: About your father, Helio Gracie, does he still train?
A: Yes, he still training until today! He has always been an example for all of us. He is a person who leaves me without words to define him.

"I have even lost count of the number of grandchildren and great-grandchildren in our family. It's evident that in a family so large, among the great many different types of people, some differences are going to appear, which is normal in any family."

Q: In Japan, ju-jutsu (preferred Japanese spelling) was the main martial art until the 40's. Afterwards they developed judo and karate, right?
A: In the olden days, jiu-jitsu was the only art used by the Japanese people. When the Japanese had swords, they fought to kill with the sword. Whenever they lost the sword, they fought to kill with their hands, using different techniques, but always with the objective of ending the fight. This is the purpose of jiu-jitsu, whose literal translation is "soft art." This art was altered a bit. As time went by, with the war and invasion of the

"Good jiu-jitsu doesn't use strength, it doesn't have to be brutal. Jiu-jitsu is supposed to be a beautiful art. It's a matter of skill. You are supposed to feel it, and appreciate and enjoy it, and want to move your body and mind in oneness. That's what's you want to do. Unfortunately, that is not what people want to see today. That's the jiu-jitsu's old school of thinking, isn't it?"

Occidental world into the Japanese culture, the Japanese hid this superior art and began to export a sportier side to the Occidental world. This is where judo and karate come in: arts that are purely sport. The objective of these arts is not to kill your opponent, but to gain points. Even Japan itself, in order to maintain itself competitively in sports in the international arena, forgot the old jiu-jitsu and began to enter into a type of training that was a lot stronger than that developed for the world. They completely forgot the traditional jiu-jitsu, that has as its predominate objective the victory over its adversary. And today, I am certain that long ago Japan had already forgotten the jiu-jitsu that was made and developed by my family.

Q: Why is such a dangerous art called a "soft" art?
A: It is soft because it is based on the movements of leverage. It does not have brutality stamped on the movements that are used; the movements are "gentle." Good jiu-jitsu doesn't use strength, it doesn't have to be brutal. Jiu-jitsu is supposed to be a beautiful art. It's a matter of skill. You are supposed to feel it, and appreciate and enjoy it, and want to move your body and mind in oneness. That's what's you want to do. Unfortunately, that is not what people want to see today. That's the jiu-jitsu's old school of thinking, isn't it?

Q: What is so different about Brazilian jiu-jitsu as opposed to conventional jiu-jitsu?
A: There is only one jiu-jitsu in Brazil. It was all created by my family. Some have a bit more technique, others have less, but basically it's the

same thing. Here in the United States there are perhaps fifty different types of jiu-jitsu, but they are totally based upon wrist locks and hip throws. It is as if they were aikido; they do not have much efficiency in the sense of a real personal defense or fighting. People from other styles of fight are really impressed with the efficiency our jiu-jitsu has shown.

Q: In Rio, you are a famous man; everyone knows who you are. How do you feel now in Los Angeles, a city of many famous people?
A: In Brazil I felt that a sequence of tradition that was implanted by my predecessors. I feel very proud of being part of this tradition, this clan; but I never stopped being part of the sequence of work that has been

"I've breathed jiu-jitsu since the day I began to understand myself as a person. Jiu-jitsu has given me everything I need: not only recognition, not only money, not only health and dignity, but everything I need as a man."

developed for over 70 years. When we moved to the United States, few people knew what Gracie jiu-jitsu was; few people knew our potential. This has changed slowly, until we got to the point of giving classes to police academies and to the Marines. The events which are being promoted by pay-per-view are giving us great recognition. We came here to implant jiu-jitsu and it has been a great success in the United States. I feel like a pioneer of jiu-jitsu who has been very successful.

Q: What is most important for you: success, recognition, or money?
A: I've breathed jiu-jitsu since the day I began to understand myself as a person. Jiu-jitsu has given me everything I need: not only recognition, not only money, not only health and dignity, but everything I need as a man. Naturally, one thing is linked to the other—if you really like something and

251

"I always try to do my best and I always believe everybody has value. I respect everyone; my honor is more important than my body. If I feel I must do something and I might die, I don't care about my physical body. My spiritual body is more important."

are interested in developing whatever you do to the highest level, money comes as a consequence.

Q: Was it the money that brought you to the United States? Were you feeling difficulties, or was it the desire to expand your jiu-jitsu throughout the world?

A: I had reached all of my goals in Brazil. It was a routine for me to win all of the competitions. My academy was full of students. With the inflation and political problems of the country, with the difficulty of actually getting money together, I thought it was the best option. Not only to expand the art, but also for my personal benefit I would come to the United States. It was said and done.

Q: What about challenging well-known sports figures, like Mike Tyson?

A: I believe that each one has his sport. For example, Mike Tyson: I think that he was the best boxer in the world. Understand? I do not see anyone who could in his prime face him in the world of boxing. But one day I picked on him for having said he was the best fighter. Since that day I began to look for him, saying I wanted to fight with him in all my interviews. He had to prove that he was the best fighter if he truly felt that he was, because I believe he was not. Mike Tyson would not last three minutes in my hands. In relation to this, jiu-jitsu mixes all of the arts in an event that combines everything.

Q: Do you have a personal code of Bushido?

A: Yes, I have it. For me, this is something very clear in my mind. I always try to do my best and I always believe everybody has value. I respect everyone; my honor is more important than my body. If I feel I must do something and I might die, I don't care about my physical body. My spiritual body is more important. I just believe one hundred percent in keeping my dignity. I can't be bought, and nobody can change my ideas. My philosophy is also to always support the people who stay with me. I never turn my back on a friend.

Q: Are you a religious man?
A: I believe in God and in a higher energy. I believe in energy. I believe in good vibrations. But I do not go to church. I do not see a connection between God and church.

"Fear is always present. If you're not afraid, you're not intelligent. It's very important that you respect your opponent and be afraid of what he can do. But this goes back to emotional control. Don't let the fear get strong. It's there, but you keep it in a shell. As soon as things start, you turn on the automatic pilot. Just do it and don't think about it or your fear. Only the stupid don't feel fear."

Q: A long time ago during a press conference in Denver, Colorado they asked your age and you responded that you were "ageless." What did you mean by this?
A: What happens is that people are very labeled by their age. I have a philosophy of life that compensates my age, not by the fact of being afraid of getting old, but because I think that people have to live the moment intensely. With time, you can lose resistance but gain experience, so you gain energy.

Q: In your opinion, what role does fear play in a real fight?
A: Fear is always present. For me that's good. You must be afraid. If you're not afraid, you're not intelligent. It's very important that you respect your opponent and be afraid of what he can do. But this goes back to emotional control. Don't let the fear get strong. It's there, but you keep it in a

"My family has fought in the dojo, in the ring, in the streets and on the beaches of Brazil. We are always training and always ready for the challenge. Yes, everyone can be beaten, and I know this. But as of yet, I have not been."

shell. As soon as things start, you have to believe in what you know and in yourself, and turn on the automatic pilot. Just do it and don't think about it or your fear. Only the stupid don't feel fear.

Q: What is the most important aspect of Rickson Gracie jiu-jitsu in terms of the students?
A: Our jiu-jitsu is something you can do for your entire lifetime. My father ensured that our philosophy and techniques would work whether you are big and very strong or small and frail. It is all about leverage and feel. It is simple. You must be able to defend yourself at all times, under all physical conditions. Today you are feeling good, you are a large and strong man. Today you might get into a fight and be able to, if nothing else, simply overpower your opponent because of this. But what if next week you are sick with the flu? Then you would not be so strong, and your thinking might not be as clear. Still, you must defend yourself successfully. Kicks and punches when you are feeling good are easy, if you are in reasonable shape and have stamina and power. But if you are sick, all of this changes. In my jiu-jitsu you can still defeat most opponents quickly with little effort, no matter how you are feeling at that moment.

Q: Why is it so hard for anyone, regardless of style, to match up against a Gracie family member? Do you think you will ever be beaten?
A: You cannot practice grappling, or ground fighting, or jiu-jitsu for six months and believe that, because you can execute a few techniques very well, you will beat us on the mat. We have been studying our art for over 70 years. I began training when just a young boy. My family has fought in the dojo, in the ring, in the streets and on the beaches of Brazil. We are

always training and always ready for the challenge. Yes, everyone can be beaten, and I know
this. But as of yet, I have not been.

**Q: What is the reason behind proposing or
accepting challenges?**
A: Every fighter, everyone who has spent his/her
life searching and training deserves all my
respect. But if you open any magazine, you're
going to see some people claim, "I believe this
is the best" or "I'm the best at what I do." So if
they really believe 100 percent in what they do,
then they should be always ready to prove it. So
I'm open to fight anyone at anytime just to reinforce my beliefs. It doesn't make sense to say, "I
believe in what I'm doing, but I'm not going to
fight." So we are always accepting challenges
and we are always ready to fight to prove we
believe 100 percent in what we do.

The only guy I ever challenged was Mike
Tyson because he said in a magazine that he's
the best fighter in the world. And I don't believe
that; being the best boxer in the world doesn't
mean he is the best fighter.

*"I am very serious, very professional,
and I try to prepare myself the best I
can mentally and physically by putting
everything in God's hands. I surrender
to God. If it is my time to lose or even to
die, then it's a good time. I'm always
prepared for whatever happens."*

**Q: What would happen if you ever lost a chal-
lenge match?**
A: It's hard to say. Of course I'm undefeated
even today, but something could happen and I
may lose some day. But if I lose, I'm not going
to relate this to the techniques; it's going to be a personal mistake. It's
going to be something I should have done and I didn't. I think at that
point my opponent would deserve to win. I don't have any pressure on
my back because the only commitment I have is to do my best. So I am
very serious, very professional, and I try to prepare myself the best I can
mentally and physically by putting everything in God's hands. I surrender
to God. If it is my time to lose or even to die, then it's a good time. Every
day I wake up, thinking it's an excellent day to enjoy a day on the beach,
an excellent day to fight, or an excellent day to die. So I'm always pre-

*"My personal training involves the physical part
—including the conditioning and jiu-jitsu techniques—
and the spiritual or mental. I have been always
mentally prepared to fight so the spiritual aspect
is not something that takes me a long time.
I can get into that mood in a very short time."*

pared for whatever happens. I don't feel pressure, ever. No matter how many fights I did before, I'm willing to do it over again.

Q: How do you see jiu-jitsu in the future? As a universal art?
A: I believe jiu-jitsu will unify all martial arts. For a fighter to really feel complete, he needs to have the vision that a jiu-jitsu fighter has: of being able to live with whatever problem, whatever surprise. He/she has to be able to adapt to any situation that may appear. The jiu-jitsu fighter is always ready in this way. A boxer and a karate fighter cannot adapt to variation.

Q: Define the qualities and attributes—both mental and physical—of the complete fighter?
A: The bottom line is that a complete fighter has to have a balance between the mental, physical and spiritual aspects. It's a combination of heart and skill.

Q: When do you know you're fully prepared for a fight?
A: It's impossible to know when you are fully prepared for a fight. That's something that you never know. All you can do is to have a complete approach to your training and preparation where you cover all the basics, both physical and mental, and put yourself fully into it. My personal training involves the physical part (including the conditioning and jiu-jitsu techniques) and the spiritual or mental. I have been always mentally prepared to fight so the spiritual aspect is not something that takes me a long time. I can get into that mood in a very short time. The physical, although I always try to be in top shape, would take me around three months to be at the level I consider appropriate to face a well-prepared

opponent in the ring. A major aspect of my preparation is my diet. I follow my family diet and depending how close the fight is I eat more protein or carbohydrate. The food you eat is the fuel of your body, so you should pay attention to your nutrition. Depending on how well you eat, you'll perform not only during the fight but during the training for the event. Personally I love to eat fresh fruits, vegetable and white meat and I try to avoid heavy foods and pork.

Q: Would you elaborate more on your diet?
A: You shouldn't be eating all the time because this takes energy away from you. If your body is constantly digesting, you are wasting energy. It's that simple. One important aspect is how you combine the food you take. If you don't know the right combinations you may suffer of headaches, joint problems, insomnia. If you combine them incorrectly you may create a chemical imbalance which brings other major problems later on. The idea is to eat light but get all the important nutrients. I try not to eat at least three hours before going to bed. I do eat red meat although my family doesn't. As a fighter I think is important, I do it twice a month, which is not a lot though.

"I don't need to punch my opponent into pulp to feed my ego. I don't need to hurt anyone to prove that I can win a fight. My main strategy is to protect myself and avoid getting hit. After I cover that aspect, then I try to adapt to what my opponent gives me. Jiu-jitsu is based on exploiting the opponent's weaknesses."

Q: Let's talk about some technical aspects of a fight. What is your main strategy in the ring?
A: The final goal is to win. It's a sport. I will do whatever it takes to win but no more. I don't need to punch my opponent into pulp to feed my ego. I don't need to hurt anyone to prove that I can win a fight. My main strategy is to protect myself and avoid getting hit. After I cover that aspect, then I try to adapt to what my opponent gives me. Jiu-jitsu is based on exploiting the opponent's weaknesses. Sometimes I face really big opponents, then I have to do things accordingly. Once you have an understanding of what your opponent can do, the idea is to limit the

257

"For me, destroying someone is not a victory. This boils down to respect and sportsmanship. Fighting is something violent, but we are athletes who practice a combat sport. We are there to test our skills, with regulations and sportsmanship. I like the Japanese approach."

elements he can use. By doing this, his possibilities of attack and defense are restricted. It's here when he's in trouble. At that moment I already have my answers ready to whatever he does. I believe in 100 percent defense. I use the counter. I'm not an aggressor. I use the opponent's mistakes, and believe that I can get him just as soon as he tries something against me. I always give him the first option. In other words, he will choose how he's going to be beaten. It takes patience to do that. When you're fighting you shouldn't go after your opponent at full speed. Physical training is not the only part of the equation to be a good fighter.

Q: To do the minimum damage to an opponent requires a lot of skill, right?
A: Unfortunately, we all see these events where the fighters try to destroy the opponent instead of winning. For me, destroying someone is not a victory. This boils down to respect and sportsmanship. Fighting is something violent, but we are athletes who practice a combat sport. We are there to test our skills, with regulations and sportsmanship. I like the Japanese approach. Their organizations are not interested in brutal, brawling kind of fights. We don't need to make it brutal and bloody. We can leave that for street fights where our lives are at stake. That's a whole different story.

Q: Why do you think that is?
A: Maybe because of the Bushido, the "code of the warrior." In Japan they respect you if you win, but to gain their deepest respect you must behave as a real warrior, like a samurai. You need to display class in all your acts. And I like that.

Q: How important do you think it is for a specialist in grappling to learn how to use his hands and feet for striking?
A: If you are strictly a jiu-jitsu or wrestling competitor, adding punches and kicks to your arsenal won't do any good because you are not going to need it. On the contrary, if you are a vale tudo fighter then you need punching and kicking skills to complement your grappling skills. To be a well-rounded fighter you need both components of the equation. This is the only way a grappler will be fully prepared for a no-holds-barred or vale tudo competition.

Although your main goal is still to take your opponent down and defeat him on the ground, you need an understanding of the punching and kicking techniques because you need to know how to counter these aspects of combat. To counter these techniques you must understand how they work and what their timing is. Otherwise, you are going to be surprised by them. Your understanding of how they work will allow you to shoot in for that takedown and to avoid the punishment your striking opponent will try to inflict as he is fighting to avoid being taken down.

"I only concentrate on today. Age is not a factor to me, the determining factor is my body. I don't think how old I am because it's irrelevant to me. If I want to do something, I just do it."

In my fights, I use punching and kicking but if you look closely I don't use these elements as the final tool to finish my opponent. I punch and kick so these techniques open a way to use my jiu-jitsu. If I punch the guy too much my hands will be damaged and that's not what I want. I look for a better way to defeat my opponent without unnecessary violence. I'd rather use jiu-jitsu to do that then punch the guy until the end. From a technical point of view, I use punching and kicking to work for my jiu-jitsu, and from a moral point of view you could say that I try to be as gentle as possible.

Q: Once you are on the ground, what position do you prefer?
A: My technique is based on my opponent. I try to stay in what I call the "zero zone." From there, I'm ready to read what my opponent gives me

"Training with a gi gives you more possibilities as far as techniques are concerned. When your opponent has no-gi, the fight becomes a little more physical due to the fact that you have to control his body in a different way."

to react. It takes a very strange balance to fight that way, but in the very end you don't know what you are going to do; you simply wait to see what the opponent gives you and then you take it. I go with the flow of the movements and actions my opponent gives me.

It's true that I like to keep my opponent in my guard. The reason is that sooner or later he is going to make a move to try to escape, and that action will open a door for me to counter. It's like having an answer for everything he may try to do. You just have to control and wait for him to move. Of course, it sounds simpler that it is in real action, but the underlying principle is to stay in that "zero zone," control your opponent so you are safe and wait for his move. Then react to it in the best possible way.

Q: There are the differences of fighting with a gi and without gi. How does the whole strategy change?
A: Yes, there are differences and a good fighter needs to know what these are. Training with a gi gives you more possibilities as far as techniques are concerned. You have more choices for choking, getting an armlock or controlling your opponent. In any grappling activity, getting a good grip is a relevant part of the fight and with a gi it is easier than when your opponent isn't wearing one. When your opponent has no-gi, the fight becomes a little more physical due to the fact that you have to control his body in a different way. You have to look for the major limbs and areas that you can hold consistently like his head, trunk, et cetera. If you compete in sport jiu-jitsu (gi), you'll need to know all the variables because your opponent can use many different grips that will end up putting you in a very difficult

position. There are more techniques, more variables; therefore, it
takes more time to become skilled
in the art. Fighting without a gi cuts
the number of possibilities down so
the basics can be mastered in a
shorter period of time. Don't get
me wrong; it doesn't mean it's easier. Unfortunately, I have seen some
good jiu-jitsu fighters enter vale
tudo events and lose due to the fact
they used the wrong approach to
the no-gi situation. When you go
from gi to no-gi, you need to know
how to change and adapt your
guard, your controls, your clinch, et
cetera, otherwise you are going to
be defeated.

*"Unfortunately, I have seen some good jiu-jitsu
fighters enter vale tudo events and lose due
to the fact they used the wrong approach to
the no gi situation. When you go from gi to
no gi, you need to know how to change."*

There are several considera-
tions for each type of situation but
in vale tudo I don't like to use the gi because that would give my opponent the advantage of more options to control me. I might use it in some
special conditions, though. But basically if I don't have a gi on, I limit my
opponent's possibilities of holding onto it and the "stalling" factor can be
very important in a fight. Of course, I'd love all my opponents to wear a
gi, but they are smart guys, too!

**Q: How do you approach your jiu-jitsu when teaching a women's
class?**
A: Well, things are changing these days. In the past you didn't have too
many women competing in jiu-jitsu so the classes were focused more on
self-defense aspects than in competition techniques. I truly believe that
everybody can get benefits from training in the arts and I try to focus my
classes so women develop self-confidence and self-esteem by training in jiu-
jitsu. My programs are designed to give women specific ways of defending
themselves in dangerous situations. The main idea for a women being
attacked is to create space and run. A woman doesn't want to stay there
and trade blows with her attacker. The bottom line in teaching a class is not
whether the student is a man or a woman but their level of ability to per-

"The main difference between a fighter and a teacher is that a fighter does it for himself and a teacher is able to change people's lives through his teachings. As a teacher you influence your students' lives in many ways."

form the techniques. If a woman student has previous jiu-jitsu experience then I can put more pressure and go at full speed. Not with the intention of hurting her but to make her feel the pressure of a consistent attack. This is the same thing I would do with a man.

Through my years teaching the art, I have found that sometimes it's beneficial for a woman to learn and train jiu-jitsu from another woman. They feel more "in tune" for obvious reasons. Because of that, my wife Kim often helps me with the instruction, which makes the student feel more comfortable and confident. What is very important is to incorporate training with men so the female student has the opportunity to experience the power and strength of a man doing the attack. In women's self-defense the goal is not to get the aggressor in a choke or arm lock. The idea is to protect yourself and escape safely. Don't stay there trying to overpower the attacker. Use common sense and you'll be safe.

Q: You are an exceptional fighter but you are also considered an excellent teacher. What do you think is the secret of a successful transition from fighter to teacher?

A: Competition is something good, especially when you are young. After years of competition the main reason for me doing jiu-jitsu slightly changed. I had nothing to prove anymore. Winning trophies was not an important issue and I truly began to enjoy the art in a deeper way. I matured and my overall approach and perception of the art did too.

The main difference between a fighter and a teacher is that a fighter does it for himself and a teacher is able to change people's lives through his teachings. As a teacher you influence your students' lives in many ways. The goal is different and more relevant. As far as I'm concerned, having been a fighter first allowed me to understand things first hand and have real experience to pass onto my students. It's my responsibility now to transmit these experiences and knowledge to my students in the proper way.

I know some excellent fighters are not good teachers but I guess this is because the love for sharing what they know is not inside of them. It boils down to the individual's personality. But the opposite is also true. I have seen people who weren't fighters but they have an exceptional ability to teach and share the art. They know all the little details, the angles, the positioning, the correct application of strength, the knowledge of why and how the technique and the movement works,

"As a teacher you must be connected to the overall philosophy of incorporating martial arts into your life and not necessarily with the fighting aspects or elements of competition. It's not about what you can do in front of your students to impress them but what you can do to make the students good."

etc. And they are capable of creating champions as well. Being a good teacher has to do with your passion to live the art and share your knowledge with others. You need patience and understanding. The approach is totally different and in some way the fighter must transform himself to become a teacher. If he doesn't know how to switch the mode, then he will end up either hurting the students or not having good disciples.

Q: Should the teacher have a different philosophical approach as well?
A: Yes, of course. The main objective is not yourself but your student. As a teacher you must be connected to the overall philosophy of incorporating martial arts into your life and not necessarily with the fighting aspects or elements of competition. It's not about what you can do in front of your students to impress them but what you can do to make the students good. If you don't have the passion to share and spend time taking care of people, then teaching is not for you. It's that simple. As a teacher you have to give the student everything you have: your experience, your knowledge

"My philosophy of life is to respect everybody and everything, trying to do my best in whatever I'm involved at that particular time. Being a Gracie is the only way I have to live my life."

and your time. You can't give him your talent or your feeling for the art because this is very personal and something that he has to develop on his own. You do your half and the rest is on the student's shoulders.

Q: How much pressure is involved in being a Gracie?

A: Although the Gracie family didn't create the art of jiu-jitsu, the Gracie name has become a symbol of effectiveness in using the art. Because of the reputation of many members of my family, past and present, there is definitely a responsibility. To a certain extent every member of the family has the obligation to meet those expectations and this is a hard task. To answer your question, yes, there is a pressure being a Gracie but at the same time I can't conceive my life without that pressure. I've had to live with it since the day I was born so I can't imagine my existence without having the name "Gracie," and all that goes with it, attached to my daily life. My philosophy of life is to respect everybody and everything, and trying to do my best in whatever I'm involved at that particular time. Any human being, if he is responsible and tries to maintain high expectations for himself, has that kind of pressure, regardless of his name. Any high level athlete has pressure every time he performs. Being a Gracie is the only way I have to live my life. There is no way out for me!

Q: Have you ever gotten bored with jiu-jitsu?

A: No never. It's true that, like everybody else, I need a change in direction to keep myself motivated. It's normal and human. Teaching provides me with that "direction" within the same field. When I teach, for me it's something very special. I do it with love. I'm sharing an art created by my family so in a way I'm sharing one of my family assets. And I want to do it in the right way. I believe the main reason I don't get bored or lose motivation in what I do is because I don't put pressure on myself about what I must do.

My workout must be fun not torture. If it's fun I can truly enjoy it and don't get burned out. The key is doing it in a enjoyable way.

Q: Who would you like to fight?
A: I know a lot of people would like to fight me. I fight those who the promoters think are good for business. It's not about me saying who I want to fight. People think that I choose my fights. That's not true. Who you fight is based on many different factors, most of them out of my hands.

"If I'm not in 100 percent physical and mental condition, I won't fight. That can happen tomorrow or in twenty years. I only concentrate on today. Age is not a factor to me, the determining factor is my body."

Q: When are you planning to retire?
A: I don't plan. I live in the present. As long as I can feel my body working the way it is now, I won't retire from fighting. But I'm aware one day I won't feel the same and I won't take a chance to get hurt. If I'm not in 100 percent physical and mental condition, I won't fight. That can happen tomorrow or in twenty years. I only concentrate on today. Age is not a factor to me, the determining factor is my body. I don't think how old I am because it's irrelevant to me. If I want to do something, I just do it. I don't think about my age. We all are aware that one day we'll start feeling physical limitations, but as human beings what is really important is not to have mental limitations. That's what I strive for. ↻

Masters Techniques

Rickson Gracie faces his opponent (1), and uses his left leg to close the distance (2). Avoiding his opponent's punch (3), Rickson clinches and sweeps the left leg (4), in order to get his opponent to the ground (5). Rickson then applies pressure (6), forcing the attacker to turn around (7), which allows Rickson to apply a finishing back-choke (8).

Rickson Gracie faces an opponent (1). As the aggressor tries to punch, Rickson ducks (2), and closes the distance to get into a clinch (3). Grabbing his opponent by the hips (4), Rickson lifts him up (5), and takes him to the ground (6), where he places his right knee on the stomach (7). The attacker then tries to punch (8), which causes him to extend his arm (9), allowing Rickson to finish him with an arm-lock (10).

Rickson Gracie sees his opponent's punch coming (1), and avoids it by ducking under (2). He then grabs both of the attacker's legs (3), takes him to the ground (4), where he maintains control over one leg (5), and applies a finishing leg-lock (6).

Rickson Gracie faces brother Royler Gracie (1). As Royler tries to kick, Rickson lifts his right leg to block the attack (2). He then grabs the attacking limb (3), takes Royler to the ground (4), where he begins to punch (5), to finish him (6).

Rickson Gracie faces brother Royler Gracie (1). When Rickson tries to take Royler down (2), Royler sprawls to avoid it (3). Rickson immediately drops his left knee to the ground (4), and moves to the side (5), to position himself behind Royler (6). Passing his right arm under Royler's arm and hooking Royler's left arm with his legs (7), Rickson applies a finishing choke (8).

269

Rigan Machado

The Force of Submission

BORN IN RIO DE JANEIRO, RIGAN MACHADO IS ONE OF BRAZILIAN JIU JITSU'S MOST STO-
RIED FIGURES. A CHAMPION IN BRAZIL, RIGAN WAS ONE OF THE FIRST BLACK BELTS TO
COME TO THE UNITED STATES AND INTRODUCE AN ENTIRE GENERATION TO THE LOST ART
OF GROUND FIGHTING. IN SO DOING HE HELPED CHANGE AMERICAN MARTIAL ARTS FOR-
EVER. THE FACT THAT HE IS ONE OF THE MOST FAMOUS AND RESPECTED INSTRUCTORS IN
THE WORLD KEEPS HIM EXTREMELY BUSY TEACHING IN SOUTHERN CALIFORNIA OR TRAVEL-
ING TO SPREAD THE ART AND PHILOSOPHY OF MACHADO JIU-JITSU. HIS EASY-GOING ATTI-
TUDE REFLECTS HIS RELAXED APPROACH TO THE ART DEVELOPED BY HIS UNCLE, CARLOS
GRACIE. A PERPETUAL STUDENT OF ANY KIND OF SUBJECT RELATED TO HIS BELOVED ART,
RIGAN MACHADO ALWAYS STRIVES TO BE BETTER AT WHATEVER HE DOES. AND THE BEST
IS YET TO COME.

**Q: You've been considered one of the top submission fighters in the
world for many years but yet have refused to do no-holds-barred
events. Why is that?**

A: You see, I only like to do things that are fun for me—that I enjoy and
get pleasure from. I love jiu-jitsu and I love to compete in jiu-jitsu so that
is what I have done. Professional fighting is a much different step. You
have to love, 100 percent, the fighting game. I feel like I still have a lot to
accomplish as a grappler. A professional fight does not give me the same
feelings that I get from Brazilian jiu-jitsu. For me, it is going to be more
something that I want to do to see the other side. The reason I didn't do
no-holds-barred fights is because I didn't have enough hunger to be in a
competition like that. To fight NHB, I want to have the same hunger as
when I compete in grappling or Brazilian jiu-jitsu.

Q: So have you trained punching and kicking?

A: Yes, but that's a complete different aspect of my personal training. I'm
from a different world that uses takedowns, clinches, and finishing
holds—my approach has to be different. And everything I learn has to fit

"In Brazil you see many good fighters, but hunger and determination is what makes a champion. But it is not only the mind. There are many pieces to the puzzle: speed, strength, flexibility, endurance, and attitude."

into my scheme. I'm not going to change the things I like just for the money.

Q: What kind of rules do you like the most?
A: It's hard to say. There are many styles of grappling. But when you step onto the mat it is just going to be one style—grappling. The people who have more grappling skills are the ones who will have the best chance in the fight. It doesn't matter if the guy is a sambo player, or a judo fighter, or this or that. The good grapplers will do fine. But I still believe the jiu-jitsu fighters own the ground. Some of the other styles are not as used to being on the ground.

Q: Do you feel that the style is more important that the person?
A: No. How you fight is still based on the individual—how hard he trains, how hungry he is. That is what makes the fighter. In Brazil you see many good fighters, but hunger and determination is what makes a champion. But it is not only the mind. There are many pieces to the puzzle: speed, strength, flexibility, endurance, and attitude. They all work together but it is based on personal motivation, which cannot be taught. You have it inside or you don't.

Q: Are the Brazilians still as dominant as they used to be?
A: No. Brazil was just the beginning of the modern grappling movement. I believe from there that seeds have been spread all around the world. I believe that in the future it will be more and more difficult for Brazil to dominate so much, due to how many Brazilians are teaching around the world. But that is how it should be. For me, I want to be the best teacher

I can be. I want to build a good school, good students, and a good environment for everyone, regardless of where they're from. That's my job. If a student is not from Brazil and he becomes good, then that makes me a good coach and makes me happy. That is my future goal—to train more champions.

Q: So you're more focused on your students than yourself?
A: In life you have many different goals. My goals right now are to concentrate 50 percent on myself and 50 percent on my students. But in the future I will be concentrating almost 100 percent on the students. I want to build up many great fighters for many types of events: for professional fights or for Brazilian jiu-jitsu, or submission, or for anything. But right now, to do that, I have to concentrate a lot on myself. What's hard for me is that I have to work very hard teaching, doing seminars, and shooting movies. So to be focused I have to stop teaching, I have to stop movies and other things to try and concentrate on my training. When I'm training I like to only focus on myself and use all my energy to try to improve my skills and to get the mental and physical sides of myself to 100 percent. What used to be better for me in Brazil is that I only used to train. I

"When I'm training I like to only focus on myself and use all my energy to try to improve my skills and to get the mental and physical sides of myself to 100 percent. What used to be better for me in Brazil is that I only used to train."

never had to work or do anything like that because my work was my training. But now, in the United States, I have to teach a lot and do a lot of classes and travel a lot for seminars. So that bugs me more than anything as far as making my training harder. When I'm getting ready for a fight, I wish I only had to train.

"A proper submission, whether it is an arm lock, knee bar, or whatever, is all a result of a proper opening and that is where the gi is most helpful. When you don't have the gi, you have to use a lot of speed and strength. It is not so much a technical match as it is a physical match."

Q: Do you think it's possible to train submission and no-holds-barred at the same time?

A: To begin with, you have to train in two different worlds and keep them separate because both are so technical. Later then you can put them together, but it depends a lot on your personal ability and level of understanding of what you're doing. So when I teach students then I will teach the things that I am good at. Then I can bring in others who are good at punching or whatever, to teach the students to be a complete fighter. Kind of like the way Dan Inosanto does.

Q: What is the difference between training with or without the gi?

A: The difference is that with the gi, the submission game is much more technical. When you wear the gi, you have many more chances to catch your opponent. You have a chance to use the gi to your advantage. You have a much better control for your opening moves. You can tighten up different points on your opponent's body, which set him up for the move to follow. A proper submission, whether it is an arm lock, knee bar, or whatever, is all a result of a proper opening and that is where the gi is most helpful. When you don't have the gi, you have to use a lot of speed and strength. It is not so much a technical match as it is a physical match—many of the techniques are either limited or completely eliminated. The number of chokes you can attempt are greatly reduced; arm locks are harder to get, because you lose so much leverage that you have to get much tighter to your opponent. So there are negatives to not having a gi. However, depending on your strategy, there are also potential advantages to both.

*"I believe today that it is very important to train both with and without a gi.
The way I train is the way I like to teach. I have trained with the gi
most of my life. But I like sometimes to challenge myself by adapting
the techniques I learned with the gi to grappling without the gi."*

I believe today that it is very important to train both with and without a gi. The way I train is the way I like to teach. I have trained with the gi most of my life. But I like sometimes to challenge myself by adapting the techniques I learned with the gi to grappling without the gi. In this way, I keep myself from getting too comfortable with one way of training—because then you stop learning.

Q: But don't most top no-holds-barred fighters train exclusively without the gi?
A: Yes, that's true I suppose. But in my academy, for example, I have 200 students, but maybe only 10 percent of them want to go into professional fighting. The rest, 90 percent, want to learn jiu-jitsu for fun, for fitness, for self-defense, or to compete in sport tournaments. That's why the sport rules were invented—it's a way to give the students goals for their training. Tournaments are something to shoot that aren't as violent or

"You have to change your approaches to a move, but you should still be trying to hit the move. In other words, don't let the fact that you have or don't have a gi throw you off your grappling strategy—don't let it take you out of your game."

intense as professional fighting. And the gi is better for tournaments because it creates more options for the students who are competing in them.

Q: Do you use different grips when you're using or not using the gi?
A: Sure. With the gi, sometimes you can do a lot of different set-ups in order to expose your opponent to a submission. You can keep a comfortable distance from your opponent, stay loose, and still grab the lapel, or the material around the elbow, or even the gi at the hip or the knee, and still control him. But with no-gi, the game is much different. You can't control your opponent from a distance and still set him up for a finishing hold because a grip that would work with a gi will be quickly broken without one. There is no lapel to grab, for example, and if you try to hold the neck, the opponent just has to turn his head a little and you slip off. So instead of grabbing for specific points on the body, you have to think about controlling entire regions of the body. For example, instead of controlling the lapel from a distance, you have to get close and control his entire upper body by circling your arms around his body, or by trapping his arm under your arm.

But in either situation, you have to think like a grappler. You have to change your approaches to a move, but you should still be trying to hit the move. In other words, don't let the fact that you have or don't have a gi throw you off your grappling strategy—don't let it take you out of your game. Control the situation rather than letting the situation control you. You must adapt the details, but keep the big picture the same. Use all the same tools, just in different ways.

Q: So chokes are easier to apply with the gi?

A: Actually, it really depends on the situation. For example, to do the basic rear naked choke, or the back choke, is much easier without the gi, because your arms get real slippery in a match because of the sweat and you can slide your arm in much easier and get deeper penetration with less effort. When you have the gi it is sometimes more difficult because the material adds a lot of friction and the arm won't slide in as easily. The gi actually stops the back choke many times. With the gi, when you have the back, I think the collar choke is a much better technique to use. So you have to adapt your entry while keeping the ultimate goal the same—to give your opponent a little nap. It's just with the gi, there are more options.

Q: So you learn more techniques with the gi?

A: There are more techniques because there are more options for each move. For example, when practicing take-downs, you have a chance to try a judo throw, to use the gi to block when someone tries to sweep you, or to open someone up for you to sweep them. But when you take away the gi, you pretty much take away all the

"When you take away the gi, you pretty much take away all the judo throws—or at the very least they are severely limited. It's much easier for you to slip in, go low, and shoot for the legs with a freestyle wrestling technique than it is to try a judo hip throw."

judo throws—or at the very least they are severely limited. It's much easier for you to slip in, go low, and shoot for the legs with a freestyle wrestling technique than it is to try a judo hip throw. So right there you're eliminated the option of the judo throw.

But this is a very relative thing, and it goes both ways depending on what art you've been practicing. When you put a wrestler in a gi, for example, they can easily get lost because they have no idea what to do when someone grabs them by the clothes instead of the body. So a jiu-jitsu man

"A lot of people just do jiu-jitsu for fun or self-defense, so I think not letting students use that move is a way of protecting them and keeping the training safe. That's the big advantage of jiu-jitsu, you can train really, really hard and not get hurt."

can use that to his advantage. The guard is another example where I use the gi to keep him close to me. Without the gi, a wrestler will have a lot more room to operate. But with the gi I can control him by controlling the gi with my arms, without having to clinch. I can keep him from going to the side more effectively, or in the mount I can keep him from escaping from the bottom. There is much less chance to slip away.

So when I train with the gi, I practice those types of moves that would be to my advantage, and then training without the gi I also focus on those things that will help me the most. However, the key thing to remember is that the angles are always the same. The only thing that changes is the grip—the way you control your opponent for the entry. But everything else is the same.

Q: Why don't you see a lot of leg locks in jiu-jitsu tournaments? Does Brazilian jiu-jitsu have many leg locks?
A: That is a good question. For a long time you didn't see a lot of leg locks because of the rules. In the tournaments in Brazil, 10 or 20 years ago, those things were not allowed. Now, though, they are legal and you see a lot more knee bars, heel hooks, and foot locks. The heel hook, though, which puts so much pressure on the knee and the hip, and can cause very serious damage, is the one that jiu-jitsu schools in general, I think, don't like to see in day-to-day training. No one wants to get their ligaments torn up and their knee destroyed. A lot of people just do jiu-jitsu for fun or self-defense, so I think not letting students use that move is a way of protecting them and keeping the training safe. That's the big advantage of jiu-jitsu, after all, over other martial arts—you can train really, really hard and not get hurt. So I think that jiu-jitsu teachers want to preserve that concept.

But little by little you see more different types of leg locks added to the jiu-
jitsu arsenal. Jiu-jitsu has four different
belt levels: blue, purple, brown, and
black. People at the brown and the black
belt level are those that have started to
use more leg techniques. And that is
spreading to the lower belts now.

I believe jiu-jitsu grows a little every
day. The real purpose of grappling, in the
Brazilian jiu-jitsu way, is to be able to
apply the moves in a real situation. So
you have to use moves that can cause
damage. But you don't have to damage
other students to practice them. So even
non-leg-lock moves, such as neck cranks,
are not things that I like to see students
use on each other. If I see someone doing
excessively dangerous moves to other students then I will tell them to stop. If they
continue, then I will ask them to leave the
school before anyone gets hurt.

Q: What is your overall philosophy of training?

A: You can train a martial art, or a martial
sport, such as jiu-jitsu, which is both, for
sportive uses. But while you're doing this
you always have to think about reality.
You have to train the sportive methods,

*"I believe jiu-jitsu grows a little every day.
The real purpose of grappling, in the Brazilian
jiu-jitsu way, is to be able to apply the moves
in a real situation. So you have to use moves
that can cause damage. But you don't have
to damage other students to practice them."*

but then always keep adapting them and yourself to be able to use them
in real situations. You can't lose sight of that or you lose sight of jiu-jitsu
itself. That is the base idea of Brazilian jiu-jitsu—practice for sport, but be
able to apply it for real.

Q: How do you usually train for an event like Abu Dhabi or a jiu-jitsu championship?

A: I tried to focus on my jiu-jitsu skills by doing a lot of drills with my students and my brothers. I also did a lot of cardio workouts and also a lot of

"When I was growing up, a coach I used to have who has since died. This coach, for me, is my biggest motivation I have in my whole life. My dream is to come close to being like him. His name was Rolls Gracie."

wrestling training for my stamina. The techniques of wrestling are different. They help a lot because the jiu-jitsu skill involves training a lot of techniques with your back on the ground, passing the guard, side control—things like that. When you train standing, you're training takedowns. Things like tie-ups, shoot the legs—single and double. You need to learn a game-plan to develop your balance, skills, and posture. For me it's like two different worlds I'm trying to put together.

Q: Are there any fighters you look up to?
A: I admired, when I was growing up, a coach I used to have who has since died. This coach, for me, is my biggest motivation I have in my whole life. My dream is to come close to being like him. His name was Rolls Gracie. He died a long time ago in a hang-gliding accident. He is the person that I really admire and who still inspires me to train hard.

Q: You must consider him one of the all-time best fighters.
A: I do—but I also admire many other fighters. Not only from jiu-jitsu but also many different styles from many different generations. Rolls, in his time, used to just be unbelievable. But I also admire Rickson Gracie. Rickson is a little bit older than me and I used to watch him fight when I was a purple belt and he was already a black belt. He inspired me to train. I have great respect for Carlson Gracie—he was a truly amazing fighter. I admire even wrestlers such as Dan Gable—he's the technician of coaching. Dave Schultz is another guy. When I came to the United States, I

really admired. Mike Tyson and Sugar Ray in boxing were other guys who inspired me to become an athlete.

Q: You have a close relationship with Chuck Norris and have appeared on his show, "Walker, Texas Ranger." What is he like?

A: I look upon Chuck Norris as a brother. I don't look at him and see a movie star—I look at him and see a friend. When he invited me and my brothers to work on his TV show we had a great time. He made us feel very relaxed and very welcome. He is just a real nice guy. He helped us to come to United States and has supported us 100 percent. He is one of the best things you have in the United States. He's also a real tough fighter. He's still hungry. He wants to train morning, noon, and night—any chance he has. He wants to train very hard. That proves why he is Chuck Norris. He trains hard, even when he works every day. He always come up to me and asks me to train. He's an amazing guy.

"I just want to be a good fighter, a good person, and to be respected by people. What makes me real sad, sometimes, is when people play politics and say bad things about you. That doesn't make sense to me."

Q: Where do you see yourself in the future?

A: I just want to be a good fighter, a good person, and to be respected by people. What makes me real sad, sometimes, is when people play politics and say bad things about you. That doesn't make sense to me, because how can you talk about people who have done so much to promote the sport and make it better. People say things because they're jealous, or just to make themselves look better in comparison. ↻

Rigan Machado is mounted on his opponent (1). As his opponent moves his arm to protect against a choke, Rigan grabs the right wrist (2), pushes the hand down to the floor (3), under-hooks the arm with his left arm (4), and applies a bent arm-lock (5).

Rigan Machado's opponent, trying to protect himself (1), lifts his arms to grab Rigan's neck (2). Rigan places both of his hands over his opponent (3), and begins to turn (4), so he can control the arms (5), and gain proper position (6), to apply a straight arm-lock (7).

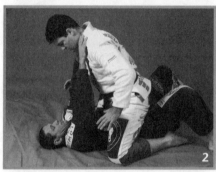

283

Masters Techniques

Rigan Machado is in side-control on Andre Lima (1). Rigan uses both of his hands (2), to push himself up (3), and place his left knee on his Andre's stomach (4). As Andre moves his left arm to protect against the choke (5), Rigan grabs his arm and turns around (6), to gain the proper position (7), to apply a finishing straight arm-lock (8).

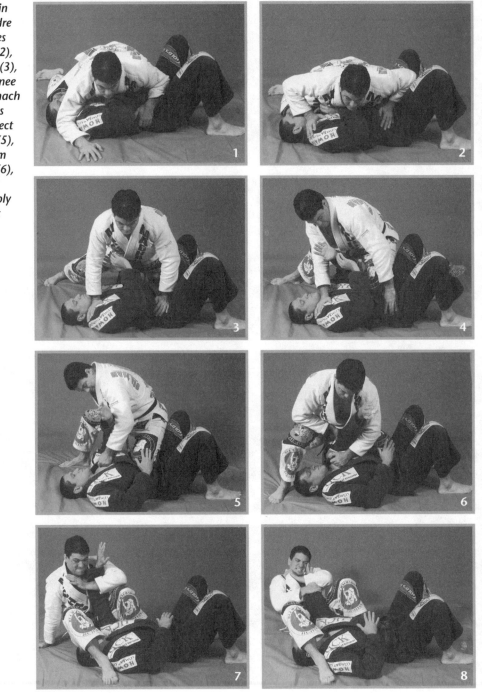

Rigan Machado faces Andre Lima (1).
Rigan moves his left leg (2), puts it
between Andre's legs (3), and grabs
under (4). Spinning around (5), Rigan
controls the body (6), and finishes
with a straight leg-lock (7).

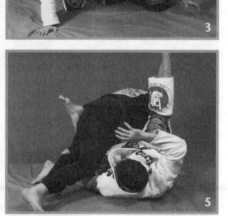

Rigan Machado controls his opponent from the open guard (1). As the opponent tries to grab his collar (2), Rigan moves his right arm under his opponent's left arm (3), pulls in as he pushes with his legs (4), and applies a straight arm-lock (5).

Andre Lima tries to pass Rigan Machado's guard (1). Rigan pulls Andre's sleeve (2), inserts his right leg under the arm (3), and begins twisting his body (4). Rigan then applies pressure with his leg (5), and sits-up to apply a bent arm-lock (6).

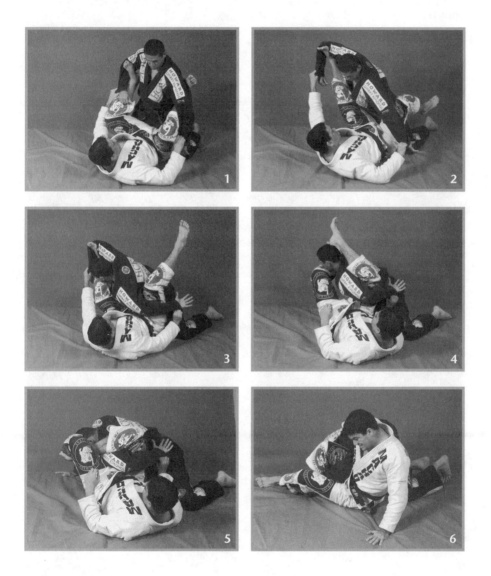

As Andre Lima tries to pass Rigan Machado's guard (1), Rigan controls his movements by placing one foot on his hips and the other on his biceps (2). Rigan then pulls Andre down and moves his right leg inside (3), so he can hook Andre's neck (4), and under-hook his right instep under his own left leg (5). Rigan then applies pressure to execute a triangle choke (6).

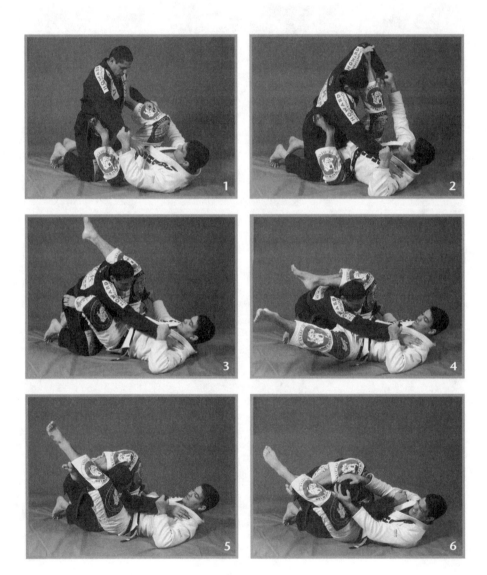

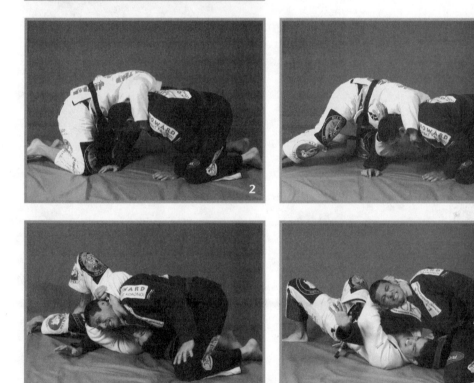

Rigan Machado controls his opponent's collar with his right hand (1). He then he slips his left hand under the collar (2), starts to apply pressure (3), by turning his hands to gain leverage (4), and chokes his opponent out (5).

Rorion Gracie

Testing Reactions

You may like him or dislike him, hate him or love him, agree or disagree with him—but there is no middle ground when it comes to Rorion Grace. The truth of the matter is that this eldest son of jiu-jitsu legend Helio Gracie is one of the most influential figures in the world of martial arts in the modern era. He took martial arts by storm when he created the Ultimate Fighting Championship in 1993, broadcast it on television, and opened the doors for a horde of his countrymen to teach the art his father created and developed over the past 70 years. Rorion brought a new approach to martial arts and changed the worldwide scene forever. The modern history of martial arts is written before and after the UFC—and before and after Rorion Gracie. He created a new way of looking at reality fighting, and his vision and way of doing things brought him into the spotlight.

There is something about Rorion Gracie that places him above any other jiu-jitsu teacher. Not only is Rorion an expert in the art his father taught, but he also combines his technical knowledge with a charismatic personality and a professional attitude in business as well. For Rorion Gracie, however, whatever he has accomplished in the past, stays in the past. He has no time to look back because for him, the best is always in the future.

Q: When did you begin your training?
A: I was practically born on the mat. I can't think of any period of my life when I was not training or teaching jiu-jitsu. The oldest recollection I have of my involvement with jiu-jitsu is a demo I did with my father. I was so little that the backs of the chairs were taller than me as I walked down the aisle towards the stage where he stood. The most significant memories I have, however, are those of my father teaching. His ability to explain with passion and dedication was unique and entertaining. When I began teaching, although I was very young, I knew I couldn't go wrong if I followed his footsteps. So I used his words and told his stories—and sure enough my students loved it. As I grew up, I started adding my own sto-

"The reason I came to America is that the Gracie name was extremely popular in Brazil, and because of my A+ personality I didn't want to stay there and live off my father's accomplishments. I wanted to build upon them."

ries and experiences. By then I had learned the perfect way to teach.

Q: You earned a law degree in Brazil. Why did you quit law and come to the United States?
A: Well, first and foremost I am a jiu-jitsu teacher. When I decided to go to law school, I was not searching for a new profession. I simply believed that going through college would be a way to expand my possibilities. I teach jiu-jitsu because I love it, not because I can't do anything else. Besides, I'd rather wear the belt around my waist instead of around my neck! The reason I came to America is that the Gracie name was extremely popular in Brazil, and because of my A+ personality I didn't want to stay there and live off my father's accomplishments. I wanted to build upon them. So I set out to spread the word of the Gracie legend. After all, if you want something to happen and the world to see you—you have to do it in America.

Q: What was it like in the beginning?
A: A little rough. There was a time I found myself panhandling and sleeping on the streets. Not for a moment, however, did I have any doubt that I would reach my goal of convincing the martial arts community that they all needed jiu-jitsu. Groundfighting was too important to be ignored! Then there were those challenge matches in the garage during the early days, which would convince one non-believer at a time. Month-after-month, and year-after-year I endured, until finally starting the UFC. After that everyone understood what I was talking about. It took me 25 years but I accomplished my goal.

Q: What made you issue the famous Gracie Challenge?

A: There has always been a lot of talk about how a certain style will teach you how to destroy someone with one hand—and this other style will enable you to pulverize three people with one finger, et cetera. Although there were instructors who knew their styles well, there were some who would capitalize on the mystic aspect of the martial arts and claim to be able to do some unbelievable things—some of them so deadly they could not be shown!

To know how to punch and kick is great, but we can't close our eyes to the most crucial aspect of a real fight—which is that 95 percent of all fights end up on the ground. The Gracie Challenge had the objective of demonstrating the effectiveness of what we teach. I owed it to all my students. It was the only way to prove my point.

"To know how to punch and kick is great, but we can't close our eyes to the most crucial aspect of a real fight—which is that 95 percent of all fights end up on the ground. The Gracie Challenge had the objective of demonstrating the effectiveness of what we teach."

Q: Why is it so important to be effective? Doesn't this produce bullies?

A: If you teach any subject you should be able to demonstrate your knowledge. In the world of martial arts, knowledge equals effectiveness—which in turn gives you confidence. For example, what if a three-year-old child came up to you and said, "I want to beat you up." Since he represents no threat, you would smile and say, "How cute! Now go play, baby." But if his father, a big and strong guy, came at you and said the same thing, you may get worried because you are not sure that you can handle him. Gracie jiu-jitsu enables you look at that big guy as if he were the child. The only reason why a person takes on the attitude of a bully is because deep down he is an insecure individual. Aggressiveness is used to try to intimidate the other party. If you lock that bully in a room with someone who he *knows* can beat him up, that bully will change into a really nice guy. When you reach a certain level of effectiveness, it changes your prospective. You start trusting yourself. That is the confidence that will make you more tolerant and even-tempered. It

*"When I arrived in America in the late '70s,
I began teaching in my garage and decided to call it
Gracie jiu-jitsu to differentiate from the Japanese
jiu-jitsu some people here had heard about."*

was this quest for genuine effectiveness that motivated my father to improve his fighting system and which has been the inspiration for the whole Gracie family.

Q: How did your father Helio became involved in jiu-jitsu?
A: The Gracie family was first exposed to it almost 100 years ago when a Japanese jiu-jitsu instructor came to Brazil to aid a Japanese immigration colony. It was then that my uncle, Carlos Gracie, had his first taste of this martial art. Carlos, the oldest, taught his brothers the traditional Japanese jiu-jitsu he had learned. Helio's frail health, caused regular fainting spasms and kept him off the mat. But it did not prevent him from watching the classes day-in and day-out and eventually learn the stuff. One day, Carlos was not around for a class and Helio, then 16, offered to step on the mat and teach the class. The student liked it. When Carlos showed up very apologetic, the student said, "No problem, but I would like to have classes with Helio from now on." On that day, the history of jiu-jitsu changed forever. Due to his small stature and light bodyweight, Helio could not make some of the moves work. So he found himself modifying them little-by-little to fit his needs, figuring out ways to use more leverage and less strength. As he got more and more into it, Helio developed new ways of controlling bigger opponents and getting them into submissions. Amazingly enough, to this date, he is still studying jiu-jitsu.

Q: What is the difference between Gracie and Brazilian jiu-jitsu?
A: When I arrived in America in the late 70's, I began teaching in my garage and decided to call it Gracie jiu-jitsu to differentiate from the Japanese jiu-jitsu some people here had heard about. I always told the same story: "Uncle Carlos was the first Gracie to learn jiu-jitsu and Helio

perfected it." Fifteen years later, I created the UFC, which was the turning point for establishing Gracie jiu-jitsu on top of the world. That brought a lot of attention and value to the Gracie name. Some of my cousins felt that if they could convince the people that Uncle Carlos, their father, was the one who had perfected the system and that they were the "keepers of the flame." As such, they could make easy and quick money selling instructor's certifications of Gracie jiu-jitsu to anyone. However, I owned the registration on the trademark, "Gracie jiu-jitsu." This is why the term "Brazilian jiu-jitsu" came into the scene. It was the next best thing. They are not different styles and they don't teach you different techniques. The arm-locks, chokes and foot-locks are exactly the same. Only recently did the U.S. Trademark Office determine that based on the huge and highly successful marketing campaign I have been doing all these years, Gracie jiu-jitsu became a generic term. It cannot be registered now and is therefore a style of martial art, just like judo or karate. Now my relatives and their affiliates have a dilemma—should they keep call-

"The credit for the refinement of the traditional Japanese system, which gave birth to what is known today as Gracie or Brazilian jiu-jitsu goes to the one-and-only Helio Gracie. Let's face it—Helio Gracie is the embodiment of jiu-jitsu!

ing their style "Brazilian jiu-jitsu" because they have been using it for a while, or start calling it "Gracie jiu-jitsu" since that is what they learned and is its true name? Time will tell.

Q: But some people in the family insist that Carlos not Helio was the one responsible for your family's system.
A: I loved and admired my Uncle Carlos. He was the man who managed Helio's career and was the spiritual leader of the family, leaving us the priceless legacy of his life's work—his knowledge in the field of nutrition. However, let's be reasonable. Uncle Carlos did not wake up one morning and say, "I am going to perfect a whole new style of fighting for a couple of years before I spend the next 70 years of my life developing the Gracie Diet." Give me a break! The credit for the refinement of the traditional Japanese system, which gave birth to what is known today as Gracie or Brazilian jiu-jitsu goes to the one-and-only Helio Gracie. Newspaper clip-

"Let me remind you that those who today wrongly insist that it was Carlos who perfected the style were not even born at that time. It is obvious that jealousy has affected their reasoning."

pings, photographs and other priceless memorabilia, now on display at the Gracie Jiu-Jitsu Museum in Torrance, California, will take you back in time and put you ringside at some of his incredible fights. This will clear any doubts and answer all questions. Furthermore, let me remind you that those who today wrongly insist that it was Carlos who perfected the style were not even born at that time. It is obvious that jealousy has affected their reasoning.

As if all that was not enough, take a look at Helio Gracie, who did nothing but jiu-jitsu his entire life. Today at age 90 he is as ready, as always, to step on the mat and demonstrate to anybody, a simpler and more technical way to apply a move. Let's face it—Helio Gracie is the embodiment of jiu-jitsu!

Q: Your father challenged the great boxer Joe Louis, right?
A: Yes, but Joe Louis declined! Joe Louis was on tour in Brazil and my father issued a challenge to pit boxing against jiu-jitsu. Joe Louis was to fight without gloves, just tape to protect the knuckles. It is true that a good punch from Joe Louis would have knocked my father out—but he was confident that he could get into a clinch. Of course with both men in a clinch, the fight would very much favor my father. Anyway, Joe Louis' manager, Marshall Miles, sent a letter declining the offer. He also challenged Primo Carnera and Ezzard Charles. It is all at the Gracie Museum.

Q: Years later you issued the same challenge to Mike Tyson, right?
A: Yes. The idea was to demonstrate that being the boxing champion of the world doesn't make you the best fighter. People always had that misconception until the UFC. Everybody knows that the only chance a boxer has in a NHB fight is that one punch. The boxer can't afford to miss or

get caught in a clinch. With the odds of 95 percent of all fights ending on the ground, pure boxers better stay out of the NHB arena.

Q: You don't bow in the traditional way of martial arts, why is that?
A: It is not necessary. Orientals bow to each other as a cultural habit. I don't teach Oriental culture, I teach Gracie jiu-jitsu, and a simple handshake is good enough.

Q: You drastically changed the face of martial arts when you started the Ultimate Fighting Championship. Why did you start it?
A: I grew up with the certainty that most real fights end up on the ground. The knowledge of jiu-jitsu has enabled me to protect myself effectively even against bigger and stronger adversaries. That is a priceless feeling. I have also seen thousands of people grow in confidence and improve their self-esteem when they were introduced to this wonderful art. Since my arrival in America a quarter-of-a-century ago, my primary goal has been to alert people to the importance of groundfighting. I wanted everyone to learn the art that did so much for me, the entire Gracie family, and thousands of students in my homeland of Brazil. I saw in the UFC an opportunity to expose to the world the truths and fallacies inherent in contemporary martial arts theory.

"I saw in the UFC an opportunity to expose to the world the truths and fallacies inherent in contemporary martial arts theory. Prior to the UFC, striking reigned supreme. With victory after victory, jiu-jitsu as a grappling art has dominated the editorial and technical articles of every major martial art magazine in the world."

Prior to the UFC, striking reigned supreme. With victory after victory, jiu-jitsu as a grappling art has dominated the editorial and technical articles of every major martial art magazine in the world. More importantly, everyone is doing it, just like I hoped for.

Q: Why are you against time limits?
A: When you impose a time limit, you are in effect giving a fighter a psychological "safety net." You are saying to him, "No matter how bad it

"When you impose a time limit, you are in effect giving a fighter a psychological 'safety net.' They can't help but alter their strategy to include an imposed time limit into their chances of victory."

gets, if you can hang on for X minutes you will be OK." The existence of this "light at the end of the tunnel" completely changes the physiological and emotional state of mind of the fighter. They can't help but alter their strategy to include an imposed time limit into their chances of victory. With the security of a scheduled conclusion ticking in the back of his head, a fighter's level of anxiety is greatly reduced.

Q: So you think the time limit affects the fighter's state of mind and mental approach to the fight?
A: Definitely. Take two men to separate but identical remote desert locations. To the first man you say, "I know this is difficult, but all you have to do is last 24 hours until we pick you up again. If you play it safe, if you don't expend too much energy, or take any risks, you should make it." This doesn't sound like anyone's idea of a great vacation, but I think most of us—secure in the knowledge of rescue—could manage to hang on. Fair enough.

Then go to the second man and tell him, "You are on your own. No one is coming to save you—ever! Your only hope lies in your own skill and ingenuity. Survive or perish—it's up to you. No playing it safe." The way the second man is going to act is totally different to the first one. That's why I tried to prevent eliminating the time limits in the UFC. Stripping away the pretenses, the judges, the scores, and the games. Two men enter—one man leaves. Let's find out what works and what doesn't. It's that simple.

Q: At your academy you encourage private classes. Why?
A: The effectiveness of our system is due to its simplicity—and it's far better to learn them one-on-one where we can coach the student individu-

ally instead of telling a whole class to play follow the leader and hope they can keep up. We want them to practice with us, to ensure the development of the proper reflexes. We don't want the students to memorize the moves. We teach their subconscious to react, which is faster than the conscious mind. It's like when you are driving down the street and a kid runs out in front of your car—your reflexes make your foot hit the brake. If you had to think about what to do with your conscious mind, there might be a tragedy. It's a simple matter of developing strong basics—the kind of foundation that eventually allows the student to become really efficient.

"A sincere teacher, a devoted teacher, does not stand aloof and in judgment as his pupil struggles along his path. The sincere teacher walks shoulder-to-shoulder with his charge, traveling the same path, sharing its difficulties and challenges."

Q; What attributes and qualities make a good teacher?
A: He must know the subject very well. He must have a genuine interest in helping the student improve. He must love teaching. The motto here at the Gracie Academy is, "There is no such a thing as a good or a bad student. All the students are the same. There is such a thing as a good or a bad teacher. All teachers are not the same. We only have great teachers. Here, everyone learns."

Properly performed, revealing knowledge to another is a deeply involving, almost symbiotic exercise. A sincere teacher, a devoted teacher, does not stand aloof and in judgment as his pupil struggles along his path. The sincere teacher walks shoulder-to-shoulder with his charge, traveling the same path, sharing its difficulties and challenges. The genuine teacher is there to help the student identify obstacles; discuss possible solutions. He shouldn't be comfortably perched upon some distant pedestal. True teachers are very rare.

"Although we all learned from the same source, not everybody in the Gracie family follows my father's guidelines. His teaching method is focused on self-defense, which involves the little known but extremely demanding stand-up aspects of jiu-jitsu."

Q: Are all the members of the Gracie family teaching the art in the same format and methodology developed by Helio Gracie?

A: Although we all learned from the same source, not everybody in the Gracie family follows my father's guidelines. His teaching method is focused on self-defense, which involves the little known but extremely demanding stand-up aspects of jiu-jitsu. It is a tough act to follow because it requires lots of: falling, getting choked and having your limbs turned and twisted in all directions countless times and then some. It is hard work on the teacher's part. If the motivation is money, no one will keep it up, regardless of how much they are making. You have to do it for love. It is much easier to let the students to roll with each other, and push the sparring for competition approach which is OK, I guess. But here at the Gracie Academy our primary goal is to increase the student's effectiveness in self-defense. That means that the teacher will be on the receiving end of every technique so he can give feedback to the student on the execution of each move. There is no doubt that many people are happy with the sportive angle. However I know my father's intention was not to develop a sport but a method of self-defense. That is why we do it his way.

Q: What's your opinion about mixing styles. Does the practice of one nullify the effectiveness of the other or can it be beneficial?

A: Of course, I think it would be important to have a strong base in jiu-jitsu because most fights will end up on the ground. It is not a bad thing to learn the other aspects of combat to help you to better apply your main art. What I have seen sometimes is people who have been training in jiu-jitsu for 20 years, start training in a striking art for a couple of years and when they fight they put their 20 years of jiu-jitsu in the back burner and rely on punches and kicks against a fighter who has been practicing strikes for 15 years. This is not smart and they are digging their own graves.

Q: You are the man who started it all with the creation of the UFC. What are your thoughts on the future of NHB events and what do you think should be done to improve the sport?
A: I don't think it will ever go back to what it was before. My idea at the time I created the UFC was to compare styles. Today, everybody does the same style of fighting—punching and kicking with some variation of jiu-jitsu. Now is not about the style, but about the athlete. As far as the events go, the current rules are making it too sanitized. I would take the gloves off and the put time limits out of the game. When that happens I will tell you the rest (laughs).

Q: What do you see in the future of jiu-jitsu and the Gracie family?
A: There is no reason why jiu-jitsu can't be an Olympic sport—but for that to happen there must be a complete overhaul within the worldwide jiu-jitsu community. And this must start with the rules currently used in jiu-jitsu tournaments. These rules are not bringing out the best in the sport. They are subjective, hard to understand, and encourage stalling. The Gracie family started the jiu-jitsu revolution and through their associates and students

"My idea at the time I created the UFC was to compare styles. Today everybody does the same style of fighting—punching and kicking with some variation of jiu-jitsu. Now is not about the style, but about the athlete. I would take the gloves off and the put time limits out of the game."

continues to be a major influence in the way the sport grows. The International Gracie Jiu-Jitsu Federation is being created with my father's blessing to organize events with a new set of rules that will revolutionize the practice of jiu-jitsu. As for future competitors, there is a new generation of Gracie family members growing tall and strong—so the best is yet to come. ○

Masters Techniques

Rorion Gracie faces his opponent (1), who attacks with a stick that Rorion deflects using his left forearm (2). Close-up (3). Rorion then wraps the attacker's arm and closes the gap (4), moves his right foot in front to square his hips (5), throws his opponent to the ground (6), and finishes with an arm-lock (7).

Ryron Gracie grabs Rorion Gracie's neck with both hands (1). Rorion controls
Ryron's right hand with his right hand and places his left hand over Ryron's left
shoulder for better control (2). Rorion then stabilizes his base, twists his hips to
create momentum (3), and applies a finishing arm-lock (4).

Royler Gracie

The Heart of a Champion

ONE OF BRAZILIAN JIU-JITSU'S MOST ENDURING CHAMPIONS, ROYLER GRACIE HAS NEVER RESTED ON THE LAURELS OF HIS FAMOUS FAMILY, BUT HAS LET HIS FIGHTING RECORD AND RING ACCOMPLISHMENTS SPEAK FOR THEMSELVES.

HE HAS BEEN INVOLVED IN MARTIAL ARTS HIS ENTIRE LIFE AND HAS BEEN COMPETING CONSTANTLY SINCE HE WAS 7 YEARS OLD. HAVING FOUGHT IN MORE JIU-JITSU EVENTS THAN PERHAPS ANY OTHER BRAZILIAN JIU-JITSU FIGHTER IN HISTORY, ROYLER HAS ATTAINED THE STATUS OF BEST IN THE WORLD. HIS CAREER HAS SPANNED OVER 28 YEARS AND THREE GENERATIONS. DURING THAT STRETCH HE HAS BEEN A FOUR-TIME BJJ WORLD CHAMPION, A TWO-TIME ABU DHABI COMBAT CLUB (ADCC) WORLD SUBMISSION WRESTLING CHAMPION, A PAN AMERICAN GAMES CHAMPION, A BRAZILIAN NATIONAL CHAMPION, AND RIO DE JANEIRO STATE CHAMPION. HE ALSO MANAGED TO FIGHT IN SEVERAL MEMORABLE NO-HOLDS-BARRED (NHB) MATCHES ALONG THE WAY, SOME AGAINST MUCH BIGGER MEN. UNDISPUTEDLY, ONE OF THE MOST SCIENTIFIC FIGHTERS IN THE WORLD, ROYLER WON THE MOST TECHNICAL AWARD AT BOTH THE 1997 BJJ WORLD CHAMPIONSHIPS AND AT ADCC 2000, MAKING HIM THE ONLY MAN TO HAVE EVER CAPTURED BOTH PRESTIGIOUS AWARDS.

IN AN ERA IN WHICH MOST FIGHTERS ARE WORRIED ABOUT THEIR RECORDS AND WON'T FIGHT OUTSIDE THEIR WEIGHT DIVISION, ROYLER HAS OFTEN TAKEN ON MUCH HEAVIER OPPONENTS. HIS REASONING IS SIMPLE AND SPEAKS VOLUMES ABOUT THE MAN HIMSELF: "I JUST WANT TO SEE HOW THE MATCH WILL TURN OUT AND HOW I WILL DO. MORE THAN ANYTHING ELSE I WANT TO LEARN MORE ABOUT JIU-JITSU, AND IN ORDER TO DO THAT I HAVE TO CHALLENGE MYSELF."

Q: Tell us a little bit about yourself.
A: I started to train BJJ when I was 3. At the time I really didn't know what I was doing, I'd go to the academy to play soccer dressed in a gi. It was fun, Brazil is the land of soccer and you generally give your kids a soccer ball, but I was given a gi. So my father and my cousin Rolls, in order to get me and the other kids interested in coming to class and to the academy, made us play soccer dressed in a gi. It was really fun then. All my

305

"We practically ate, slept, and breathed jiu-jitsu then, so the sport took over my life very early on, but very naturally because all the other kids in the family did it too."

brothers were at the academy also, so it was the gathering place. We practically ate, slept, and breathed jiu-jitsu then, so the sport took over my life very early on, but very naturally because all the other kids in the family did it too.

Q: When did you start to fight?
A: For my first competition I was only 7 years old. My dad came to me and said, "I want you to go there and have fun. If you win I am going to give you five dollars—but if you lose I am going to give you ten dollars." So I thought, "What a deal, if I win I make a little money and get the medal, and if I lose I get even more money." So I always looked forward to competitions because it was always a win-win situation. Now I see the wisdom of this, because no one enters a competition or a fight to lose; everyone wants to win. So in order to take away the pressure from me, he devised this reward. Because when you think about it, being that my family had many champions, the pressure for us to win was naturally stronger than for other kids. I believe it had a great effect on me and is why I still look forward to competing and why I thrive during pressure situations. In my mind, I just need to do my best—before and after the competition. I mention before the competition because if, for some reason, I didn't prepare myself correctly, I would feel bad. But that's never happened before and I hope it never will.

Q: How many times did you fight?

A: I started at 7 years old, but I have lost count of how many times I have fought in tournaments. But just as a black belt, I have approximately 300 fights recorded on video and film. But I didn't record all my fights as a lower belt so that number is much higher.

Q: Who were the big names when you started to compete?

A: I fought many people: Peixotinho, Marcio Simas, Marcio "Macarrao", Carlson Gracie Jr., Ricardo de La Riva, Amauri Bitteti, and so forth.

Q: So you have crossed several generations?

A: I believe that I have fought three generations of fighters.

"I started at 7 years old, but I have lost count of how many times I have fought in tournaments. But just as a black belt I have approximately 300 fights recorded on video and film. But I didn't record all my fights as a lower belt so that number is much higher."

Q: You also have fought several fights, including underground fights, like the time you fought Eugenio Tadeu. How old where you then?

A: I was 21.

Q: Was that your first vale tudo match?

A: Yes. That fight happened at our academy and it sort of happened without warning. I was teaching at the academy and my brother Rickson called and said, "Hey, Royler, tomorrow you have a vale tudo against a *luta livre* (free fighting) guy." At the time, jiu-jitsu and luta livre fighters had a real strong rivalry going so I accepted. Rickson called late in the afternoon and when I asked when, he answered, "Noon!" I then asked him if it was OK, if I took the rest of the evening off and rested, and he agreed. So it was on the spur of the moment, at least for me, with no preparation.

"So I showed up the next day to do a "fight-train" as Rickson called it, with Eugenio Tadeu, who at the time weighed about 25 lbs more than me. So we fought just to see who was the better fighter. I left the fight feeling great because I had never done a vale tudo before and it was a new experience in my life."

So I showed up the next day to do a "fight-train" as Rickson called it, with Eugenio Tadeu, who at the time weighed about 25 lbs more than me. We fought for 46 minutes with kicks and punches, all done for free, because at that time there was no money in vale tudo fights—so we fought just to see who was the better fighter. There were six people from my team watching and six people from his team. I left the fight feeling great because I had never done a vale tudo before and it was a new experience in my life.

Q: Tadeu already had a few matches prior to that, right?
A: He had a few fights, was used to street fighting, and he really liked fighting.

Q: Then after that you had a series of vale tudo matches?
A: Over a period of time. I fought one in Brazil, then I fought in Japan Vale Tudo 1996 against Noburo Asahi who was ranked number one in the Shooto organization at the time. Then I fought in Pride 2 against Yuhi Sano in 1998. After that I did the fight with Sakuraba in October 1999 and just recently in Deep 2001 against Japanese fighter Murahama. During that same time I was also fighting the world BJJ tournaments. I was the champion four years running in 1996 through 1999. I also fought in the ADCC championships and won both in 1999 and 2000. I fought in a few *Brasileiros* (Brazilian national tournaments). I also did a few special

events like the Copa Pelé. The Copa Pelé had special jiu-jitsu matches in an outdoor arena that was set up every summer on the beach in Rio.

Q: Describe the Deep 2001 match.

A: During the first round I was able to get Murahama's back right away, I believe by the third minute I was on his back. He was, however, an experienced fighter with many professional stand-up matches and he knew how to protect himself. The fact that he was only 5'2" made it easier for him to protect his neck. I spent about six minutes of the first round on his back trying to submit him. Around the ninth minute I decided to try an arm attack but we ended up too close to the ropes and his arm was wrapped around the ropes and the more I tried the harder it got.

In the second round he was

"Because the fight is never over until it's over, one mistake with a good striker can be fatal. A grappler, however, has to work a lot harder to get the precise moment to sink in the submission."

feeling more confident and we exchanged some punches while standing up. I got a little tired and I started to have a harder time taking him down. I finally took him down and attempted a foot lock but it was quickly defended by him. I believe that the fight was pretty even—he is a good striker and only needs to connect with one good shot to end the fight. Because the fight is never over until it's over, one mistake with a good striker can be fatal. A grappler, however, has to work a lot harder to get the precise moment to sink in the submission. The draw was a fair result. I have no complaints. I think that we both deserved the draw, but I also believe that the rules favored a draw.

"To my way of thinking, if a fighter who is my size draws with me after 20 or 30 minutes, then it is fair to say that we are even. I believe that from a promotion and entertainment standpoint you have to limit the matches to under one hour—and my preference is 30 minutes."

Q: Why was your fight two rounds of 10 minutes each?

A: Well, my fight was the main event so I believe that the promoters decided to make it longer. I think this would have been better for the other fights also, because it gives the fighters more time to develop a strategy and positioning. The person with the least amount of endurance would prefer a shorter fight, and the person who is more technical prefers a longer match. I am not talking about a three-hour fight, but I prefer two ten-minute rounds or even three rounds of that length. I believe anything longer than one hour makes for a boring fight. To my way of thinking, if a fighter who is my size draws with me after 20 or 30 minutes, then it is fair to say that we are even. Of course, if you go another round then anything can happen, but it can happen just as much to me as to him, so it goes both ways. I do not believe in saying that if a fight had gone longer I would have won. I believe that from a promotion and entertainment standpoint you have to limit the matches to under one hour—and my preference is 30 minutes.

Q: It seems that the Gracie family is always accused of going to an event and changing the rules at the last minute. Is there any truth to this?

A: I really don't understand that criticism. I always leave for an event with the rules already agreed to by both parties far in advance. As a matter of fact, when I arrived in Japan for Deep 2001 a reporter asked me that

*"I remember the time I fought with Sakuraba, who was 40 pounds heavier
than me, and all that I asked was for longer rounds. I don't think that
that was an unreasonable request. I have never had the chance to fight
someone who was 40 pounds lighter than me. I don't know where
these stories about last-minute changes come from."*

same question and I turned around to him and said that I didn't know of
any changes and asked him to tell me what had changed. He couldn't
answer. I remember the time I fought with Sakuraba, who was 40 pounds
heavier than me, and all that I asked was for longer rounds—two rounds
of 15 minutes instead of 10 minutes. I don't think that was an unreasonable request. I have never had the chance to fight someone who was 40
pounds lighter than me. But if that ever happens and he asks for three
rounds of 20 minutes each, I am going to agree. If he asks for 20 rounds
of three minutes each I'll also agree! The fact of the matter is that the
contracts are drawn way in advance and the rules are set before anyone
signs a contract; so I don't know where these stories about last-minute
changes come from.

"People may love the attention and the exposure and the perks, but no one in his right mind likes to hit someone or to get hit in a fight. You may love the challenge that is fighting but I don't believe that you can love to fight NHB. Fighting is something that traumatizes the body."

Q: What motivates you to keep fighting?

A: I have always loved fighting. After a while it becomes a natural part of your life. I live exclusively from fighting and teaching jiu-jitsu, grappling, and NHB. So I eat, sleep and breathe it. I look at it as a way to measure myself and to make a living at the same time. I focus on my work which involves teaching at academies that I have in Rio, doing seminars that I conduct everywhere in the world, and then fighting. The fights give me an extra income. So today I see NHB as a way to broaden my career, while at the same time making extra income. I don't believe that anyone will tell you that they love to fight NHB. People may love the attention and the exposure and the perks, but no one in his right mind likes to hit someone or to get hit in a fight. You may love the challenge that is fighting but I don't believe that you can love to fight NHB. Fighting traumatizes the body and is not something that anyone should do just for the pleasure of it.

Q: You are known for your ability to think and adjust your strategy during a fight. How did you develop that mental skill?

A: I have read the book, *The Art of War*, at least 50 times. It has influenced me a lot. One of the things that it says is, "If you know yourself but don't know your enemy, for each victory you will have a defeat. If you don't

*"I was also lucky to have been born into a family of fighters and was
fortunate enough to have grown-up around fighting. So I learned from
watching and absorbing the experience of many champions—
and not just those from my own family."*

know your enemy and you don't know yourself then you will lose every
battle. If you know yourself and your enemy then you don't have to fear
the result of 100 battles." I was also lucky to have been born into a family
of fighters and was fortunate enough to have grown-up around fighting.
So I learned from watching and absorbing the experience of many champions—and not just those from my own family.

"I believe that BJJ had a tremendous influence in the media in turning public attention to the idea of wrestling and submission styles being a legitimate combat art. There is not a top-level fighter today who doesn't have BJJ knowledge."

Q: What do you think of the evolution of submission grappling? Since the early days of Brazilian jiu-jitsu, when you taught out of a garage in L.A., it has become an established sport with a huge number of followers. Are you surprised?

A: Not really. Think about it. Years ago there wasn't a magazine dedicated to grappling alone; nowadays you have *Grappling* magazine in the U.S., *Gracie* Magazine in Brazil, and many other magazines totally dedicated to the sport. I think this whole thing has been because of the success that BJJ had in NHB. I believe that BJJ had a tremendous influence in the media in turning public attention to the idea of wrestling and submission styles being a legitimate combat art. All of a sudden, out of nowhere, there was something very different and fresh and very effective that changed the way people viewed fighting. There is not a top-level fighter today who doesn't have BJJ knowledge. Likewise the world of stand-up fighting has made BJJ practitioners look to develop skills that complement their style as well. But when BJJ came into the scene it really created a revolution. Judo is very important, luta livre is very important, wrestling is very important, and *sambo* is very important—but it was BJJ that initially showed that ground fighting is at least as important as stand-up striking in a fight.

Q: How do you approach the different elements (cardiovascular, strength and technical) in your training program?

A: Training for me is part of my life, the thing that I try to do is to adapt my lifestyle depending on what I am training for. I strongly believe that you have to be extremely fit to be ready for battle. So I have different routines depending if I am going to fight a BJJ tournament, a no-gi grappling event like ADCC, or an NHB match. The only common ground in my training is the aerobic part. I believe that you have to have strong endurance in order to perform at high level. For that I do a lot of running and biking. I like biking a lot because you get to see a lot of things and the exercise is more fun. If I am going to be in an NHB match, then I will lift weights according to a specific routine set up for me by my

"If I am going to compete in BJJ, which means fighting with a gi, then I will do a lot of judo and do a different series of weight training than I do for NHB. I will focus more on repetitions with lighter weights rather than fewer reps with heavier weights."

trainer Jaime Rousso and also take supplements according to the advice of my orthomolecular nutrition advisor Dr. Osvino Peña. I also train boxing with Professor Claudio Coelho.

If I am going to compete in BJJ, which means fighting with a gi, then I will do a lot of judo and do a different series of weight training than I do for NHB. The emphasis is more on endurance rather than strength, so I will focus more on repetitions with lighter weights rather than fewer reps with heavier weights. Also, I will train more the auxillary muscle groups rather than just the main muscle groups of the chest, arts, legs, et cetera. I find that combination strength training, when you are working several muscle groups together at the same time, is more realistic to how the body will work during a fight. This is especially true with the gi, because of the unlimited positions that can result from the grabbing of the gi. I

"Becoming a champion requires personal sacrifice. I am very lucky to have a very understanding and supportive wife who has made my life easier rather than make it harder."

also believe in focusing mentally in order to truly achieve peak performance. The mental aspect is at least as important as the physical. I sometimes focus so hard that I get cranky and irritable. So after the training is done and the event is over I sometimes had to apologize to a lot of people! In the past I have rented an apartment and left my house so that I could concentrate 100 percent on training for events. That of course is really hard because I love my family and I miss them. But becoming a champion requires personal sacrifice. I am very lucky to have a very understanding and supportive wife who has made my life easier rather than make it harder.

Q: Do you approach training differently if you are going to fight a vale tudo or straight grappling tournament without the gi?
A: If I am training for a grappling event then the training is similar to what I would do for a BJJ tournament but the emphasis is once again different. Grappling is a much more slippery fight than BJJ, because of the fact you don't wear a gi, and the need is for quick explosive motion rather than slow and methodical techniques. Because of this, I adjust my weight training and my cardio exercise accordingly. I do explosive repetitions with heavier weights and other things like that. As far as techniques go I concentrate more on takedowns and on getting to the back for a choke, as arm bars are harder to get without a gi. I also try to avoid practicing the guard, because in grappling you don't want to be laying on your back

waiting to react to your opponent, but rather attacking him and forcing him to react to you. In grappling without a gi, you need to be very active and be constantly on the move—so I train for this by constantly shifting positions with my training partners. The important thing to keep in mind is that you need to do your homework and find something that works for you and then keep improving it. I truly believe that fights are won or lost outside of the limelight, way before you step into the arena. That is what I keep in mind and that is what motivates me to train.

Q: Finally, did you ever think when you fought Eugenio Tadeu for free, that NHB would become so well-established and popular?

A: Vale tudo has become a money-making machine for an elite few. However, there are many athletes who are fighting for very little. There are many people that are not getting what they deserve. Fighters need to be able to get a fair payment; but for various reasons, some of which are the fighters' own fault, they will fight for any amount. I believe that anyone that fights deserves to get more than they are getting now. Luckily, the events are getting more popular and the new promoters are people who love the sport and who are visionaries. They are making big strides to fairly compensate the fighters. That will be very good for the sport. ○

"The important thing to keep in mind is that you need to do your homework and find something that works for you and then keep improving it. I truly believe that fights are won or lost outside of the limelight, way before you step into the arena."

Using the open guard (1), Royler Gracie pulls opponent Kid Peligro down (2), grabs his belt (3), then throws him (4). Rolling on top (5), Royler puts his knee on the stomach (6), and then wraps his arm around the opponent's head, securing control (7).

Kid Peligro grabs Royler Gracie's gi with both hands (1). Royler lifts both arms (2), breaks the grip (3), and wraps both of the attacker's arms (4), to control him (5). Royler then moves his right leg (6), throws his opponent onto the ground (7), and gains final control (8).

319

Masters Techniques

Grabbed from behind by Kid Peligro (1), Royler Gracie holds the attacker's arm to protect his neck (2), steps to the side (3), throws his opponent over his back (4), traps the arm (5), and applies a finishing wrist-lock/choke combination (6).

Royler Gracie chokes Kid Peligro, who keeps pushing forward to avoid the submission (1). Royler pushes and moves back (2), hooks his opponent's leg (3), throws him over the top (4), and mounts him and applies a finishing choke (5).

Wallid Ismael

The Desire to Win

YOU MIGHT NOT LOVE WALLID ISMAEL, YOU MIGHT NOT CARE ABOUT HIM, OR YOU MIGHT JUST PLAIN DISLIKE HIM. BUT WHATEVER YOUR FEELINGS ABOUT HIM, YOU HAVE TO RESPECT HIM. BORN IN THE AMAZON RAIN FOREST, ISMAEL, THROUGH THE SHEER FORCE OF HIS DESIRE TO BETTER HIMSELF, WORKED HIMSELF INTO A POSITION WHERE HE COULD PULL-OFF ONE OF THE GREATEST UPSETS IN THE MARTIAL ARTS HISTORY. IN BEATING ROYCE GRACIE, A TRULY GREAT FIGHTER IN HIS OWN RIGHT, WALLID PROVED THAT DESIRE AND HARD WORK COUNT FOR AT LEAST AS MUCH, IF NOT MORE, THAN NATURAL TALENT OR PHYSICAL STATURE. THE BIGGEST THINGS ABOUT THIS WORLD JIU-JITSU CHAMPION ARE HIS HEART AND HIS FIERCE DESIRE TO WIN. WITH THE KIND OF WORK ETHIC THAT SURROUNDS HIS LIFE IT IS NO WONDER THAT HE FEELS SO CONFIDENT EVERY TIME HE STEPS ONTO THE MAT. ALL WHAT HE HAS ACHIEVED, HAS NOTHING TO DO WITH LUCK. HE SIMPLY BELIEVES IN HIMSELF. THERE IS A LESSON THERE FOR ALL OF US.

Q: How old are you and how long have you been training jiu-jitsu?
A: I am thirty-years old and have trained jiu-jitsu for twenty years.

Q: Do you believe jiu-jitsu to be superior to the other martial arts?
A: Let me tell you this: jiu-jitsu is an exceptional art. I respect all arts, but if you don't know jiu-jitsu, your art is not complete. Everyone who fights standing needs to know some of it, the same way a jiu-jitsu fighter also needs to know some boxing, some taekwondo or karate. I can box, I can wrestle a little and I've studied taekwondo. One art complements the other. I love martial arts and I love to fight! But every fight ends up body against body. Nowadays lots of people are training jiu-jitsu. Do you know Frank Shamrock's arm lock? That's jiu-jitsu! Mark Kerr can defend the armlock because he also trains jiu-jitsu. If a fighter doesn't know jiu-jitsu he is like a defenseless child. Why? Because, like I said before, every combat ends body against body. You see this in boxing matches, don't you? They clinch. Every fight will end on the floor.

"It used to be that a jiu-jitsu fighter did not need to work out a lot since no one knew jiu-jitsu and it was easy to win any fight. Nowadays, everyone is training jiu-jitsu. Without good physical conditioning the defeat will be certain!"

Q: Would you describe your training routine?

A: I train vigorously. I run three-times a week for 45 minutes. I train eight-hours a day: four hours of jiu-jitsu and four hours of working out. It used to be that a jiu-jitsu fighter did not need to work out a lot since no one knew jiu-jitsu and it was easy to win any fight. Nowadays, everyone is training jiu-jitsu. Without good physical conditioning the defeat will be certain! And that's true for sport jiu-jitsu and vale tudo as well. I also practice yoga. That's a very important part of my training. I do it for relaxation and breathing, since I am by nature a very agitated individual.

Q: What about your diet?

A: For a while I did the Gracie diet but mine is a little more radical. I keep a vegetarian diet. For protein supplements I use protein shakes and a lot of egg whites and soy. I've followed this diet for fifteen years.

Q: What are your best jiu-jitsu techniques?

A: I am good at passing people's guard, and I train how to defend my guard a lot. Sometimes people say I only like the game from the top. At the academy, Carlson makes me train the guard all the time. My trainers and Bebeu, always make me do the guard. But when the fight is on I go right to the top. It's a warrior's thing, you know?

Q: What are your best submissions?

A: The side arm-lock and the back submission are my best. That's how I finished Royce.

Q: Why do you do so well fighting the Gracies when they are feared by so many?

A: I don't just do well fighting the Gracies, I do well fighting anyone. The Gracies are just like any others for me. I do well because I train and study jiu-jitsu a lot. It is the chess of the body for the very intelligent. I do five or six fights a year. My best fights were not even against the Gracies. I've been world champion at the IBF, the Ultimate Japan Superfight and the Luta Livre. I've always been a champion. I've lost a few, but that's normal.

Q: Do you think the fact that some of the Gracies have been defeated will lead to the end of the Gracie dynasty?
A: Absolutely not! A few defeats will not end seventy-five years of tradition. Hopefully what I did was to end the myth that you have to be a Gracie to be a great jiu-jitsu fighter. That is an absurd idea. I believe as a result of this last fight, jiu-jitsu will grow in popularity in America because it showed Americans that they can be as good as a Gracie without being one. The Gracies still have their place, but I also want mine. I've always thought it to be wrong when they boasted to be the only ones who could teach jiu-jitsu. This is the greatest lie! I've shown them I can beat them, and will go on winning many other fights. That's the reason I'll fight Royce again.

"What I did was to end the myth that you have to be a Gracie to be a great jiu-jitsu fighter. That is an absurd idea. Americans can be as good as a Gracie without being one."

Q: Can you describe your fight with Royce?
A: The fight lasted almost five minutes. It was a tough fight. Royce has very good technique. We started standing, one trying to drop the other down. When I went for his legs he threw me down. I fell underneath but turned quickly, held his legs, and put him down. Tough fight. His technique is good. I tried to go behind his back and he placed me under his guard. He defended his guard and tried to get me in a triangle and to choke me, while I kept trying to go to one side then another. Suddenly, when I was trying to go to one side, I reversed direction and went the other way. I finally got to his side and he turned his back and stood up. I brought him down with a leg hook—I don't remember exactly—at one point he gave me his back. When he stood up I tried a hook to bring him down; I was on his back and fell with my hand reaching for his neck. I got hold of his neck with one hand on the collar, coming

"I got hold of his neck with one hand on the collar, coming from underneath the arm, and the other hand on the collar on the neck. All I did was squeeze and squeeze. He tried to get away by doing everything right, everything by the book."

from underneath the arm, and the other hand on the collar on the neck. All I did was squeeze and squeeze. He tried to get away by doing everything right, everything by the book. However, it is part of the game: one wins, one loses. I went on and finalized it, but he never tapped out. He tried to fight it to the last minute and then fell quiet and fainted. I didn't realize that he had fainted, neither did the referee, until Rorion stormed into the mat and begged the referee to stop the fight.

Q: Did Carlson Gracie teach you any specific techniques to beat him?
A: No, he did not teach me anything specific. It was all strategy. Royce had been invincible for so many years because he is a very intelligent, good fighter. I was also invincible for 15 years. But we are, after all, human and sometimes we fail. I won the fight not because of luck. I won because my jiu-jitsu is a great deal superior to his.

Q: Would you fight Royce again?
A: Of course I'll fight him again! He is an excellent fighter; I have to give him another chance. He may believe that his defeat was just an accident, but I want to show him the truth: my superiority. I'll win again! I hope, contrary to people's beliefs, he will take up the challenge of fighting me again this year or next. We have been negotiating a match, but he wants a million dollars.

"Royce had been invincible for so many years because he is a very intelligent, good, fighter. But we are, after all, human and sometimes we fail."

Q: What were your expectations? Were you surprised at your swift victory?
A: I had no doubt I would win! I was well prepared. I train jiu-jitsu eight-hours a day. When Royce said at a press conference that this fight against me was just a training session I warned him: "Remember Ralph? Remember Renzo? I am going to finish you up. You think you're leaving L.A.'s cold weather to warm up on Brazil's beaches, but you've got another thing coming. I am going to show you some bad weather, man." This is what I always say to my adversaries.

Q: What other Gracies have you fought and beaten?
A: Very few people know I defeated Ralph and Renzo Gracie before Royce. These were the three greatest Gracies. Listen, I love to fight. I am from the Amazon rain forest, which means I grew up with nothing. Everything I have came from jiu-jitsu. My home was at the jiu-jitsu school. There I slept at night and trained all day. All I wanted to do was to fight. I had been on a winning spree for a while which provoked some jealousy from the Gracies. They never want to see anyone do well but themselves. So they prepared Ralph to fight me. We had a ten-minute fight, which I won without much difficulty. Three years later Renzo came along. He was training a lot and winning many competitions. With all the titles he earned, the word went out that he was better than I was. They dared me to fight him and I took up the challenge. I am not one to be afraid. Renzo

327

"I love to fight. I am from the Amazon rain forest, which means I grew up with nothing. Everything I have came from jiu-jitsu. My home was at the jiu-jitsu school. There I slept at night and trained all day. All I wanted to do was to fight."

soon wanted to impose conditions. First he said he wanted a 30-minute match, to which I said yes. Then he changed his mind and wanted a one-hour match. I said, fine! I drive them crazy because I accept any condition they come up with.

I fought him for an hour. It was an unbelievable match. Renzo remained under me like a child, not able to move! There were no rounds and I scored 12 and he nothing. So the one everyone expected to win spent one hour on the defensive. It was like I was fighting alone! Then my name exploded in Brazil and I became the most popular jiu-jitsu fighter. After that I won many vale tudos, and lost a few, but I kept on fighting.

Q: Since your victory there has been a lot of criticism of Royce. Do you think that's fair?
A: That's a very good question. After the match some fighters began to put Royce down. I believe they are cowards! When Royce went to Brazil and challenged them for a fight, with no time limit and no scoring, nobody wanted to fight him. The only requirement was a world title. So now I don't think they should be saying anything against him. Only the one who took up the challenge has the right to say anything.

Q: Do you feel a part of Gracie jiu-jitsu or do you feel like a traitor? After all, you defeated the most famous member of the Gracie family.
A: I am glad you asked that! I am a jiu-jitsu fighter and I fight for Carlson Gracie. While his family has tried to hide his name, I have always tried to bring the name Carlson Gracie to the forefront. But there is only one jiu-jitsu, Brazilian jiu-jitsu. There is no difference between Brazilian and Gracie jiu-jitsu. This is all a marketing strategy invented by the Gracies. There are

several excellent jiu-jitsu teachers in the U.S.—Carlson, Franco, and teachers from the Carlson team, to name just a few—who do not carry the Gracie last name. Bill Goupa once said, "Hey, Carlson, now is the time for Walid Ismail Jiu-Jitsu!" I said, "No! It is the time of the one and only jiu-jitsu, the one we all know, Brazilian jiu-jitsu!" And I hope it will become the world's jiu-jitsu, because if we limit it we'll lose it. If the Americans, the French, or any others start to get good at it, it will just keep improving and growing. Only the incompetent, the ones who don't want to train a lot, want to keep it a secret.

"I am a jiu-jitsu fighter and I fight for Carlson Gracie. While his family has tried to hide his name, I have always tried to bring the name Carlson Gracie to the forefront. But there is only one jiu-jitsu, Brazilian jiu-jitsu. There is no difference between Brazilian and Gracie jiu-jitsu."

Q: Some of the best jiu-jitsu fighters train with Carlson Gracie. Do you believe him to be the best teacher in the world?
A: I don't think there is any doubt about that. It has been proven again and again. Show me a good fight and you'll be see the Carlson team right there. The Carlson team doesn't pick fights, we just fight them!

Q: Which would you rather fight: jiu-jitsu or vale tudo?
A: I would rather just fight anything. But I love to fight in vale tudo because I love to punch. Funny thing about me, I love to punch. Sometimes I even cause my opponent to loose consciousness. The times I lost were because I wanted to punch when I should be using jiu-jitsu technique. Vale tudo is in my blood and I'm not afraid. A fighter is not the one who knows only how to hit, but knows also how to be hit.

"If the Americans, the French, or any others start to get good at it, it will just keep improving and growing. Only the incompetent, the ones who don't want to train a lot, want to keep it a secret."

Q: You have a reputation of winning the most difficult fights but loosing the easiest ones. What do you say to that?

A: I haven't lost many times. It is an interesting question because I realize I only lost when I was sure of the victory. But that's the way, that's just life. I have, though, challenged these same adversaries for a rematch but they did not want it. If I were given that opportunity I would then fight totally focused as I would on my more important fights.

Q: How do you think you would do in a fight against Rickson Gracie?

A: Good question, but I'd have to say fighting is even easier than analyzing. When I am in the ring I believe in myself, and the tougher my opponent the more confident I feel.

Q: Is there anyone you would like to fight?

A: I'll be straight with you. I don't pick and choose my opponents. I'll fight anyone. I'd like to fight the guys I lost to at vale tudo, but they run from me like the Devil from the Cross. But that's all right, I like to remember only the good fights and I've had a lot of them.

Q: In your opinion, who are the five best jiu-jitsu fighters and the best vale tudo fighters in the world?

A: I don't want to answer that because I may leave somebody out. Besides, it's not a good idea to point to one or the other as being the best. I'll end up contradicting myself since I've always said the best is really God. There will always be fighters who are better than others at any given time, but to me the best will always be God.

Q: What was the hardest fight you've ever had?
A: I think the hardest fight is the everyday fight of training—the fight to give up parties and the other temptations of life. Especially for a successful fighter the opportunities for going the wrong way are always there: the parties, the alcohol, the drugs, and the women. A strong spirit is necessary to choose the right way and not the bad. I only believe in my success if I'm still training hard. I respect everybody who fights and doesn't run away from fights.

Q: What was the hardest time in your career as an athlete?
A: I always see a fighter's career as a roller coaster: one day you may be at the top, the other at the bottom. One needs to have a strong spirit not to be taken by the extremes: at the top not

"The times I lost were because I wanted to punch where I should be using jiu-jitsu technique. Vale tudo is in my blood and I'm not afraid. A fighter is not the one who knows only how to hit, but knows also how to be hit."

to let it go to your head and at the bottom not to let it defeat you. One needs to keep balanced. That is what I told my wife when, at my first defeat, people tried to put me down. People tried to denigrate my name, the way they did to Royce. That's why I defend him today. These people are like hyenas. They don't attack the lion when it's healthy and strong. They lurk in the shadows, waiting for the day the lion has been hurt. I'm going to continue to train really hard, keeping my body in shape. ⟲

Wallid Ismael is mounted on Franco de Camargo (1). He begins to turn to the side looking for a choke (2). When his opponent defends the choke (3), the opponent leaves his left arm vulnerable for Wallid to trap (4), and apply a finishing arm-lock (5).

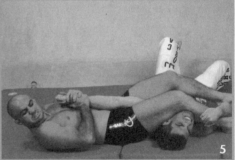

Wallid
Ismael

Wallid Ismael defends Franco de Camargo's attempt to pass the guard (1). As Franco tries to punch him, Wallid controls the arms with his legs (2), and pushes Franco's right arm to the side (3). This opens an angle for Wallid to put his right leg around Franco's neck (4), and apply a finishing triangle choke (5).

Wallid Ismael has his opponent in side control (1). He stands up and puts his left knee on his opponent's chest (2). As his opponent pushes the knee to protect himself, Wallid grabs his wrist (3), puts his right leg over his opponent's head (4), and applies a finishing arm-lock (5).

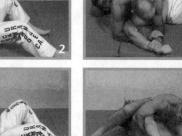

Wallid Ismael controls Franco de Camargo from the side mount (1). Wallid under-hooks Franco's left leg (2), stands up to grab the left ankle (3), and applies a finishing ankle lock (4).

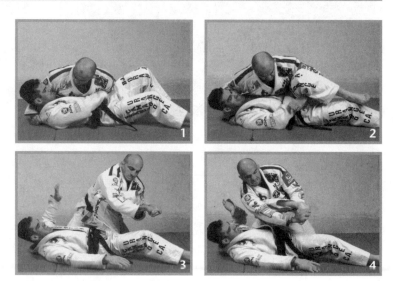

334

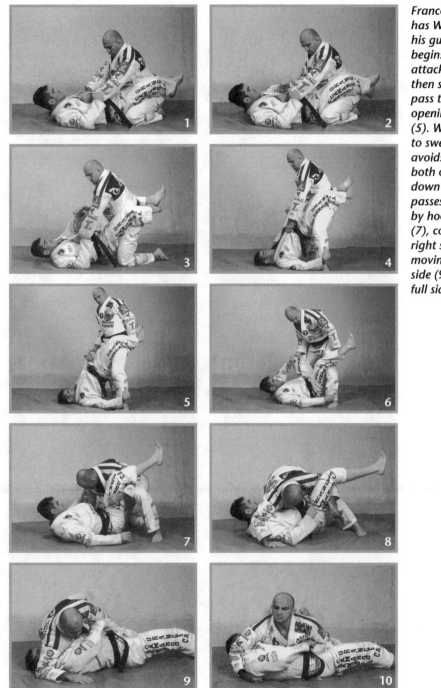

Franco de Camargo has Wallid Ismael in his guard (1). Wallid begins to move to attack Franco (2), and then stands up (3), to pass the guard (4), by opening Franco's legs (5). When Franco tries to sweep him, Wallid avoids it by pushing both of Franco's legs down (6). Wallid then passes Franco's guard by hooking his left leg (7), controlling his right shoulder (8), and moving his legs to the side (9), ending up in full side-control (10).

Franco de Camargo tries to choke Wallid Ismael from behind (1). Wallid grabs Franco's pants and pulls him (2), unbalancing Franco and bringing him forward (3), giving Wallid space to spin around (4). Ending up on Francos's back (5), Wallid mounts an attack (6), gets Franco in a vulnerable position (7), and applies a finishing choke (8).

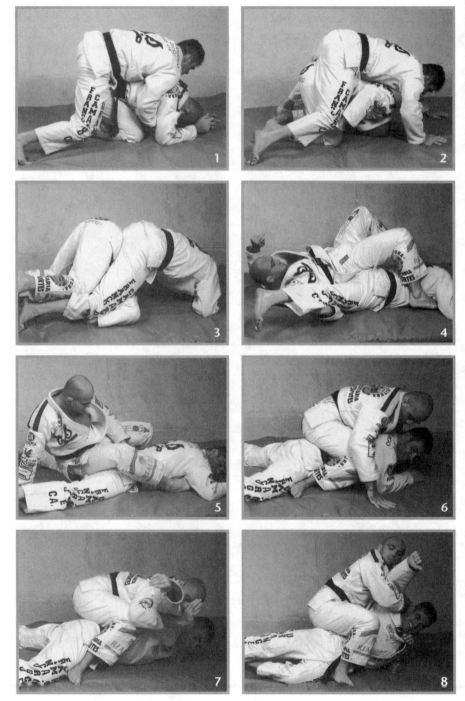

Wallid Ismael faces Franco de Camargo (1). Franco attacks with a roundhouse kick (2), that Wallid blocks and grabs to unbalance Franco (3). Wallid then kicks Franco's supporting leg (4), brings him to the ground (5), puts his left leg over Franco (6), and applies a finishing ankle lock (7).

337

Wally Jay

A Revolution of One

PROFESSOR WALLY JAY IS ONE OF THE MOST REVOLUTIONARY MARTIAL ARTISTS OF THE 20TH CENTURY. HIS MOTTO COULD BE THAT HE DOESN'T BELIEVE IN KEEPING TRADITION FOR TRADITION'S SAKE. HE MOVED FROM JAPAN TO HAWAII AT THE AGE OF 17 AND HIS MARTIAL ARTS CURRICULUM IS COMPRISED OF JUDO, JIU-JITSU, BOXING, FILIPINO ARTS, WRESTLING, OKINAWAN KARATE AND EVEN KUNG-FU. WHILE IN HONOLULU HE LEARNED THE FINE POINTS OF BOXING AT MCKINLEY HIGH SCHOOL FROM JAMES HARADA.

IN 1941, HE RESUMED HIS JIU-JITSU TRAINING UNDER JUAN GOMEZ, A DISCIPLE OF MASTER OKAZAKI, AND IN 1944 HE EARNED HIS BLACK BELT, BEING PROMOTED TO INSTRUCTOR'S LEVEL A YEAR LATER. BEFORE OPENING THE KAHILI JU-JUTSU CLUB, JAY BEGAN HIS TRAINING UNDER MASTER HENRY S. OKAZAKI HIMSELF. MANY YEARS LATER AND USING HIS VAST JIU-JITSU KNOWLEDGE, HE PRODUCED ONE OF THE BEST JUDO TEAMS EVER. BRUCE LEE WAS SO IMPRESSED WITH PROFESSOR JAY'S STUDENTS THAT ASKED HIM ABOUT IT. "YOU HAVE TO GO OUTSIDE OF YOUR SYSTEM TO GET THE ADVANTAGE, BRUCE," ANSWERED JAY. HE DEVELOPED SMALL CIRCLE JIU-JITSU, CREATING AN ORIGINAL AND COMPLETE SYSTEM BY BLENDING HIS KNOWLEDGE OF DIFFERENT MARTIAL ARTS. HE HAS NOT STOPPED TEACHING HIS ART FOR A SINGLE DAY OF HIS LIFE, AND IS RECOGNIZED WORLDWIDE AS ONE OF THE GREATEST ALL-TIME MASTERS OF MARTIAL ARTS.

Q: You trained jiu-jitsu under Henry S. Okazaki, right?
A: Yes. He was a Kodenkan master and was very uncommon for that time. He was the founder of danzan-ryu jiu-jitsu and liked to teach everybody, regardless of race or religion. Of course, from a traditional point of view, this was against the Japanese philosophy.

Q: It is true that he also taught massage?
A: Yes. Knowing how to massage was a requirement for second degree black belt. You needed to know how to heal the body, not just harm it.

Grappling Masters

"I quit Okazaki's organization because they wanted me to teach the same things he was teaching in the '20s. I didn't believe in those things anymore, because I wanted to be practical in my approach to jiu-jitsu."

Q: Why did you quit Master Okazaki's school?
A: Well, you don't fight World War II with World War I weapons, right? You have to know how to change and adapt to different environments and circumstances. I've always disagreed with adhering to tradition just for tradition's sake. Master Okazaki developed his own system because he felt the other systems were lacking something. That's exactly how I felt at the time. I quit Okazaki's organization because they wanted me to teach the same things he was teaching in the 20's. I didn't believe in those things anymore, because I wanted to be practical in my approach to jiu-jitsu.

Q: Did you tell them their techniques were unpractical?
A: Of course I did! I kept telling them that you have to constantly change and improve all the time and that their stuff was out of date. I really feel sorry when people stay locked in tradition.

Q: Have you seen many changes in the way the martial arts are taught today?
A: Many changes! And there are different reasons for that. William Chow used to punch his students in the leg, causing swelling and a great deal of pain. We can't do that now!

Q: Who were your role models as a young martial artist?
A: In boxing it was Jimmy Mitchell, the P.E. teacher at the junior high school, and James Harada, a great young boxer who rated very high in the Hawaiian boxing scene. In jiu-jitsu was Professor Henry S. Okazaki. In judo my role models were Ken Kawachi, who was my sensei, and Yamamoto Sensei. Yamamoto Sensei taught a great humbling lesson. He told me to *randori* (spar) with Yamamoto Sensei who was a visiting teacher. The first move he made was a foot sweep. I lifted my foot in time to evade the attack then I cracked a smile. Yamamoto Sensei tried again and I did the same thing. And I cracked another smile. After that,

Yamamoto Sensei must have thrown me over a hundred times. I told him that I had enough and he said, "I will tell you when you have enough." After another few minutes of hard throws he dismissed me. I had learned a lesson of humility, the hard way.

Q: You once said, "The more martial arts you know, the better." Still think that?
A: Definitely. To begin with, you have to know where you're going and what you're looking for. That's the hard part. A lot of people just cross-train for fun. That's not the goal. You have to go outside of your base system to gain knowledge and become

"To become your best, you cannot stay locked in your system—you cannot confine yourself to only one system. You have to study different things and find out the best way they might work for you, for what you're doing. Constant change, improvement and evolution is the hallmark of a truly great martial artist."

more unpredictable. To become your best, you cannot stay locked in your system—you cannot confine yourself to only one system. You have to study different things and find out the best way they might work for you, for what you're doing. Your brain is like a room. You can put in a lot of furniture when it's empty but after reaching a certain point you have to rearrange the distribution in order to find room for the new furniture you've just acquired. Constant change, improvement and evolution is the hallmark of a truly great martial artist.

Q: Do you think this approach can be confusing?
A: Only if you don't have a base system to grow from, and don't know where you're going. I remember telling Dan Inosanto that people are

"Once you start with a system, stick to it. Don't go jumping from one system to another. This is a big mistake. Each art has its strong and weak points so you have to analyze those and see whether the art fits you or not."

built differently so they need different martial arts systems. You have to find what fits you and what you're compatible with. I know this philosophy can be confusing and I don't want people to misunderstand me. Once you start with a system, stick to it. Don't go jumping from one system to another. This is a big mistake. Each art has its strong and weak points so you have to analyze those and see whether the art fits you or not. You can't train a St. Bernard to run. Well you can, but he'll never be a greyhound—it doesn't matter what training method you use.

Q: How do you remember Bruce Lee?
A: He was a great guy. When I met him he was young, but he was very fast. I couldn't believe how fast he was at that time and how hard he could hit. I met him at World's Fair in Seattle in 1962. In the very beginning I thought Bruce knew a lot but as I got to see him more, I came to

realize that he didn't know as much as I had first thought.

Q: How old was Bruce at that time?

A: He was around 22. His secret was that what he did know, he knew very well. He was able to use it in combat. He never made the mistake of accumulating a lot of things. It was very difficult to estimate his whole knowledge, because he always looked for the quality of what he was doing not the quantity.

Q: It is true that you told him to change the direction of his punch?

A: Yes. In wing chun, the direction of the force is upwards because of the wrist action. The late Chris Case, who was a Taky Kimura student, told me that Bruce was planning to change the punch so he could make contact in a downward direction.

"Judo instructor Ken Kawachi told me that the two-way-action principle (push and pull) is very important. I've tried to apply the same concept by pulling with my fingers and pushing with my hands. This doesn't require a big motion, only two-way action."

Q: What is small circle ju-jitsu?

A: The idea came from a very old book about impact and inertia called *Sports Medicine*. It cost me 45 cents but I got a lot of knowledge from that book. I began to apply principles described in that book to judo and jiu-jitsu. Judo instructor Ken Kawachi told me that the two-way-action principle (push and pull) is very important. I've tried to apply the same concept by pulling with my fingers and pushing with my hands. You have to locate and secure the fulcrum and move around it instead of moving just one part of the lever. This doesn't require a big motion, only two-way action. All the big movements are wasted energy. The whole idea is very

"I've spent my whole life researching, and I'm still learning new ways of making the things better and more effective."

scientific and you don't need to use a lot of strength but just find the fulcrum and create a base for applying pressure. That's it! The idea in jiu-jitsu is to control the opponent rather than maim him. You have to learn to apply the right amount of pressure because if you overdo it you're going to dislocate his joint and if you cause too little pain, the aggressor is going to punch or kick his way out of the hold. In my art, size doesn't make the difference.

Q: When you're doing the palming action, isn't it easy for the opponent to punch?
A: The other person's mind is on the pain and can't focus on being offensive until the pain goes away. I apply the lock and then stick to the opponent. You have to learn how to stay with him, applying the right amount of force to keep the lock or if he tries to escape. If I miss the first one, I shift to the next one. I like to work on the tendon because I don't want to hurt the guy, just control him.

Q: Why do you apply pressure to the nerves and tendons?
A: After years of training it is easy for me to locate the nerves and tendons so I can apply a small pressure. There are some weak points in the human body that if you know how to manipulate and dig in with your knuckles and fingers, there's nothing the opponent can do. He's under control because it hurts too much to resist.

Q: What are the basic principles of small circle theory?
A: Proper direction of force in the smallest point, no head-on collision of forces, create a base, right way of transferring the energy, balance, mobility and stability, rotation momentum, transitional flow, and sticking.

Q: A lot of great martial artists have come to you for knowledge, haven't they?

A: Yes, and I'm really happy about that because it's a sign of recognition. I'm happy to share what I have with all those great teachers. I've spent my whole life researching, and I'm still learning new ways of making the things better and more effective. I like to say that I'm still going through the trial and error process. I look at small circle ju-jitsu as something very revolutionary, not just evolutionary. The whole world is changing so we have to evolve and improve in order to keep up with the new things.

Q: Is the skill level of the teachers in the West as high as in Japan or China?

A: I think it is. I believe that in United States we have very good instructors, second to none. I also feel that our teaching methods are much better than those used in the Orient.

"I look at small circle ju-jitsu as something very revolutionary, not just evolutionary. The whole world is changing so we have to evolve and improve in order to keep up with the new things."

Q: How do you think martial arts can make a person a better human being?

A: If the person doesn't want to improve, there's nothing anybody can do. But going through the demands of training can improve the person's attitude. I know that people, after training in martial arts, don't have to prove themselves anymore. They become better human beings. ○

NOTES

"A true martial arts practitioner—like an artist of any kind—be they musician, painter, writer or actor—is expressing and leaving parts of themselves in every piece of their craft. The need for self-inspection and self-realization of who they are becomes the reason for a journey in search of that perfect technique, that great melody, that inspiring poetry, that amazing painting or that Academy Award performance. It is this motivation to reach that 'impossible dream,' that allows a simple individual to become an exceptional artist or master of their craft."

—Jose M. Fraguas

MASTERS SERIES by the same author

MARTIAL ARTS are among the most popular yet mysterious physical activities in the world. In this *Masters Series*, through conversations with the world's foremost masters of arts such as karate-do, kung-fu, taekwondo, kali-eskrima, kenpo, judo, Brazilian jiu-jitsu, and more, the threads of martial arts learning and legend are woven together to complete an integrated view of the fighting and philosophical aspects of these arts. For the first time ever, interviews with historical masters such as Brendan Lai, Masatoshi Nakayama, Leo Giron, and Ed Parker, as well as contemporary masters such as Hirokazu Kanazawa, Hee Il Cho, William Cheung, Jun Chong, Bong Soo Han, Ben Largusa, Rickson Gracie, Dan Inosanto and more, have been gathered into one outstanding collection.

WITH INFORMATION that has never appeared anywhere else, the interviews contain intriguing thoughts, fascinating personal reflections, revealing philosophies and historical recollections. In these interviews, each master reveals a true love for the art and a deep understanding of every facet of the practice and spirit of martial arts. No matter how well you think you know these masters, you haven't truly experienced their wit, wisdom, and insight until you've read *Masters Series*.

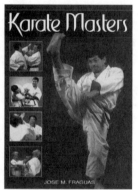